2023 Turkish Elections in All Aspects

Ozan Örmeci

2023 Turkish Elections in All Aspects

PETER LANG

Lausanne - Berlin - Bruxelles - Chennai - New York - Oxford

Library of Congress Cataloging-in-Publication Data
A CIP catalog record for this book has been applied for at the
Library of Congress.

**Bibliographic Information published by the
Deutsche Nationalbibliothek**
The Deutsche Nationalbibliothek lists this publication in the Deutsche
Nationalbibliografie; detailed bibliographic data is available online at
http://dnb.d-nb.de.

ISBN 978-3-631-90775-7 (Print)
E-ISBN 978-3-631-90797-9 (E-PDF)
E-ISBN 978-3-631-91348-2 (E-PUB)
10.3726/b21743

© 2023 Peter Lang Group AG, Lausanne
Published by Peter Lang GmbH, Berlin, Deutschland

info@peterlang.com - www.peterlang.com

This publication has been peer reviewed.

Table of Contents

Author Ozan Örmeci 9

Foreword 13

Ozan Örmeci
Turkey's 2019 Local Elections: Latest Polls 15

Ozan Örmeci
Turkey's 2019 Local Elections: Ak Parti Is Damaged 21

Ozan Örmeci
2019 Istanbul Local Election Will Be Renewed 27

Ozan Örmeci
CHP's Ekrem Imamoğlu Is Re-elected 31

Ozan Örmeci
New Political Party Initiatives in Turkey 35

Ozan Örmeci
Current Situation of Political Parties in Turkey 41

Ozan Örmeci
Early Projections for Turkey's Presidential Election 45

Ozan Örmeci
Turkish Politics: President Erdoğan Needs A Miracle 51

Ozan Örmeci
A New Political Star in Turkey: Ekrem Imamoğlu 65

Ozan Örmeci
Turkey in Three Blocs 71

Ozan Örmeci
Could Mansur Yavaş become a Presidential Candidate? 75

Ozan Örmeci
The Changing Status of Hagia Sophia 79

Ozan Örmeci
Caliphate Discussions in Turkey 89

Ozan Örmeci
Turkish Politics in Critical Conjuncture 99

Ozan Örmeci
Key Issues for 2023 Turkish Elections 103

Ozan Örmeci
Could Turkish Elections Be Postponed? 107

Ozan Örmeci
Growing Polarization in Türkiye after the Earthquakes 113

Ozan Örmeci
Crack in the Opposition Might Secure Victory for Erdoğan 119

Ozan Örmeci
Explaining the Rise of Erdoğan from Huntington's Perspective 125

Ozan Örmeci
Türkiye Will Hold Its Elections on May 14, 2023 131

Ozan Örmeci
Turkey's Boss: Recep Tayyip Erdoğan 137

Ozan Örmeci
Kemal Kılıçdaroğlu: The Opposition's Candidate 147

Ozan Örmeci
2023 Turkish Elections: 46 Days Left 157

Ozan Örmeci
2023 Turkish Elections: Erdoğan Victory Is Expected 167

Ozan Örmeci
2023 Turkish Elections: Erdoğan Clinches Victory 173

Ozan Örmeci
CHP's Electoral Performance Over the Past Years 179

Ozan Örmeci
Erdoğan's New Cabinet: Fresh Names But Low Hopes 185

Ozan Örmeci
What Happens in Türkiye in the Post-Election Process? 191

Ozan Örmeci
Secular Opposition Is Weak in Türkiye 197

Ozan Örmeci
Erdoğan's Successor? 203

Ozan Örmeci
Tragedy in Gaza and the Republican Centennial 213

Ozan Örmeci
Türkiye's Main Opposition Party Elected A New Chair: Özgür Özel 217

Ozan Örmeci
Türkiye Is Heading Toward 2024 Local Elections 223

Conclusion 231

Author Ozan Örmeci

Dr. Ozan Örmeci was born in 1981 in Bornova-Izmir. His father's family is from Senirkent-Isparta. He finished primary school in Izmir Turk College (ITK) and had a middle school and lycee education in Izmir Saint-Joseph French College. He graduated from Bilkent University's Political Science and Public Administration department in 2004 as high-honour student. In 2011, he earned PhD degree from Bilkent University Political Science department with his thesis entitled "Portrait of a Turkish Social Democrat: Ismail Cem", under the supervision of Dr. Berrak Burçak, from a distinguished jury composed of Prof. Metin Heper, Prof. Ergun Özbudun, Prof. Ayşe Güneş Ayata, and Dr. Nur Bilge Criss. He worked as Lecturer in Uşak University's Public Administration department between 2009 and 2012. Between October 2012 and January 2016, he worked as Assistant Professor and headed the department of Political Science and Public Administration (English language) at Girne American University (GAU) in Northern Cyprus (TRNC). Between March 2016 and September 2018, he worked as an Assistant Professor in the department of Political Science and Public Administration (English language) at Beykent University in Istanbul. He became Associate Professor in June 2018. He began to work as Associate Professor in the department of International Relations (English language) at Istanbul Gedik University in September 2018. He was appointed Associate Professor in the department of Political Science and Public Administration at Istanbul Gedik University in June 2019 and served as the Head of the

Department for a while. Between October 2020 and June 2023, he worked as Associate Professor for Istanbul Kent University and headed the departments of Political Science and Public Administration (Turkish and English). He has been working as Associate Professor at Istanbul Aydın University's Political Science and International Relations (English) department since July 2023. He has previously published many scientific books and articles in Turkey and abroad. He is the editor of some academic books specialized on Turkish Foreign Policy including *Turkish Foreign Policy in the New Millennium* (Peter Lang, 2015), *Mavi Elma: Türkiye-Avrupa İlişkileri* (Gazi Kitabevi, 2016), *Historical Examinations and Current Issues in Turkish-American Relations* (Peter Lang, 2020), *Turkish-French Relations: History, Present, and the Future* (Springer, 2022), *Cumhuriyet'in 100. Yılında Nasıl Bir Dış Politika?* (Nobel Akademik Yayıncılık, 2023) and the author of *Türk-Amerikan İlişkileri* (Urzeni Yayıncılık, 2021) and *Türkiye-Fransa İlişkileri* (Urzeni Yayıncılık, 2022). In addition, he wrote books in Turkish language analyzing the political system and foreign policy of countries including the United States, the Russian Federation, the People's Republic of China, France, the United Kingdom, and Germany. He can speak fluently and write academically in French and in English. He also works as a specialist for the Turkish Political Psychology Association (PPD) and the General Coordinator of UPA (International Political Academy) initiative. In addition, he is the owner of the *UPA Strategic Affairs* academic journal. His main research interests are; International Politics, Comparative Politics, Great Power Politics, Political Psychology, Turkish Political History, Leftist Movements in Turkey, and Turkish Foreign Policy. Dr. Ozan Örmeci is married to Cansu Örmeci (Karakoç) since 30 September 2011 and is the father of two children. He is also a congress member of Karşıyaka Sports Club.

Website: http://www.ozanormeci.com.tr

Email: ozanormeci@gmail.com

Twitter: @ozanormeci

Facebook: https://www.facebook.com/officialozanormeci

Blog: http://ydemokrat.blogspot.com

Linkedin: http://tr.linkedin.com/in/ozanormeci

Academia: https://ikent.academia.edu/OzanOrmeci

Amazon.com: https://www.amazon.com/-/e/B073PZ1KSY

Goodreads: https://www.goodreads.com/author/show/7245759.Ozan_Ormeci

Kaynakça: http://kaynakca.info/kisi/95857/ozan-ormeci

Google Scholar: https://scholar.google.com/citations?user=HSpF-ykAAAAJ&hl
ResearchGate: https://www.researchgate.net/profile/Ozan_Oermeci
Scopus: https://www.scopus.com/authid/detail.uri?authorId=39262224900
Web of Science: https://www.webofscience.com/wos/author/record/11905550
ORCID: https://orcid.org/0000-0001-8850-6089

Foreword

The Republic of Türkiye or Turkey with its most common name was established in 1923 by Mustafa Kemal Atatürk. The year 2023 marks the 100th year anniversary of the foundation of Türkiye. It is interesting that, at the end of its 1st century, Türkiye had very critical elections in 2023. These elections took place between two blocs or camps proposing very different future perspectives for Türkiye. In that sense, we can claim that there was a struggle for setting the conditions of the 2nd century between two large blocs fighting for the soul of the nation. From my perspective, 2023 Turkish elections were extremely important and interesting for three reasons.

First of all, the competition between two political blocs advocating divergent visions for the future of Türkiye had become a pivotal determinant in shaping the country's trajectory. On the one hand, incumbent President Recep Tayyip Erdoğan and his bloc upheld an authoritarian-leaning presidential system and espoused a nationalist/Islamic worldview as a substitute for conventional Kemalist secularism. In the foreign policy domain, Erdoğan sought to position Türkiye as a more assertive regional power by leveraging the growing significance of the national defence industry and supporting Ankara's confrontational stance against Western policies in various realms, including the Kurdish Question (PYD/YPG in Syria) and the Eastern Mediterranean (by adopting a more assertive stance in the Cyprus Problem and towards Greece), through forging close partnerships with authoritarian states such as Russia and China. On the other hand, Kemal Kılıçdaroğlu and his opposition bloc advocated a return to a parliamentary regime, restoration of the conventional Western-oriented foreign policy, implementation of democratic and secular policies inside, revitalization of Türkiye's bid for European Union (EU) membership in addition to renegotiated terms for Customs Union and the Syrian immigrants deal, and a democratic negotiation process involving all stakeholders in determining the future of Kurds and the Eastern Mediterranean Question.

Secondly, 2023 Turkish elections had quickly transformed into a battleground between the West and the East over the future trajectory of Türkiye. While Russia, along with other authoritarian regimes, openly backed President Erdoğan and even delayed Türkiye's natural gas debt to Moscow to bolster his prospects before the election, the United States (U.S.) and the EU also exhibited a clear preference for the opposition to emerge victorious in the polls. Prior to becoming the 46th

President of the United States, Joe Biden even stated that democratic means should be employed to topple Erdoğan by supporting the opposition.

Thirdly, Turkish elections were not conducted in a standardized democratic context. The competition took place between highly polarized social groups forming two large political blocs and the victory of one side was largely perceived as the beginning of a new period of political pressures and legal sanctioning of the other. President Erdoğan and his bloc, in particular, were seen as fighting for their survival against an opposition that sought to punish the regime's controversial and unjustified actions over the past 21 years.

To commemorate and in a sense immortalize these critical Presidential and parliamentary elections on the 100th year anniversary of Türkiye and to make a new contribution to growing academic literature on Turkish Politics, in this book, I tried to collect my articles written on 2023 Turkish elections in Uluslararası Politika Akademisi/International Political Academy (politikaakademisi.org) platform starting from 2019. The book starts with articles about the local elections in Türkiye in 2019, which led to the flourishing of high hopes on the opposition to topple down the government after winning the municipalities of three biggest cities of the country. The book continues with the most important political developments taking place in Türkiye since then and ends with the concluding comments and analyses on the results of 2023 presidential and parliamentary elections as well as some post-election developments.

I hope the book will reach the audience and will help future generations to remember this critical and special year in Turkish political history.

Lastly, I want to dedicate this book to my newborn daughter Lina Su Örmeci…

Ozan ÖRMECİ

20.09.2023
Kartal, Istanbul

Ozan Örmeci[*]

Turkey's 2019 Local Elections: Latest Polls

Abstract The chapter analyzes contemporary developments in Turkish politics before the 2019 local elections with a particular focus on the strategy and candidates of two big parties, namely; AK Parti (Justice and Development Party) and CHP (Republican People's Party).

Keywords: *Turkish Politics, 2019 Turkish local elections, AK Parti, CHP, Recep Tayyip Erdoğan.*

Turkey's local elections will take place on March 31, 2019 in 81 Turkish cities (30 of them are metropolitan cities). Turkey's long time ruling Islamic-oriented party Justice and Development Party (AK Parti) decided to keep its electoral alliance called *"Cumhur İttifakı"* (People's Alliance) with the Turkish nationalist Nationalist Action Party (MHP) before the elections. Accordingly, MHP will support AK Parti candidates in 27 metropolitan cities including three biggest and most developed cities of Turkey (Istanbul, Ankara, and Izmir) and AK Parti will support MHP candidates in return in 3 other metropolitan cities (Adana, Mersin, and Manisa)[1]. In addition, in other 21 cities, People's Alliance electoral coalition will contest with only one candidate[2]. That means, in 51 out of 81 Turkish cities, AK Parti and MHP will contend together. Moreover, the Great Unity Party (BBP), a small Islamist-Turkish nationalist party also declared that in 30 metropolitan cities and Kurdish populated Southeastern Anatolian cities, it will support the candidates of the People's Alliance[3].

Opposition parties also decided to keep their electoral alliance in order to have chance against People's Alliance. The main opposition party, the pro-secular Kemalist/Social democratic Republican People's Party (CHP) decided to maintain its electoral alliance *"Millet İttifakı"* (Nation Alliance) it has established

[*] Associate Professor in the department of Political Science and International Relations (English) at Istanbul Aydın University, Istanbul, Türkiye.
Email: ozanormeci@aydin.edu.tr / ozanormeci@gmail.com.
ORCID: 0000-0001-8850-6089.

1 https://www.haberler.com/ak-parti-kars-ta-adayini-geri-cekti-11758463-haberi/.
2 *Ibid.*
3 https://tr.sputniknews.com/turkiye/201902171037707424-bbp-yerel-secimler-cumhur-ittifaki-destekleyecek/.

during the 2017 Presidential election campaign with the center right-Turkish nationalist İYİ Parti (Good Party). Two secular-oriented parties made an agreement for presenting only one candidate in 23 metropolitan cities and 27 ordinary cities[4]. CHP limited itself with 19 metropolitan candidates (including three biggest cities) and 38 other candidates[5]. İYİ Parti on the other hand was able to dictate its candidates in important metropolitan cities including Balıkesir, Trabzon, Denizli, and Gaziantep[6]. Other important parties that will contest in the local elections are Islamist Felicity Party (*Saadet Partisi*) and pro-Kurdish Peoples' Democratic Party (HDP). However, HDP did not present candidates in some cities including Istanbul, Izmir, Adana, Ankara, Mersin, Aydın, Bursa, and Antalya[7] in order to support the Nation Alliance against increasing authoritarian practices of the government[8].

If we look at the popular political themes before the elections, we see that opposition parties often use the recent slowdown of Turkish economy and the devaluation of Turkish lira as major points of criticism towards Erdoğan government. Turkey's failed Syria policy and deteriorating relations with the European Union and the United States are also within the menu of opposition leaders such as Kemal Kılıçdaroğlu and Merak Akşener. The AK Parti government and MHP on the other hand present these local elections as a matter of survival (*bekâ* in Turkish) to Turkish voters, a highly exaggerated approach for local elections which have nothing to do with national security issues. President Erdoğan uses his personal charisma and populist attacks towards the opposition as well to win the hearts of the electors. For instance, he recently blamed the Nation Alliance for acting on behalf of the terrorists[9] by using a Schmittian (Carl Schmitt) approach to politics. President Erdoğan also threatened Kurdish voters by saying that if they continue to vote for HDP candidates, Turkish government might annul the election and appoint a trustee for such municipalities[10].

---

4 https://www.bbc.com/turkce/haberler-turkiye-47296568.

5 *Ibid.*

6 https://www.yeniakit.com.tr/haber/iyi-parti-belediye-baskan-adaylari-2019-turkiye-geneli-iyi-parti-belediye-baskanlari-listesi-573230.html.

7 https://www.bbc.com/turkce/haberler-turkiye-47296568.

8 http://haber.sol.org.tr/turkiye/hdpnin-aday-cikarmayacagi-il-sayisi-artiyor-millet-ittifaki-icinde-yer-almak-istedik-ama.

9 https://www.takvim.com.tr/guncel/2019/02/28/Erdoğan-cumhur-ittifaki-ile-zillet-ittifakini-kiyasladi.

10 https://www.memurlar.net/haber/781886/Erdoğan-hdp-ye-belediye-kaptirma-yin.html.

Especially in three big cities, both electoral alliances put forward very good candidates. In Istanbul, the heart of Turkey's economy with more than 16 million residents and former Byzantine and Ottoman capital, AK Parti and MHP will endorse Binali Yıldırım, Turkey's former -and the last- Prime Minister and Minister of Transportation. With his experience, successful career, and connections within Turkey and abroad, Mr. Yıldırım seems to be a perfect choice. However, CHP and İYİ Parti's joint candidate Ekrem İmamoğlu is also a very good choice with his democratic stance and proven success at Beylikdüzü municipality. Recent polls made by Gezici Company in the last week of February suggest that, Mr. Yıldırım will win the election with a margin of 4 to 6 points (52.1 % against 46.6 %)[11]. I also think that Binali Yıldırım has more chance to win Istanbul for several reasons. First of all, losing Istanbul would be a great damage to Erdoğan's new regime and might even a signal the decay of his government; a factor which guarantees that AK Parti will use every means to win the election. Secondly, Istanbul has become a very conservative city in the last few decades due to rural-to-urban migration from Anatolian cities, a notion that has changed the classical multicultural and cosmopolitan atmosphere of the city and created a new -unofficial- Islamist capital. Thirdly, Binali Yıldırım is a very famous and trusted politician for the majority of Turkish people contrary to enigmatic (unknown) İmamoğlu. It is true that a young and successful politician like İmamoğlu could create a difference right place at right time; but CHP leader Kemal Kılıçdaroğlu's choice still seems risky. Lastly, the voting pattern of the Kurdish voters in Istanbul will be the decisive factor due to large Kurdish population in the city and it seems like Kurdish voters do not hate Mr. Yıldırım or adore Mr. İmamoğlu, a fact that shows Kurdish votes might not go to İmamoğlu as a bloc.

In Ankara, according to the word in the street, the opposition has more chance. CHP and İYİ Parti chose Mansur Yavaş, a Turkish nationalist politician coming from MHP tradition as their common candidate. Yavaş is a good choice for preventing populist attacks coming from the government and especially from President Erdoğan thanks to his ultranationalist background. Erdoğan's criticism towards Mr. Yavaş for supporting pro-Kurdish groups and terrorist circles makes non-sense for Turkish voters who know Yavaş for several years. Moreover, in Ankara, unlike Istanbul, the number of Kurdish voters is relatively low and Turkish nationalists' voting preference is the key factor for winning the election. Both Mansur Yavaş and Mehmet Özhaseki are successful municipal leaders that

---

11 https://www.ensonhaber.com/gezici-arastirmanin-son-anketi.html.

Turkish people have confidence. Recent polls suggest made by Gezici Company in the late February suggest that, Mr. Özhaseki will win the race with 51.8 % against Yavaş's 46.3 % [12]. However, I still think anything could happen in Ankara due to reactions towards the AK Parti government's poor economic performance as well as MHP leader Devlet Bahçeli's decreasing popularity among the Turkish nationalist voters in recent years.

In Izmir, CHP is confident of its victory. Although CHP's coalition partner in Nation Alliance -İYİ Parti- is not satisfied from the choice of Tunç Soyer[13], former municipal leader of Seferihisar, it would be a great surprise for everyone if Soyer is beaten by People's Alliance candidate and former Economy Minister of Turkey Mr. Nihat Zeybekçi. Nihat Zeybekçi's job is really difficult since he represents the "*other*" in a highly secularized city like Izmir. Although Zeybekçi tried everything to present himself as a secular Muslim candidate and even said that he is not against the production of vine[14], it seems like this would not be enough for changing the voting preference of large majority of people in Izmir.

Among other important cities to be mentioned, especially Antalya will witness a tight race between People's Alliance candidate and current municipal leader Menderes Türel and Nation Alliance candidate Muhittin Böcek. Gezici Company's recent poll points out that Türel would win the election, but the difference will not be larger than % 5 points[15]. I think CHP might still have a chance in Antalya since the city is based on tourism industry and secular parties in general perform better in terms of tourism due to Islamist parties' tendency to ban alcohol and night-life. In Bursa also, Nation Alliance could win with Mustafa Bozbey against People's Alliance candidate Alinur Aktaş. Recent polls also strengthen this view. In Aydın, polls suggest that People Alliance candidate Mustafa Savaş will topple down current municipal leader endorsed by Nation Alliance, Mrs. Özlem Çerçioğlu. However, due to her successful performance and good reputation as an exemplary female mayor, I think Çerçioğlu could also win one more time.

If we look at the general picture, I think local elections will not be helpful to Turkish democracy, which is in sharp fall in recent years in terms of freedoms and the rule of law. Considering the fact that there will not be a Presidential

---

12 https://www.ensonhaber.com/gezici-arastirmanin-son-anketi.html.

13 https://www.gazeteduvar.com.tr/politika/2019/01/28/iyi-partiden-tunc-soyer-aciklam
    asi-tabanimiz-ve-teskilatimiz-tepkiyle-karsiladi/.

14 https://tr.sputniknews.com/turkiye/201902141037652910-zeybekci-sarabin-destek
    lenmesi-bir-ticarettir-diyanet-isleri-baskani-degilim/.

15 .https://www.ensonhaber.com/gezici-arastirmanin-son-anketi.html.

election scheduled until 2023, it would be too optimistic to claim that everything will be good if CHP could increase its votes. As far as I am concerned, only if CHP could win both in Istanbul and in Ankara, in addition to Izmir, we can talk about a meaningful transition of power taking place at the electorate base. However, this does not seem realistic especially in Istanbul. So, we have to wait until Turkish voters send a strong signal by supporting the opposition parties in order to improve Turkish democracy. Another solution is the return of the AK Parti to its reformist and pro-Western agenda. However, this does not seem realistic and possible for the moment. Finally, I should add that there are political discussions in Turkey right now about the necessity of a new centrist party, which will be established by former political stars and leaders of the AK Parti including previous President of the Republic Mr. Abdullah Gül, former Economy Minister Mr. Ali Babacan, and former Turkish Foreign Minister and Prime Minister Mr. Ahmet Davutoğlu.

Ozan Örmeci[*]

Turkey's 2019 Local Elections: AK Parti Is Damaged

Abstract The chapter focuses on the results of Türkiye's 2019 local elections with a special attention given to three big cities' municipalities, namely; Istanbul, Ankara, and Izmir.

Keywords: *Turkish Politics, 2019 Turkish local elections, AK Parti, CHP, Recep Tayyip Erdoğan, Ekrem İmamoğlu, Mansur Yavaş, Tunç Soyer.*

Turkey's 2019 local elections took place on March 31, 2019 Sunday in a relatively peaceful atmosphere. Except for deadly local feuds in Malatya[1] and Gaziantep[2], no serious clashes happened and elections were organized in a free and fair manner. The voting turnout rate was high (84.52 %) as usual.[3] Turkey's governing (2002–) -Islamist-oriented- right-wing AK Parti (Justice and Development Party) took 44.42 % of the total votes, whereas the main opposition party -pro-secular and social democratic- CHP (Republican People's Party) garnered 30.07 % of the votes. It seems like electoral coalitions helped these two parties to monopolize the left (it is widely associated with secularism in Turkey) and the right-wing politics in the country. However, AK Parti lost three most populated and developed cities of Turkey; Istanbul, Ankara and Izmir, a serious blow to President Erdoğan's power and a new hope for the opposition.

---

[*]   Associate Professor in the department of Political Science and International Relations (English) at Istanbul Aydın University, Istanbul, Türkiye.
       Email: ozanormeci@aydin.edu.tr / ozanormeci@gmail.com.
       ORCID: 0000-0001-8850-6089.
1   https://t24.com.tr/haber/sandik-musahitleri-arasinda-kavga-cikti-olu-ve-yaralilar-var,814767.
2   https://www.cnnturk.com/video/turkiye/gaziantepte-muhtarlik-kavgasi-3-olu-1-yarali.
3   Statistical information is taken from http://secim.ntv.com.tr/ and https://www.cnnturk.com/.

TÜRKİYE GENELİ
AÇILAN SANDIK
(%99.01) 192.742 / 194.678

PARTI / OY	OY ORANI
AK PARTİ ▲ 20.421.254	%44,42
CHP ▲ 13.823.738	%30,07
İYİ PARTİ ▲ 3.429.937	%7,46
MHP ▲ 3.330.708	%7,25
HDP ▲ 1.938.064	%4,22
SAADET PARTİSİ ▲ 1.231.587	%2,68
DSP ▲ 454.280	%0,99

Election results[4]

Election results show that Turkey's economic slowdown in recent months and increasing authoritarian practices of President Erdoğan's government reduced his party's voting rates in urbanized and more secular parts of the country. In my opinion, AK Parti also made some mistakes in choosing appropriate candidates. For instance, they chose Mehmet Özhaseki as their candidate in Ankara (a successful municipal leader coming from Kayseri) against a local politician of Ankara and former municipal leader of Ankara's Beypazarı district Mansur Yavaş and eventually lost the election. However, AK Parti was still able to keep its superior and unchallenged position in Turkish politics thanks to its electoral coalition with the Turkish nationalist MHP (Nationalist Action Party) and loyal electoral base supporting the party and its undisputed leader Recep Tayyip Erdoğan for cultural (strong Islamist cultural identity of Turkish people) and historical reasons (opposition to CHP's authoritarian single-party period and left-wing politics due to Cold War legacy). AK Parti won 39 of 81 Turkish cities, whereas CHP won in 21 cities. MHP took municipalities of 11 cities with 7.25 % of the total votes and pro-Kurdish HDP (Peoples' Democratic Party) won in 8 municipalities with only 4.22 % of the votes. CHP's electoral coalition partner İYİ Parti (Good Party) on the other hand took 7.46 % of the votes and became

---

4   Taken from http://www.cnnturk.com.

the third largest party in Turkey, but could not win a municipality in any of 81 Turkish cities. These three parties' (MHP, HDP, and İYİ Parti) voting rates should not be misleading; because these parties engaged in electoral coalitions and supported AK Parti (MHP made an electoral pact with AK Parti) or CHP (İYİ Parti made an electoral pact with CHP and HDP supported CHP candidates in many cities) in most of the cities. Lastly, Islamist *Saadet Partisi*-SP (Felicity Party) took 2.68 % of the votes and the left-wing *Demokratik Sol Parti*-DSP (Democratic Left Party) had 0.99 %.

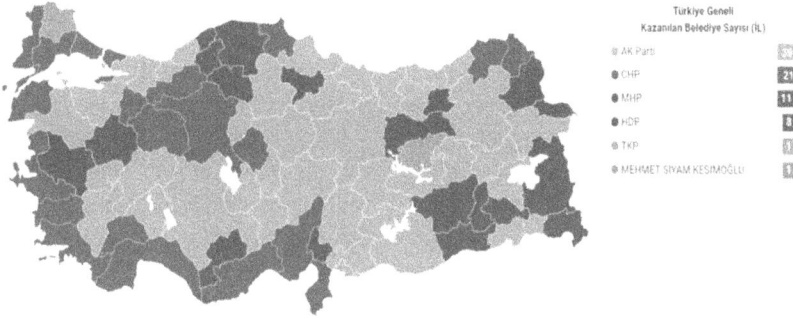

Electoral map[5]

The biggest shock for the governing AK Parti is of course the loss of Istanbul, the economic capital of Turkey. In Istanbul, both parties chose very good candidates; AK Parti convinced the former Prime Minister and the speaker of Turkish Parliament Binali Yıldırım and CHP chose the young municipal leader of Beylikdüzü, Ekrem İmamoğlu. The race was very tight in Istanbul and only a few thousand votes determined the winner. İmamoğlu won the election slightly in a shocking manner. Both candidates declared their victory on the night of the elections. However, on Monday all votes are counted and it was found out that Ekrem İmamoğlu won the election. Mr. İmamoğlu took Istanbul municipality from the hands pro-Islamist parties after 25 years and made history. Both candidates had around 48.70 % of the votes. İmamoğlu achieved this unexpected success with his humble personality and popular image of an honest, bright, and conservative young politician. His success at Beylikdüzü municipality also convinced many voters that he could rule Istanbul better than AK Parti

---

5   Taken from http://secim.ntv.com.tr/.

candidate Binali Yıldırım. In addition, İmamoğlu conducted a very good and virtuous electoral campaign; he never tried to defame AK Parti or his rival Binali Yıldırım, but rather he tried to present himself and explain his projects to the voters. It should not be forgotten that İmamoğlu was nobody for most of the Istanbul residents just three months ago. This shows the success of his electoral campaign. The loss of Istanbul is a serious damage to AK Parti since controlling Istanbul municipality also means ruling an important segment of the Turkish economy thanks to construction licenses and rents.

In Ankara also, the official capital and the second biggest city of Turkey, CHP's Turkish nationalist candidate Mansur Yavaş defeated AK Parti's candidate Mehmet Özhaseki with 50.09 % of the votes against 47.06 % and made a historical win by taking the capital of Turkey from the hands of Islamist parties after 25 years. Mansur Yavaş was able to do this by unifying pro-secular left-wing and Turkish nationalist voters with his unique political identity as a secular and modern politician supporting the local development and coming from MHP background. Moreover, AK Parti's strategy of slandering Mansur Yavaş for personal issues in the last few days of the election backfired. Ankara voters did not approve the negative campaigning methods implemented by AK Parti officials including President Erdoğan, Mehmet Özhaseki, and Ömer Çelik. Although the loss of Istanbul and Ankara will not pose a critical threat to AK Parti and President Erdoğan's power in the short run, if the economic slowdown continues, call for early Presidential and parliamentary elections (Presidential and parliamentary elections will be organized in Turkey in 2023 according to regular schedule) might be increased in the following months and years.

In Izmir, CHP won a landslide victory with left-wing candidate Tunç Soyer's 58.02 % of the votes against AK Parti's former Economy Minister Nihat Zeybekçi's 38.62 %. Tunç Soyer was the successful mayor of Izmir's Seferihisar region; so, his success should not be considered as a surprise. The loss of three big cities of Turkey should be a strong signal to President Erdoğan and his party about increasing the economic performance of the government and liberalizing the political regime. Turkey is now considered as an unfree country by many political observers due to harsh treatment of Turkish and international journalists in addition to opposition voices by the Turkish State. The negative trend in three big cities should be alarming for President Erdoğan for the next Presidential and parliamentary election as well since almost all important political developments in Turkey first start in big cities (mainly Istanbul) and then spread to other parts of Anatolia. In addition, it seems like the survival (*bekâ* in Turkish) rhetoric of the government was not approved by all Turkish voters and Turkish people clearly showed their preference of economic development rather than military expeditions to the government. In this conjuncture, Turkey's military operation towards the eastern side of the Euphrates River in Syria against YPG-PYD groups might rather be limited and Turkey could try to solve the Syrian crisis by working closely with Russia, Iran, and other international powers via focusing on political and diplomatic solutions rather than military ones. However, since Turkish nationalist MHP is acting like the coalition partner of the AK Parti government, President Erdoğan will have to convince Russia and Iran for the territorial integrity and unitary state structure of Syria in order to keep MHP support. Although the loss of three big cities is a serious challenge to AK Parti's power as well as a loss of prestige for President Erdoğan, we should not forget that President Erdoğan has still 4 years of tenure in the office until the next election. So, Erdoğan might still want to take risks in Syria in order to eradicate terrorist groups completely despite the fact that this might increase risks for the fragility of Turkish economy.

If we look at other important cities, in Antalya, another surprise took place and CHP's Muhittin Böcek defeated AK Parti's candidate and previous municipal leader Menderes Türel with 50.63 % of the votes against 46.27 %. AK Parti's Islamist identity was the main cause of this defeat in the summer tourism capital of Turkey although Menderes Türel himself was a popular and successful secular mayor. In Tunceli, the Turkish Communist Party's (TKP) candidate Fatih Mehmet Maçoğlu won the election with 32.37 % of the total votes and became the first communist municipal leader in Turkish history. In Kırklareli, an independent candidate, former CHP mayor Mehmet Siyam Kesimoğlu was elected with 37.53 % of the votes. In addition, CHP made an important progress in the Black Sea (Karadeniz) region by winning in Sinop, Artvin, and Ardahan but lost Giresun to AK Parti. CHP also won in important metropolis cities including Adana, Mersin, Burdur, and Hatay. Lastly, AK Parti took Şırnak, Ağrı, and Bitlis from HDP, other surprise takeovers.

Finally, Turkey's 2019 local elections was an important test for Turkish politics and it showed that the majority of Turkish people are modern and rational individuals who look at their life standards and economic situation first rather than nationalist or religious (Islamist) ideals. In addition, President Erdoğan's polarization methods did not work this time and CHP made an important progress by winning in Ankara and Istanbul and increasing its votes above 30 %. From now on, President Erdoğan will try to straighten up things in the country to save his government. He has to recover the economy first by preventing Turkish lira's devaluation and creating new jobs, and then he should find a solution to Syrian crisis by working closely with all international powers. Another difficult task for President Erdoğan is to recalibrate Turkish foreign policy carefully between the United States, Russia, and the European Union. As far as I am concerned, President Erdoğan might try to make an autocritique of his policies and to rejuvenate his party's cadres after this election. One thing is for sure: President Erdoğan's power is still unchallenged (AK Parti and MHP's joint votes still make 51–52 %) and the rise of CHP in this election does not mean that a CHP candidate could win a Presidential election against Erdoğan (CHP and İYİ Parti's joint votes reach only 37–38 %). Another important lesson from this election is that pro-Kurdish HDP is weakened with the Turkish State's collaborative efforts motivated by this party's links with terrorist groups and without its charismatic leader Selahattin Demirtaş, HDP lost a lot of its power. Interestingly, President Erdoğan commented the election result as a success and pointed out AK Parti's progress in densely Kurdish populated Turkey's southeastern Anatolian cities (such as Şırnak, Ağrı, and Bitlis) while not mentioning the loss of Ankara and Istanbul. CHP leader Kemal Kılıçdaroğlu on the other hand commented the result as a victory for Turkey rather than CHP and thanked his electoral coalition partner İYİ Parti's leader Meral Akşener. It seems like the gaining of three big cities will secure Kılıçdaroğlu's seat as the chair of CHP until the next election. MHP leader Devlet Bahçeli also guaranteed to keep his seat with these results.

Ozan Örmeci[*]

2019 Istanbul Local Election Will Be Renewed

Abstract This chapter deals with the Turkish High Election Board's decision to renew 2019 local elections in Istanbul, which created huge reactions among the opposition circles and increased Western skepticism towards Turkish democracy.

Keywords: *Turkish Politics, 2019 Turkish local elections, AK Parti, CHP, Recep Tayyip Erdoğan, Ekrem İmamoğlu, Binali Yıldırım, Istanbul.*

Turkey's High Election Board or Supreme Election Council (*Yüksek Seçim Kurulu*-YSK) decided for the renewal of March 31, 2019 local election for Istanbul metropolitan municipality due to allegations of electoral fraud with a 7–4 decision on Monday[1]. The decision caused anger in Turkey and Western capitals since the main opposition party pro-secular CHP's (Republican People's Party) candidate Ekrem İmamoğlu had a surprising narrow victory against governing Islamist-originated AK Parti's (Justice and Development Party) strong candidate and the former Prime Minister Binali Yıldırım in the previous election. Although the decision was legitimized as a technical issue related to the non-existence of public official ballot box personnel, many authorities in Turkey suggest that this was a politically-motivated judgment that overshadowed impartiality of YSK and decreased confidence towards state institutions and legal authorities in the country. It should not be forgotten that President Recep Tayyip Erdoğan repeatedly asked for the cancellation of the previous election and claimed that "*organized crimes*" took place during this election before this decision was announced[2]. It is also highly interesting that YSK only cancelled Istanbul metropolitan municipality election and did not annul elections for Istanbul's district municipalities although all elections were conducted with the

---

[*] Associate Professor in the department of Political Science and International Relations (English) at Istanbul Aydın University, Istanbul, Türkiye.
Email: ozanormeci@aydin.edu.tr / ozanormeci@gmail.com.
ORCID: 0000-0001-8850-6089.
1 https://edition.cnn.com/2019/05/06/middleeast/turkey-Istanbul-mayor-recount-intl/index.html.
2 https://activehi.com/2019/04/08/Erdoğan-says-organised-crimes-befell-in-Istanbul-vote-information/.

same ballot box personnel. Whether it is a fair decision or not, it seems like Istanbul voters will go to ballot box again on June 23, 2019 for determining the new mayor of Istanbul.

The decision made by YSK took negative reactions from other countries. For instance, the EU's foreign policy chief Federica Mogherini and Enlargement Commissioner Johannes Hahn both reminded that *"Ensuring a free, fair and transparent election process is at the heart of the European Union's relations with Turkey"*[3]. Moreover, European Parliament's Turkey rapporteur Kati Piri, a Dutch socialist and Guy Verhofstadt, a Belgian politician who chairs the liberal ALDE group, both warned Ankara that *"This ends the credibility of democratic transition of power through elections in Turkey"*[4]. The U.S. Department of State on the other hand declared that they noted down this decision and accepting free and fair elections' results are non-negotiable in a democracy[5]. Although the declaration did not exceed diplomatic norms, it clearly showed American disappointment with the cancellation decision. The decision immediately had a negative effect over the Turkish lira which was at 6.1075 against the dollar on Monday evening. Analyzing Turkey's financial risks, Timothy Ash from Blue Bay Asset Management said *"This is damaging for Turkey's perception as a democracy and will leave Turkey's economy vulnerable, given risks to macro financial stability in the period to July"*[6].

Although the decision took harsh reaction from CHP members on the first day and some party officials resembled Turkey's political system to *"plain dictatorship"*[7], CHP's Istanbul candidate Ekrem İmamoğlu achieved to stay calm and cool. İmamoğlu commented the decision as a great injustice, but he said he will continue to use democratic methods and will win the election once again on June 23[8]. AK Parti's electoral coalition partner Turkish nationalist MHP's (Nationalist Action Party) leader Devlet Bahçeli on the other hand welcomed the decision and said that everyone should respect this decision[9]. Another right-wing

---

3   https://euobserver.com/foreign/144824.

4   https://euobserver.com/foreign/144824.

5   https://www.bloomberght.com/abd-den-Istanbul-secimleri-aciklamasi-2217853.

6   https://www.theguardian.com/world/2019/may/06/turkey-orders-rerun-of-Istanbul-election-in-blow-to-opposition.

7   https://www.theguardian.com/world/2019/may/06/turkey-orders-rerun-of-Istanbul-election-in-blow-to-opposition.

8   https://www.haberturk.com/son-dakika-Istanbul-buyuksehir-belediye-baskani-ekrem-imamoglu-ndan-tek-kelimelik-yorum-2453800 ; https://www.bbc.com/turkce/haberler-turkiye-48198506.

9   https://www.bbc.com/turkce/haberler-turkiye-48180567.

party, İYİ Parti's (Good Party) leader Meral Akşener on the contrary, resembled YSK's decision to a *"civilian coup"* against the popular will[10]. Pro-Kurdish HDP (Peoples' Democratic Party) also declared that the decision does not have democratic legitimacy[11]. President Recep Tayyip Erdoğan on the other hand said that *"the decision is an important step to strengthen our democracy"*[12]. Former AK Parti officials including the previous President Abdullah Gül and former Prime Minister Ahmet Davutoğlu however criticized the YSK after this decision. These declarations prove that no one is discussing the legality of the decision and all sides continue to perceive it from political perspectives. This shows that Turkish democracy has seriously eroded in recent years and building trust between political parties from different camps is almost impossible now.

So, on June 23, AK Parti and MHP's joint candidate Binali Yıldırım and CHP and İYİ Parti's joint candidate Ekrem İmamoğlu will contest again. İmamoğlu this time seems to be the favorite since ordinary Turkish people without strong political attachments generally prefer to support the mistreated side as the quick political rise of President Erdoğan who was imprisoned for reciting an Islamist-nationalist poem once, proves. In addition, Kurdish voters are crucial for Istanbul and I think HDP will not change its decision to support Ekrem İmamoğlu. However, I should add here that President Erdoğan is a political mastermind and he might try to make some political moves before the election in order to win the election. Despite of this fact, I think İmamoğlu will win this time more comfortably because of average Turkish people's emotional characteristic. But since the difference between İmamoğlu and Yıldırım was less than 14,000 votes in the previous election, in case thousands of CHP voters will go on holiday on the election day and İmamoğlu's victimized image will not provide him extra support in this strong polarization atmosphere, Mr. Yıldırım might still have a chance to become Istanbul's new mayor.

Whether it will be İmamoğlu or Yıldırım, one thing is for sure; Istanbul is Turkey's economic capital and it has a lot of problems to be solved starting from traffic jam to expensive prices. Moreover, losing democratic credibility will also weaken Turkey's hand in its foreign policy initiatives starting from Syria to the Eastern Mediterranean. That is why, Turkey has to solve quickly the *"Istanbul dilemma"* and focus on its economy and foreign policy troubles.

---

10 https://www.bbc.com/turkce/haberler-turkiye-48180567.
11 https://www.bbc.com/turkce/haberler-turkiye-48180567.
12 https://uk.news.yahoo.com/turkish-opposition-confident-winning-Istanbul-poll-run-lira-005111220–business.html.

Ozan Örmeci*

CHP's Ekrem Imamoğlu Is Re-elected

Abstract This chapter focuses on the renewed local elections in Istanbul in 2019, which resulted in the glorious victory of CHP's candidate Ekrem İmamoğlu.

Keywords: *Turkish Politics, 2019 Turkish local elections, AK Parti, CHP, Recep Tayyip Erdoğan, Ekrem İmamoğlu, Binali Yıldırım, Istanbul.*

After the cancellation of March 31, 2019 local elections in Istanbul, Istanbulite voters went to polls again today. Pro-secular Republican People's Party's (CHP) candidate Mr. Ekrem İmamoğlu, this time clinched a decisive victory with 54 % of the votes against the ruling Justice and Development Party's (AK Parti) candidate and former Prime Minister Mr. Binali Yıldırım's 45 %. İmamoğlu won the first election also with less than 14,000 votes, but the election was later cancelled by the Higher Electoral Board (YSK) due to the lack of public official personnel in some of ballot box committees. Amazing increase in Mr. İmamoğlu's votes (he took almost 800,000 more votes than Yıldırım this time) just in three months proves that the cancellation of the first election was not approved by Turkish people. By doing this, Turkish people also gave a strong message to President Recep Tayyip Erdoğan and to the rest of the world about their insistence on free and fair elections and democracy. In my opinion, Istanbul results show that Turkish democracy is still alive and Turkish people deserve a good functioning democratic regime.

In my opinion, this humiliating defeat for AK Parti in Istanbul's municipal election might be a turning point in Turkish politics especially concerning AK Parti and President Erdoğan's power. There are several reasons for this claim. First of all, once considered as champion of democracy for fighting against Kemalist regime's restrictive political attitude (Erdoğan was once imprisoned in Turkey for reading an Islamist poem), now President Erdoğan and his party represents authoritarianism in Turkey. President Erdoğan is even considered by the majority of people as the person who ordered the cancellation of the first

---

* Associate Professor in the department of Political Science and International Relations (English) at Istanbul Aydın University, Istanbul, Türkiye.
  Email: ozanormeci@aydin.edu.tr / ozanormeci@gmail.com.
  ORCID: 0000-0001-8850-6089.

election. Moreover, Turkish democracy is not doing fine in recent years due to increasing restrictive, authoritarian, and Islamist policies of the government. The main opposition party CHP on the contrary, is now considered as a hope for democracy with young and bright (culturally) conservative and (politically-ideologically) social democratic candidates such as Mr. İmamoğlu. CHP's hardliner secularist single-party years on the other hand are now considered as a historical period rather than a contemporary political issue by most of the people.

Secondly, Turkish political history teaches us that right-wing populist parties with charismatic leaders (Adnan Menderes' Democratic Party, Süleyman Demirel's Justice Party, Turgut Özal's Motherland Party, and lastly President Erdoğan's JDP) perform well as long as the economy is good, but once the economic downward trend begins, they can be easily dissolved or divided. Since Turkish economy is not performing well in the last two years, after the loss of Istanbul, the heartland of Turkish economy, President Erdoğan might not be able to keep his party and voters united. It should not be forgotten that the former Prime Minister and Foreign Minister from AK Parti, Mr. Ahmet Davutoğlu is ready for establishing his new party alongside with the previous President Mr. Abdullah Gül and the former Minister of Economy Mr. Ali Babacan. So, President Erdoğan has to keep his party and electorate solid and unified in the next few months in order to prevent a possible fragmentation.

Thirdly, since AK Parti's political power in Istanbul is partly based on social aid (distribution) system for needy people organized by the municipality, the loss of Istanbul might further decrease the party's popularity and electoral support. In any case, President Erdoğan has to stay confident and calm and should focus on new strategies for fixing the Turkish economy. President Erdoğan could also adopt a ultranationalist rhetoric in terms of the Cyprus Problem and the Eastern Mediterranean Question in order to keep his Turkish nationalist support alive (mainly the MHP-Nationalist Action Party). President Erdoğan might also try to rejuvenate his party by choosing new ministers and deputies.

According to the regular schedule, the next Presidential and parliamentary election in Turkey will be organized in 2023. However, the ongoing economic crisis and foreign policy troubles might force President Erdoğan to call for early elections before 2023. Moreover, CHP -long years after- for the first time now has a serious contender against Erdoğan. If Mr. İmamoğlu could perform well as the new Istanbul municipal leader, he could be a tough opponent against Erdoğan in the next Presidential election. I think CHP's current chair Mr. Kemal Kılıçdaroğlu could also endorse İmamoğlu in addition to Meral Akşener and her Good Party (İYİ Parti). So, Mr. İmamoğlu is now a potential Presidential candidate for the opposition concerning the next election. İmamoğlu showed his respect to Erdoğan after winning the election and said that he is ready to work with him in harmony. Erdoğan on the other hand accepted the defeat and congratulated İmamoğlu. This is a positive development for Turkish politics since politicians (especially Mr. Erdoğan) often use polarization methods.

Istanbul election showed once again Turkish people's support for democracy and proved that authoritarian political systems would not be stable in Turkey. That is why; I think Turkish people deserve more support from other democracies.

Ozan Örmeci[*]

New Political Party Initiatives in Turkey

Abstract This chapter deals with new political party initiatives in Türkiye led by Abdullah Gül, Ali Babacan, and Ahmet Davutoğlu, three former top figures of the governing AK Parti.

Keywords: *Turkish Politics, AK Parti, Recep Tayyip Erdoğan, Abdullah Gül, Ali Babacan, Ahmet Davutoğlu.*

As Turkey's economic problems deepen with the ongoing recession and the volatility in Turkish lira[1], dissatisfaction with the current political system increases both at the mass and political elite levels in the country. After securing a comfortable victory in the 2018 Presidential election against CHP's Muharrem İnce[2], AK Parti chair and President Recep Tayyip Erdoğan is now in difficult situation. Erdoğan has been able to keep its electoral alliance (*Cumhur İttifakı*) with the Turkish nationalist MHP solid until now; but this costs him loosing Kurdish votes and having more conflictual relations with other countries. It is not surprising that Erdoğan and his party lost a lot of votes and many municipalities in the March 31, 2019 local elections[3]. The negative trend was accelerated with the annulment of Istanbul's local election. In the repeated election, on June 23, 2019, CHP's mayoral candidate Ekrem İmamoğlu had an easier victory against AK Parti's Binali Yıldırım[4]. In addition to economic and foreign policy problems, nowadays President Erdoğan has to face with domestic political problems as well such as new political party initiatives organized by his former Ministers and close associates including the previous President of the Republic Abdullah Gül, former Prime Minister and Minister of Foreign Affairs Ahmet Davutoğlu and

*   Associate Professor in the department of Political Science and International Relations (English) at Istanbul Aydın University, Istanbul, Türkiye.
    Email: ozanormeci@aydin.edu.tr / ozanormeci@gmail.com.
    ORCID: 0000-0001-8850-6089.
1 https://www.reuters.com/article/us-turkey-economy-poll/turkeys-economy-to-contr act-in-2019-longer-recession-ahead-idUSKCN1RO19Y.
2 http://politikaakademisi.org/2018/06/24/Erdoğans-decisive-victory/.
3 http://politikaakademisi.org/2019/04/02/turkeys-2019-local-elections-ak-parti-lost-three-big-cities/.
4 http://politikaakademisi.org/2019/06/23/chps-ekrem-imamoglu-is-elected-Istanbuls-new-municipal-leader-again/.

former Economy Minister Ali Babacan. In this piece, I am going to explain recent political developments in Turkey in relation to new political party initiatives.

Due to rising reactions against the Islamist and authoritarian practices of the government and the new Executive Presidential (Executive Presidency) system (*Cumhurbaşkanlığı hükümet sistemi*), in fact two new political party initiatives are taking place simultaneously within the AK Parti right now.

The first political party initiative is organized by Turkey's former Minister of Foreign Affairs (2009–2014) and Prime Minister (2014–2016) Mr. Ahmet Davutoğlu. Davutoğlu was known as one of the leading thinkers of new generation of Islamists in Turkey in the 1990s. He worked in the International Islamic University Malaysia and taught Political Science. He later returned to Turkey and taught at Istanbul universities such as Marmara University and Beykent University. He also wrote in Turkish daily *Yeni Şafak*. He published his chef d'oeuvre *Strategic Depth* (*Stratejik Derinlik*) in 2001. With this work, he became one of the earliest geopolitical thinkers of Turkey. He advocated a more ambitious and more Islamist foreign policy strategy for Turkey in order to become a regional power. Thus, he was often called as *"Neo-Ottomanist"* or *"Neo-Ottoman"* (*Yeni Osmanlıcı*) although he never accepted this labeling[5]. He became an influential advisor to then-Prime Minister Erdoğan after AK Parti came to power in 2002. In 2007, *The Economist* called him as *"an eminence grise"*[6] due to his heavy influence over governmental decisions. He was the architect and mastermind of Turkey's *"zero problems with neighbors"* (*komşularla sıfır sorun*) strategy in the early AK Parti government years. In 2009, he became Turkey's Minister of Foreign Affairs. He tried to mediate the United States and the Islamic Republic of Iran -together with Brazil- on Iran's nuclear (uranium enrichment) program. Although he was the one who established Turkey's peaceful relations with its neighbors, due to strong waves of the Arab Spring, he later had to change his political stance and began to act together with Western powers against autocratic leaders such as Egypt's Hosni Mubarak and Syria's Bashar al Assad. During the Syrian civil war, at the beginning, he became a more influential political figure and Turkey's new Prime Minister in 2014. Together with President Erdoğan, he published Turkey's first letter of condolence to Armenia for the 1915 events in 2014[7]. He supported Turkey's bid for European Union membership and made a deal with Brussels concerning the situation of Syrian migrants with

---

5   https://balkaninsight.com/2011/04/26/davutoglu-i-m-not-a-neo-ottoman/.

6   https://www.economist.com/europe/2007/11/15/an-eminence-grise.

7   https://www.bbc.com/turkce/haberler/2014/04/140423_Erdoğan_1915_aciklama.

the hope of arranging visa free status for Turkish people visiting EU countries. He also supported the peace negotiations in Cyprus. However, due to Russian military intervention into Syria in the late 2015 as well as the emergence of ISIS, Turkey's foreign policy towards Syria became a matter of harsh international criticism after 2015. Thus, Davutoğlu had to resign in 2016 and was replaced by Binali Yıldırım.

After his resignation, Davutoğlu returned to academia. He taught International Relations courses in Japan and continued to think and write. He also made preparations for his new political initiative. On April 22, 2019, he published his first 15 pages manifesto in order to criticize the current political system[8]. After this manifesto, Turkish and international press began to publish news about his political actions by underlining his intention to establish a new (right-wing conservative) political party[9]. Few days ago, he made a speech in Elazığ and clearly showed his intention to set up a new political party by criticizing President Erdoğan's policies[10]. Although Davutoğlu is still a popular name among the Turkish Islamists/conservatives, due to Turkey's failed Syria policy, he was declared as the scapegoat by the government as well as the opposition. That is a major disadvantage for him. Aside from this, he has a large network among Turkish academics and he can easily set up a good team for policy-making. He also has close personal relations with important world leaders due to his long tenure in office as Turkey's Foreign Minister and Prime Minister. However, against President Erdoğan, still a strong, heroic, and fatherlike figure for Turkish Islamists, Davutoğlu might not have the best chance for the moment. Except for a few names, probably none of the current AK Parti deputies will join his party. So, it seems like his political party initiative might rather help the opposition (CHP and İYİ Parti) to have better chances against Erdoğan and AK Parti for now. But one thing is certain: Davutoğlu's political ambitions did not end and he will return to active politics soon.

The second political party initiative within the AK Parti is originated from Turkey's former Minister of Economy Mr. Ali Babacan. Previous President of the Republic Mr. Abdullah Gül also supports Babacan and guides him closely according to many sources. Ali Babacan was known as the most liberal and

---

8   https://medyascope.tv/2019/04/22/ahmet-davutoglundan-15-sayfalik-manifesto-cumhurbaskaninin-siyasi-parti-lideri-olmasi-sakincalidir/.

9   https://www.amerikaninsesi.com/a/davutoglundan-akpye-sert-elestiri/4885981.html ; https://www.bbc.com/turkce/haberler-turkiye-48148636.

10 https://www.bbc.com/turkce/haberler-turkiye-48816565.

"*occidentalist*" figure within the Turkish Islamist movement. He was educated in
METU and went to the U.S. on Fulbright Scholarship to make his postgraduate
studies. In 1992, he received MBA degree from the Kellogg School of Management
at Northwestern University with majors in marketing, organizational behavior,
and international business. He then worked for two years as an associate at
QRM, Inc. in Chicago, Illinois, a major financial consulting company in the
U.S. He returned to Turkey in 1994 and served as chief advisor to the Mayor
of Ankara. He was the chairman of his family owned textile company between
1994 and 2002. He became Turkey's Minister of Economic Affairs in 2002. For
many analysts, he did a very good job in implementing the IMF and Kemal
Derviş's plan to save the Turkish economy after the huge 2001 economic crisis.
Turkish economy boomed during this period. He also worked as Turkey's
chief negotiator (*başmüzakereci*) for Turkish accession to the European Union
between 2005 and 2009. He was praised as a sympathetic and polite person and
was resembled to Turkey's former Prime Minister Adnan Menderes (1950–1960)
because of his physical appearance. Later, he became the Minister of Foreign
Affairs during the 2007–2009 period by replacing Abdullah Gül who was elected
Turkey's 11th President of the Republic. Babacan became once again the chief
of Turkish economy between 2009 and 2015 as Turkey's Deputy Prime Minister
responsible for the economy. Turkish economy performed very well during this
period according to official statistics concerning the GDP growth rate, inflation,
and employment.

After 2015, he began to criticize the authoritarian orientation of the
government and gradually distanced himself from Erdoğan and AK Parti. His
outer position within the AK Parti coincided with Turkey's economic regression
after 2015 and increased his reputation as a successful statesman. He always
stayed close to Abdullah Gül and international finance circles. In July 2019, few
days ago, he resigned from AK Parti and began to work for establishing a new
political party[11]. *BBC* claims that he will start a new liberal-conservative political
party in this fall[12]. According to Abdülkadir Selvi, a Turkish journalist close
to governing party and its elite, Babacan now feels like his "*Macron moment*"
approaches after witnessing the success of CHP's young Istanbul mayor Ekrem
İmamoğlu[13]. In addition, Talat Atilla from *Milliyet* claims that, in case Abdullah

11 https://t24.com.tr/haber/ali-babacan-kurucusu-oldugu-akp-den-istifa-etti,829603.
12 https://www.bbc.com/turkce/haberler-turkiye-48784162.
13 https://tr.sputniknews.com/amp/turkiye/201906031039229580-selvi-imamoglunun-basarisinin-ali-babacani-umutlandirdigi-soyleniyor/.

Gül and Ali Babacan set up a new political party, 55 of current AK Parti deputies might join this party[14]. This might be an exaggerated guess; but this is certain: Gül and Babacan have more support within the AK Parti compared to Davutoğlu and there will be many deputies supporting this duo in case they start a new political party. It seems like Gül-Babacan duo can take more support from international financial and political circles as well due to their liberal and pro-Western stance.

Watching these developments posing -at least- potential risks to his power, President Erdoğan makes some warnings. Most recently, by referring to the party initiatives of Davutoğlu, Gül and Babacan, he said *"you don't have right to divide the umma"*[15]. However, President Erdoğan still seems confident and he thinks that he can manage this process by using his governmental power as well as his personal charisma and legitimacy in the eyes of Turkish Islamists.

Finally, although new political party initiatives (especially that of Gül and Babacan) have great potential, it should not be forgotten that Turkey's loyal right-wing voters change their preferences rarely. So, unless the governing AK Parti begins to give impressions of a breakdown, Turkish voters might not immediately prefer one of these new parties instead of AK Parti. Moreover, if these two separate initiatives will be somehow unified, Babacan, Gül, and Davutoğlu (right-wing opposition in Turkey) will definitely have more chances against Erdoğan. Lastly, all of these three important political figures make reference to Turkey's former parliamentary system that produced serious problems including three major coups (1960, 1971, 1980) and many economic crises (1994, 1999, 2001). It is a fact that Turkey's current Executive Presidential system is not the best example of democracy, but returning back to old parliamentary system might not be that reasonable or appealing for Turkish people. Thus, advocating a democratic Presidentialism like that of the United States or semi-Presidentialism like the French political system might be a better political rhetoric for the opposition. That is because Turkish society is very young and Turkish people always support new and untried alternatives in times of crisis.

---

14 http://www.milliyet.com.tr/yazarlar/talat-atilla/gul-beni-partiye-almiyorlar-dip-dal gasiyla-55-vekili-isaretledi-2795949.

15 https://www.bbc.com/turkce/haberler-turkiye-48932191.

Ozan Örmeci[*]

Current Situation of Political Parties in Turkey

Abstract This chapter is based on an analysis about approaching 2023 Turkish elections. The piece focuses on contemporary political developments taking place within the country.

Keywords: *Turkish Politics, 2023 Turkish elections, AK Parti, CHP, Recep Tayyip Erdoğan, Kemal Kılıçdaroğlu.*

Similar to other countries, due to Covid-19 (coronavirus) crisis, party politics have been forgotten for a while in Turkey. However, because of the strong political polarization in the country, the latest voting rates of political parties and the current approval rate of President Recep Tayyip Erdoğan are important indicators for understanding current state of affairs in the country. Meanwhile, although there have been discussions recently in the Turkish press about the possibility of an early Presidential election, I do not think President Erdoğan and his party (AK Parti) will be interested in calling for early elections in times of economic crisis mainly caused by the Covid-19 disease that literally slowed down -if not stopped- international economic activities. That is why; I think the next Presidential election will not take place until 2023, the 100th anniversary of the Republic of Turkey. A recent poll published by Istanbul Economics Research & Consultancy (*Istanbul Ekonomi*)[1] on the other hand underlines important domestic political developments in relation to Covid-19 pandemic, its complications, and the government's response to this crisis.

---

[*]   Associate Professor in the department of Political Science and International Relations (English) at Istanbul Aydın University, Istanbul, Türkiye.
      Email: ozanormeci@aydin.edu.tr / ozanormeci@gmail.com.
      ORCID: 0000-0001-8850-6089.
1   Official website at: https://researchIstanbul.com/.

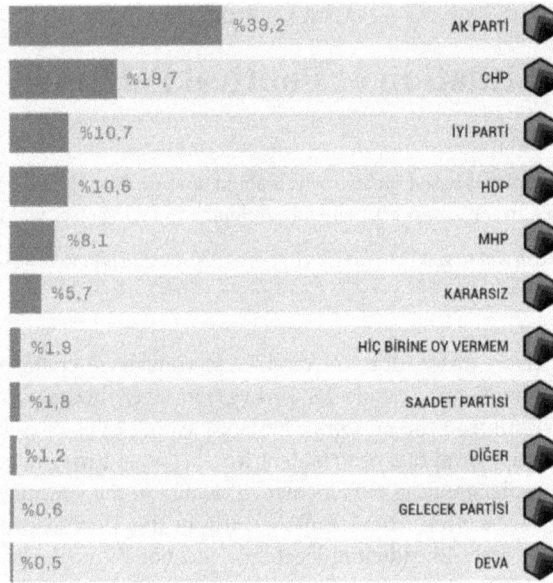

Turkish political parties' voting rates (May 2020)

According to information given by the company's General Manager Can Selçuki, a research was conducted on May 4–5, 2020 about the current voting rates of political parties with 1,537 participants from 12 different Turkish cities[2]. The research indicates that due to government's successful response to crisis, the governing AK Parti's (Justice and Development Party) voting rates increased from 35.8 % to 39.2 % in the last few weeks, whereas the main opposition party CHP's (Republican People's Party) votes fell to 19.7 %. Selçuki claims that since the Covid-19 pandemic created a chaotic environment with increasing fear and insecurity of the people, AK Parti government was able to increase its popular support with successful crisis management conducted by President Erdoğan and his successful Minister of Health Fahrettin Koca. Similar to Turkey, in many other countries as well (the U.S. and Brazil are two exceptions) existing governments were able to increase their popular support during this process[3]. The poll suggests that the Good Party (İYİ Parti) has still considerable support with 10.7 % of

---

2   For details, see; https://www.nethaber.com/siyaset/Istanbul-ekonomi-arastirma-sirk
    eti-son-anket-sonuclarini-acikladi-20826.

3   https://tr.sputniknews.com/aksam_postasi/202005081042000038-salgin-siyasi-partile
    rin-oy-oranini-nasil-etkiledi/.

the votes, whereas the Nationalist Action Party (MHP) is around 8.1 % for the moment. Pro-Kurdish HDP on the other hand has a popular support around 10.6 %. New political parties including Professor Ahmet Davutoğlu's Future Party (*Gelecek Partisi*) and Ali Babacan's Democracy and Leap Party (DEVA) have only around 0.5–0.6 % support for the moment, but Selçuki notes that this might be caused because of people's lack of knowledge about these new political initiatives since Turkish media does not give them enough chance to voice out their political views. According to this research's findings, in terms of Presidential election, AK Parti and MHP votes (*Cumhur İttifakı*-People's Alliance) reach 47.3 %, which stays a little short of the % 50+1 of the votes that is required to be elected in the first round for President Erdoğan. Opposition bloc (*Millet İttifakı*-Nation Alliance) on the other hand reaches 30.4 % of the votes for the moment; but it should not be forgotten that most of the supporters of the pro-Kurdish HDP and new parties also will be likely to support CHP's candidate in the next Presidential election. Thus, Nation Alliance's votes could be easily reaching over 40 % in the first round with considerable Kurdish support and increasing performance of the newly established political parties. This might secure a second round (in case there will be a strong third candidate) and anything is possible in the second round because President Erdoğan will be vulnerable for the first time.

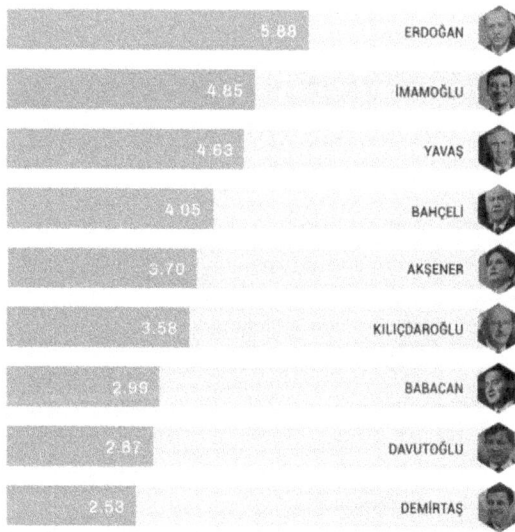

5.88	ERDOĞAN
4.85	İMAMOĞLU
4.63	YAVAŞ
4.05	BAHÇELİ
3.70	AKŞENER
3.58	KILIÇDAROĞLU
2.99	BABACAN
2.87	DAVUTOĞLU
2.53	DEMİRTAŞ

People's approval of Turkish political leaders

Another research[4] made by the same company on the other hand points out that President Erdoğan is still considered as the most successful politician in Turkey; but Istanbul Mayor (municipal leader) Ekrem İmamoğlu and Ankara Mayor Mansur Yavaş are following him at close distance and the gap is reducing between Erdoğan and CHP's new political stars. This might be a strong indicator for CHP in choosing its next Presidential candidate; so, either İmamoğlu or Yavaş could be Nation Alliance's Presidential nominee against Erdoğan while the party leader Kemal Kılıçdaroğlu could wait for return to Parliamentary system first in order to become Prime Minister.

Finally, in assessing these statistics, one should not forget that the effects of the global economic crisis caused by Covid-19 pandemic will hit Turkey hard similar to all other countries and the next months of 2020 will not be easy for the government in terms of economic performance. However, starting from 2021, if things will be returning to normal in full-scale, Turkish economy might have a good performance similar to the first quarter of 2020 (before the pandemic), during which Turkey had 4.5 % economic growth[5].

---

4   See; https://www.turkiyeraporu.com/sureklitakip.
5   See; https://www.bbc.com/turkce/haberler-turkiye-52856622.

Ozan Örmeci[*]

Early Projections for Turkey's Presidential Election

Abstract This chapter is an analysis about the approaching 2023 Turkish elections and it contains data from early public opinion polls about the possible results of the elections.

Keywords: *Turkish Politics, 2023 Turkish elections, AK Parti, CHP, Recep Tayyip Erdoğan, Kemal Kılıçdaroğlu.*

Turkish domestic politics is always dynamic and excited although the country has been passing through rather difficult times due to the Covid-19 pandemic and economic problems. In this context, it should not be forgotten that Turkey made a transition to hyperpresidentialism in 2017 via a controversial referendum[1] and Turkey's next Presidential election will determine who will be the ruler of the country on its 100th anniversary. That is why; the next Presidential election in Turkey is very symbolic and important for determining the spirit and the image of the country for the new (21st) century. In this piece, I am going to share some of my observations and projections for Turkey's next presidential election.

First of all, I should underline that the new political system Turkey adopted in 2017 transformed the post of Presidency almost into an "*elected God*" position with immense presidential powers and authorities that overshadow even the legislative powers of the Turkish parliament (Turkish Grand National Assembly-TGNA). Recep Tayyip Erdoğan, Turkey's Islamist originated conservative Prime Minister since 2003 and President of the Republic since 2014, became the 12th President in its history, but also the first President within the new Presidential system in 2018. Recep Tayyip Erdoğan now has the power of executive orders or decrees to make laws and even to ratify or abolish international agreements. For instance, recently Turkish President abolished Istanbul Convention with a

---

[*] Associate Professor in the department of Political Science and International Relations (English) at Istanbul Aydın University, Istanbul, Türkiye.
Email: ozanormeci@aydin.edu.tr / ozanormeci@gmail.com.
ORCID: 0000-0001-8850-6089.
[1] There are controversies about the referendum since the constitutional changes were approved by only 51.41 % of the people and opposition parties claimed that there were fraudulent activities during the election.

presidential decree. In that sense, the first thing to be stated about Turkey's next presidential election is that it really matters since the post of Presidency is now the highest post in the system and has immense powers.

Secondly, the adoption of hyperpresidentialism in 2017 led to the birth of bloc politics in Turkey. Turkey's governing AK Parti/AKP (Justice and Development Party) established the conservative-nationalist bloc of People's Alliance (*Cumhur İttifakı*) with the ultranationalist MHP (Nationalist Action Party), and the BBP (Grand Unity Party) before the 2018 Presidential election. As a response, Turkey's main opposition party, pro-secular and pro-European center-left CHP (Republican People's Party) established its own bloc of Nation Alliance (*Millet İttifakı*) with the center/center-right İYİ Parti (Good Party), Islamist Saadet Partisi/SP (Felicity Party), and the center-right Demokrat Parti/DP (Democrat Party). In the 2018 presidential election, People's Alliance won the election comfortably in the first round with Recep Tayyip Erdoğan's 52.59 % of the votes. Nation Alliance did not present a joint presidential candidate; so, CHP's Muharrem İnce took 30.64 % of the votes, whereas İYİ Parti's leader Meral Akşener garnered 7.29 % and SP leader Temel Karamollaoğlu took 0.89 % of the total votes. Pro-Kurdish HDP leader Selahattin Demirtaş on the other hand became a candidate for his party and took 8.40 % of the votes. So, after the failure of the opposition in 2014 to endorse a joint candidate (Ekmeleddin İhsanoğlu who took 38.44 % of the votes against Erdoğan's 51.79 % and lost the election in the first round), although this time the opposition tried to present more candidates to prevent Erdoğan to win in the first round, this strategy failed as well. This time it is still unknown whether the opposition will present a joint candidate or not. It seems to me that the opposition will again try to present many candidates in order to prevent Erdoğan to win the election in the first round. However, in case the limit for being elected in the first round is reduced to 45 %, the opposition parties might take risk and present a common candidate. 11th Turkish President Abdullah Gül could be an ideal candidate in that case. However, I do think that the Nation Alliance will not choose this strategy.

Thirdly, the timing of the election will be crucial. Normally, since the previous election was organized in 24 June 2018, the election should take place towards the end of June 2023, few months before the 100th anniversary of the Republic of Turkey[2]. However, since all sides want to take advantage of the situation and win this paramount election, President Erdoğan and his bloc might prefer to call for

---

2   The Republic of Turkey was established on October 29, 1923 by Mustafa Kemal Atatürk. This date is still celebrated with official ceremonies in Turkey as the "*Republic Day*".

an earlier election in 2022 or early 2023 if public polls would convince him that he could win in the first round.

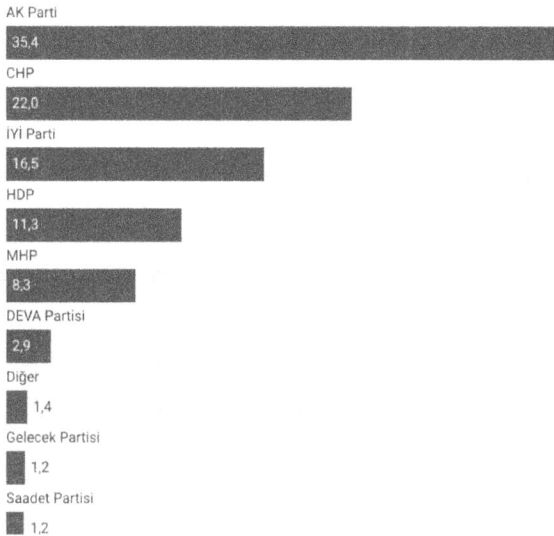

AK Parti
35,4

CHP
22,0

İYİ Parti
16,5

HDP
11,3

MHP
8,3

DEVA Partisi
2,9

Diğer
1,4

Gelecek Partisi
1,2

Saadet Partisi
1,2

Current votes of the parties

Fourthly, current public polls prove that the next presidential election will be extremely competitive and very tough. According to *Istanbul Ekonomi Araştırma*'s March 2021 study[3], the ruling AK Parti/AKP still has 35.4 % support (when the indecisive votes are also added), which should be considered as a success due to very difficult socioeconomic conditions in Turkey related to the Covid-19 pandemic and economic crisis. Erdoğan's partner Devlet Bahçeli's party MHP has also 8.3 % support, which makes almost 44 % support for the People's Alliance in total. The opposition (Nation Alliance) on the other hand seems to have equal chance this time with CHP's 22 %, İYİ Parti's 16.5 %, DEVA Party's (Ali Babacan's new party) 2.9 %, SP's 1.2 %, and *Gelecek Partisi*-Future Party's (Ahmet Davutoğlu's new party) 1.2 %, which makes around 44 % support in total. These numbers prove that the government bloc should do something to increase its votes towards 50 % to win the election in the first round. Since the

---

3   See; https://www.turkiyeraporu.com/sureklitakip.

second round of presidential election will be a totally new experience for Turkish voters, I think President Erdoğan should seek ways to win it in the first round. By the way, İYİ Parti's rise in recent months prove that Turkish people are open to alternatives and they primarily care about the trust towards the leader rather than ideological sharpness or consistencies (İYİ Parti is a populist center/center-right party with a strong and charismatic leader – Meral Akşener).

Fifthly, if we have to empathize with President Erdoğan, we can foresee that there will be important strategic political steps coming from the government in the next months. Obviously, President Erdoğan has to integrate more parties to his bloc in order to increase his support. The ideal party seems to be the SP, an Islamist party following the Necmettin Erbakan's "*National Outlook*" (*Milli Görüş*) tradition. Erdoğan already had a meeting with Oğuzhan Asiltürk[4], a very important name within this tradition although the party leader Temel Karamollaoğlu is against joining the People's Alliance. So, there could be a competition between the government and the opposition from now on in order to acquire the control of SP leadership. Erdoğan's decision to quit the Istanbul Convention in fact could be perceived as a way to impress SP voters since the SP is essentially an anti-Occidentalist political Islamist party. Erdoğan could also invite Erbakan's son Fatih Erbakan to his party, since the young Erbakan recently established a new Islamist political party, the New Welfare Party (*Yeniden Refah Partisi*)[5] that has the potential to steal some ten thousands of votes from Erdoğan's bloc in some conservative villages and neighborhoods. Recently, a former CHP politician Mustafa Sarıgül also established a new centrist political party, *Türkiye Değişim Partisi*/TDP (Party for Change in Turkey). Sarıgül gives warm messages to President Erdoğan[6] and he seems like he is interested in joining People's Alliance through political negotiations. Since all votes are important in a tight race, President Erdoğan and his party could make some strategic moves before the election.

Sixthly, I should admit that the opposition also has been implementing clever strategies to increase its votes. CHP leader Kemal Kılıçdaroğlu's tactic is simple but it is working; that is to support new right-wing parties that would decrease the vote of the governing bloc. Kılıçdaroğlu first helped the birth and the progress

---

4   https://www.cumhuriyet.com.tr/haber/Erdoğanla-gorusen-oguzhan-asilturk-aciklar sam-bolunme-olur-1809022.

5   See; https://yenidenrefahpartisi.org.tr/.

6   See; https://www.yenisafak.com/gundem/turkiye-degisim-partisi-lideri-sarigul-genel-merkezden-ak-parti-kongresini-takip-etti-3615195.

of the İYİ Parti in 2017 and now gives strategic support to two new right-wing parties; Ali Babacan's DEVA and Ahmet Davutoğlu's *Gelecek Partisi*. These parties are expected to support the Nation Alliance and they would obviously take votes mostly from either the AK Parti/AKP (Babacan's party and Davutoğlu's party) or the MHP (Akşener's party and Davutoğlu's party). Especially Babacan's party DEVA (Democracy and Leap Party) has a great potential if the AK Parti/AKP starts to fluctuate. In the meantime, although the CHP recently had a blow with the resignation of Muharrem İnce, who will soon start a new Kemalist political party called *Memleket Partisi* (Homeland Party), İnce's support for the Nation Alliance and the CHP's presidential candidate is almost guaranteed[7]. So, although İnce himself could become a presidential candidate and could take some portions of CHP candidate's votes, in the second round it seems like he and his supporters will endorse the CHP's and Nation Alliance's candidate. It should not be forgotten that İnce's rhetoric and speeches are very powerful and he could steal some votes from the governing AK Parti/AKP and MHP as well due to his nationalist/Kemalist political stance.

Seventhly, I think *"who will be the CHP's presidential candidate"* is going to be the most important question/factor for the result of the next presidential election. CHP leader Kemal Kılıçdaroğlu acts like a modest political guru and does not engage in complexness. He previously endorsed Muharrem İnce's candidacy in 2018. So, if the public polls show that CHP should definitely choose a specific candidate, Kılıçdaroğlu might not be his party's presidential candidate himself. His party already supports a return to parliamentary system and if the CHP candidate wins the presidency, Kılıçdaroğlu might try to become Turkey's Prime Minister within the new system. At this point, CHP has two strong candidates; Istanbul Mayor Ekrem İmamoğlu and Ankara Mayor Mansur Yavaş. While İmamoğlu is a pr (public relations) master and has a very good and clean image for both center-left, center-right, and Kurdish voters (he recently opposed to the banning of HDP as well), Yavaş comes from the MHP tradition (he has an ultranationalist background) and has an appeal towards the right-wing voters in Turkey. According to a recent study made by *Aksoy Araştırma*, both Yavaş and İmamoğlu could win against Erdoğan in the next presidential election; with Yavaş does slightly better than İmamoğlu[8]. In case CHP shows a weak candidate

---

7   See; https://tr.sputniknews.com/turkiye/202010291043118927-ince-millet-ittifakinin-icindeyiz-ama-bir-siyasi-partinin-yola-cikarken-ittifakla-yola-cikmamasini/.

8   See;   https://www.cumhuriyet.com.tr/haber/son-anket-geldi-Erdoğani-geciyorlar-1818848.

(not Yavaş or İmamoğlu), it is also possible that Meral Akşener might take the lead of the opposition and could have the second seat after Erdoğan in the first round of presidential election. In that case, whether Akşener could beat Erdoğan in the second round is very dubious. Yavaş and Akşener's biggest disadvantage is that they might not motivate Kurdish voters to go to polls against Erdoğan. İmamoğlu on the other hand has a better image and high chance concerning Kurdish voters. That is why; İmamoğlu could be the ideal presidential candidate for the opposition.

Lastly, I should state that the next Presidential and parliamentary election in Turkey will be about the spirit and the future of the country. If Erdoğan and his bloc wins, Turkey will be headed towards a more independent, but also more Islamist and nationalist future whereas if the opposition wins, Turkey will probably have a more democratic and Western-oriented future. I'm hoping that all sides and political actors will be respectful towards other groups' ideas, freedoms, and rights and will try to make Turkey more democratic, developed, and stable.

Ozan Örmeci*

Turkish Politics: President Erdoğan Needs A Miracle

Abstract This chapter contains an earlier analysis about approaching 2023 Turkish elections. The article focuses on contemporary political developments taking place within the country -including huge wildfires in the summer of 2021- with a particular focus on negative trends in Turkish economy and Turkish foreign policy.

Keywords: *Turkish Politics, 2023 Turkish elections, AK Parti, CHP, Recep Tayyip Erdoğan, Kemal Kılıçdaroğlu, 2021 wildfires in Türkiye.*

Introduction

Turkish people are passing through a rather difficult time these days due to disasters, economic problems, and unending political problems and disputes. The hottest problematic issue on the agenda is wildfires taking place in touristic villages. Starting from the late July, almost 163 different wildfires occurred in the Mediterranean and Aegean regions of the country. Among these, 154 were brought under control, but 9 other wildfires are still posing danger to people's lives as well as to the nature[1]. A total of three Turkish people died during the wildfires[2] and an enormous damage was done to the nature. These wildfires demoralized the whole nation and empoisoned people's short holidays during the hottest days of the summer.

The first and most notable wildfire started on July 28, 2021 in Manavgat, Antalya and burned down a great majority of the forests of this touristic location during ten days. Other important blazes took place in Muğla, Adana, Osmaniye,

---

*   Associate Professor in the department of Political Science and International Relations (English) at Istanbul Aydın University, Istanbul, Türkiye.
        Email: ozanormeci@aydin.edu.tr / ozanormeci@gmail.com.
        ORCID: 0000-0001-8850-6089.
1   *HaberTürk* (2021), "Türkiye yanıyor! Yangınlarda 8'inci gün", 03.08.2021, Date of Accession: 05.08.2021 from https://www.haberturk.com/turkiye-yaniyor-son-dakika-yanginlarda-7-nci-gun-iste-son-gelismeler-3151324.
2   *Haberler.com* (2021), "Yangında ölen var mı? Yangında can kaybı kaç oldu?", 30.07.2021, Date of Accession: 05.08.2021 from https://www.haberler.com/yanginda-olen-var-mi-14298184-haberi/.

Mersin, Kayseri, and Denizli. During the crisis, it was found that Turkey has only three fire-fighting aircrafts or tanker planes that are rented from Russia. Other three planes belonging to European countries (two from Spain and one from Croatia[3]) are also used with the permission of these countries[4]. It is hard to grasp for Turkish people to see that their state is not well prepared for wildfires although during each summer we have to face this reality. What it is more depressing that in fact Turkish Aeronautical Association (*Türk Hava Kurumu*) still possess six tanker planes, but the maintenance of these planes are neglected after Turkish government appointed a trustee (*kayyum* in Turkish) to the institution in 2019[5].

Turkish President Recep Tayyip Erdoğan's crisis management was severely criticized by the opponents. Opposition voices underlined that while Turkish Presidency has eight different jet planes[6], it is scandalous for the country to have only three tanker planes rented from Russia (Beriev BE-200s). President Erdoğan on the other hand blamed local municipalities of the regions where the wildfires took place and asserted that it was their responsibility to protect the nature against such dangers[7]. Since Turkey has a unitary system and the security issues are handled solely by the central authority, Erdoğan's defense seems groundless.

Conspiracy Theories

Turkish people and authorities in the country have begun to discuss many conspiracy theories about the wildfires recently. For instance, retired rear admiral and one of the leading theoreticians of Turkey's Blue Homeland (*Mavi Vatan*)

---

3 Hüseyin Hayatsever (2021), "Türkiye, 'yangın' konusunda AB'den yardım istedi, 'uçak' tartışmaları sürüyor ", *Cumhuriyet*, 03.08.2021, Date of Accession: 05.08.2021 from https://www.cumhuriyet.com.tr/haber/turkiye-yangin-konusunda-abden-yar dim-istedi-ucak-tartismalari-suruyor-1857425.

4 *Karar* (2021), "Türkiye'deki yangınlar neden söndürülemiyor? Türkiye'nin kaç yangın söndürme uçağı var?", 02.08.2021, Date of Accession: 05.08.2021 from https://www. karar.com/guncel-haberler/turkiyedeki-yanginlar-neden-sondurulemiyorkac-yangin-sondurme-ucagi-var-1627078.

5 *Ibid.*

6 *Sputnik Türkiye* (2021), "Fuat Oktay açıkladı: Cumhurbaşkanlığına kayıtlı 8 uçak var", 05.01.2021, Date of Accession: 05.08.2021 from https://tr.sputniknews.com/turkiye/ 202101051043511472-fuat-oktay-acikladi-cumhurbaskanligina-kayitli-8-ucak-var/.

7 *Cumhuriyet* (2021), "Erdoğan: Yerleşim bölgelerindeki yangın, büyükşehir belediyelerinin sorumluluğundadır", 04.08.2021, Date of Accession: 05.08.2021 from https://www.cumhuriyet.com.tr/haber/Erdoğandan-yangin-aciklamasi-sorumlu luk-buyuksehirlerin-1858027.

doctrine, Cihat Yaycı claimed that these wildfires are terrorist acts organized by PKK and Greece[8]. A Turkish expert on terrorism, Abdullah Ağar also pointed out that many different wildfires taking place simultaneously create serious doubts for an organized terrorist attack[9]. However, after the police investigation, it was found out that Manavgat wildfire was initiated by a 12 year old kid who has psychological (family-based) problems[10]. On the other hand, Demirören News Agency (DHA) published fake news blaming PKK for the wildfires that is later controverted by the Manisa Governorship[11]. Of course, PKK, as a dangerous terrorist organization could be one of the reasons of these wildfires. However, we have to wait for the police investigation and evidence before making such bold claims. It should not be forgotten that recently a Kurdish family was massacred in Konya in a hate crime[12]. This kind of news could agitate Turkish nationalists and lead to other provocative events in the country. Moreover, it should not be forgotten that Greece also suffers a lot from wildfires each year[13] and instead of blaming each other, Turkey and Greece could cooperate on such matters.

Another popular conspiracy theory in the country was about Turkish government's decision to allow these wildfires taking place for establishing new hotels and resorts to touristic locations. In fact, a new law entered into force these days giving the right to decide on the new settlements in forestland regions

8 *Ulusal Kanal* (2021), "Cihat Yaycı'dan flaş açıklama: 'İhmal falan yok devlet Yunan-PKK terörüyle karşı karşıya'", 30.07.2021, Date of Accession: 05.08.2021 from https://www.youtube.com/watch?v=QwzWf1oIsDQ.

9 *Haberler.com* (2021), "Yangınlar neden çıkıyor? Türkiye'de yangınların sebebi ne?", 03.08.2021, Date of Accession: 05.08.2021 from https://www.haberler.com/yanginlar-neden-cikiyor-turkiye-de-yanginlarin-14305123-haberi/.

10 *DW Türkçe* (2021), "Manavgat'taki yangını 12 yaşındaki çocuğun çıkardığı belirlendi", 04.08.2021, Date of Accession: 05.08.2021 from https://www.dw.com/tr/manavgattaki-yang%C4%B1n%C4%B1-12-ya%C5%9F%C4%B1ndaki-%C3%A7ocu%C4%9Fun-%C3%A7%C4%B1kard%C4%B1%C4%9F%C4%B1-belirlendi/a-58758463.

11 *BBC Türkçe* (2021), "Orman yangınları: Hangi iddialar ortaya atıldı, yetkililer ne yanıt verdi?", 03.08.2021, Date of Accession: 05.08.2021 from https://www.bbc.com/turkce/haberler-turkiye-58075222.

12 Hatice Kamer (2021), "Konya'da aynı aileden 7 kişinin öldürülmesiyle ilgili 13 kişi gözaltına alındı", *BBC Türkçe*, 30.07.2021, Date of Accession: 05.08.2021 from https://www.bbc.com/turkce/haberler-turkiye-58029461.

13 *HaberTürk* (2021), "Atina'daki yangın kontrol altına alındı: 12 bin 500 dönüm alan küle döndü", 04.08.2021, Date of Accession: 05.08.2021 from https://www.haberturk.com/yunanistan-da-dehseti-yasiyor-haberler-3152667.

to the Ministry of Culture and Tourism[14]. Journalist Murat Yetkin was the first person to point out this coincidence[15]. However, I do not think that Turkish government would do such a thing because the poor crisis management terribly affected the government and President Erdoğan in terms of popular support. President Erdoğan also denied this accusation[16].

What Is the Reason of These Wildfires?

Then, what could be the real reason of these wildfires? I think, although we should not speak confidently until the police provides concrete evidence, the probability of a terrorist attack towards Turkey is a reality. In each year we witness a few major wildfires in Turkey during the months of summer. But this year we have noticed an enormous rise as eight big wildfires took place by the early August. It is known that Turkey's successful military operations in Syria and Iraq and Azerbaijan's recent victory in the Nagorno Karabakh War disturbed anti-Turkey groups. However, we should be patient enough to find evidence before pointing out some groups as the responsible. That is because Turkey is fighting with a lot of different terrorist organizations (ISIS, al Qaeda, PKK, PYD/YPG, FETO) at the same time and many countries that are hostile to Turkey also support these groups.

Another reason could be the undeniable climate crisis that not only Turkey, but the whole world has begun to face with. For instance, climatologist Professor Levent Kurnaz from Boğaziçi University claimed that these wildfires are the natural consequence of global warming and climate crisis[17]. Kurnaz also

14 *Resmi Gazete* (2021), "TURİZMİ TEŞVİK KANUNU İLE BAZI KANUNLARDA DEĞİŞİKLİK YAPILMASINA DAİR KANUN", 28.07.2021, No: 31551, Date of Accession: 05.08.2021 from https://www.resmigazete.gov.tr/eskiler/2021/07/20210728-2.htm.

15 *Cumhuriyet* (2021), "Ormanlar yanarken yürürlüğe giren kanun tartışma çıkardı", 31.07.2021, Date of Accession: 05.08.2021 from https://www.cumhuriyet.com.tr/haber/ormanlar-yanarken-yururluge-giren-kanun-tartisma-cikardi-1856846.

16 *Hürriyet* (2021), "Son dakika haberi: Erdoğan'dan 'Yanan alanlar turizme açılacak' iddiasına net yanıt: Söz konusu değil", 04.08.2021, Date of Accession: 05.08.2021 from https://www.hurriyet.com.tr/gundem/son-dakika-haberi-cumhurbaskani-Erdogandan-gundeme-dair-onemli-aciklamalar-41866342.

17 Şükran Şençekiçer (2021), "SosyoPolitik (77) – Prof. Dr. Levent Kurnaz: 'İklim krizinde daha zor günler bizi bekliyor, hazırlıklı olmak durumundayız'", *Medyascope*, 01.08.2021, Date of Accession: 05.08.2021 from https://medyascope.tv/2021/08/01/sosyopolitik-77-prof-dr-levent-kurnaz-iklim-krizinde-daha-zor-gunler-bizi-bekliyor-hazirlikli-olmak-durumundayiz/.

underlines that there would be more difficult days in the future and Turkey should be ready for the climate crisis.

Foreign Help Not Wanted

Some Turkish people initiated a social media-based campaign during the crisis with the hashtag of "*#Help Turkey*". Approximately 2.7 million different tweets were shared on Twitter to create a global appeal and awareness. However, the head of Media and Communications of the Turkish Presidency (*İletişim Başkanlığı*), Fahrettin Altun showed a harsh reaction to this campaign by claiming that the real aim of social media activists is to present Turkey as a weak country to the world[18]. Moreover, the Office of the Chief Public Prosecutor in Ankara started an investigation for such Twitter posts[19].

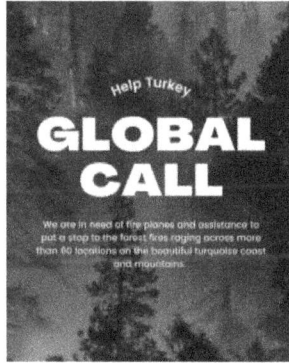

"Help Turkey" posts were considered as dangerous for the image of the country by some Turkish authorities

---

18 *SonDakika.com* (2021), "Fahrettin Altun'dan sosyal medyada başlatılan "Help Turkey" kampanyasına ilginç tepki", 02.08.2021, Date of Accession: 05.08.2021 from https://www.sondakika.com/haber/haber-fahrettin-altun-dan-sosyal-medyada-baslatilan-14303123/.

19 *Haberler.com* (2021), "Son Dakika: Ankara Cumhuriyet Başsavcılığı, "Help Turkey" başlığı altında yapılan paylaşımlar hakkında resen soruşturma başlattı", 05.08.2021, Date of Accession: 05.08.2021 from https://www.haberler.com/son-dakika-ankara-cumhuriyet-bassavciligi-help-14310197-haberi/.

Turkey's Struggle with the Covid-19 and Other Problems

Other than wildfires as well, Turkey has many problems during the summer of 2021. For instance, although the country has successfully launched a rapid vaccination campaign this year, by early August, the daily death toll reached 122 in addition to 26,822 new cases[20]. With these numbers, it will not be a surprise if the government takes another curfew decision in the near future. According to official statistics provided by Turkish Ministry of Health, more than 41.3 million Turkish citizens have received their first doses of Covid-19 vaccine, whereas over 27.8 million have been fully vaccinated[21]. Turkish State provides Sinovac (three doses required) and Biontech (two doses required) vaccines to its citizens. I should also add that thanks to the efforts of Turkish Minister of Health Fahrettin Koca, Turkish people consider the government's struggle with the Covid-19 pandemic as its most successful policy compared to its educational and economic policy during the crisis. Accordingly, by June 2021, 77.9 % of Turkish people consider the government's economic policy terrible, whereas 76.7 % of them also think the government's educational policy is also terrible[22]. However, the number of people who strongly condemn the government's health policy is only around 51.3 %[23].

Another major problem is of course the economy. The inflation in the country surpassed 17 %, which obviously reduces people's purchasing power[24]. In the meantime, the rapid depreciation of Turkish lira (TL) continues as U.S. dollar is now around 8.5 TL and euro is around 10.1 TL[25]. The rapid fall of Turkish lira is caused by political problems between Turkey and the United States after the Pastor Brunson crisis and Turkish President Erdoğan's insistence on low interest rates. This is another problem which makes Turkish people disadvantageous in

---

20 *Hürriyet Daily News* (2021), "Turkey reports 26,822 new coronavirus cases, 122 more deaths", 03.08.2021, Date of Accession: 05.08.2021 from https://www.hurriyetdailyn ews.com/turkey-reports-26-822-new-coronavirus-cases-122-more-deaths-153559.

21 *Ibid.*

22 *Türkiye Raporu* (2021), "Salgın Yönetimi Memnuniyeti", 30.06.2021, Date of Accession: 05.08.2021 from http://www.turkiyeraporu.com/arastirma/salgin-yonet imi-memnuniyeti-2-5144/.

23 *Ibid.*

24 Selva Demiralp (2021), "Enflasyon: Türkiye'de yıllık enflasyon yüzde 17'yi aştı, 'vahim tablonun' nedenleri neler?", *BBC Türkçe*, 03.05.2021, Date of Accession: 05.08.2021 from https://www.bbc.com/turkce/haberler-turkiye-56972702.

25 *Bloomberg* (2021), "Döviz Euro", Date of Accession: 05.08.2021 from https://www.bloo mberght.com/doviz/euro.

the international market. Moreover, the unemployment rate reached 13.9 %[26], which shows that the problems in the Turkish economy are structural. By the way, the unemployment rate among the youth is much higher.

Another major problem is the presence of millions of immigrants which could be easily pointed out as the scapegoat during the economic crisis. In addition to 3.6 million Syrian immigrants[27], recently immigrants from Afghanistan, where Taliban will soon seize the control following the U.S. withdrawal, began to attract Turkish people's attention and anger. While these people seem rightful in their fear of Taliban, of course, Turkey, with a stagnating economy, could not offer much to Afghan immigrants. Moreover, due to some irresponsible political statements, these people are open to racist attacks. U.S. and the EU's lack of help to Turkey in humanitarian matters also force Turkish government to take harsh measures.

Latest Polls about Political Parties

A recent poll conducted by the *Istanbul Ekonomi* in July 2021 shows that the support for AK Parti is now around 35.5 % and MHP votes are around 7.5 %. This makes the combined vote for the *Cumhur İttifakı* (People's Alliance) maximum 43 %, which would not be enough for an electoral victory in the Presidential election normally scheduled for June 18, 2023[28]. According to new electoral law, % 50 + 1 votes is needed for being elected either in the first or the second round. On the other hand, CHP's (23.2 %), İYİ Parti's (16.8 %), and *Saadet Partisi*'s (0.9 %) votes reached 41 % as part of the opposition bloc, the *Millet İttifakı* (Nation Alliance). Considering the fact that the other oppositional parties (DEVA, Future Party, pro-Kurdish HDP) will probably support the candidate of the Nation Alliance against the Erdoğan regime, it seems like President Erdoğan needs a miracle to secure another five years as the Turkish President. But since President Erdoğan is a genius of political strategy, we can say that it is not impossible, yet very difficult for him to win the next presidential election.

---

26 Hilmi Hacaloğlu (2021), "Türkiye'de İşsizlik Tarihi Rekora Yaklaştı", *Amerika'nın Sesi*, 10.06.2021, Date of Accession: 05.08.2021 from https://www.amerikaninsesi.com/a/resmi-issiz-sayisi-4-5-milyonu-asti-issizlik-tarihi-zirveye-yaklasti/5923524.html.

27 *Doğruluk Payı* (2019), "Türkiye'de Suriyeli Sığınmacılar", 24.06.2019, Date of Accession: 05.08.2021 from https://www.dogrulukpayi.com/bulten/turkiye-de-suriyeli-siginmacilar.

28 *Türkiye Raporu* (2021), "Sürekli Takip: Oy Oranları", July 2021, Date of Accession: 05.08.2021 from https://www.turkiyeraporu.com/surekli-takip/.

TurkiyeRaporu.com - Temmuz 2021

Bu Pazar genel seçim olsa hangi partiye oy verirsiniz? (%)

Kararsızlar Dağıtıldığında

AK PARTİ
| 35,5

CHP
| 23,2

İYİ PARTİ
| 16,8

HDP
| 11,4

MHP
| 7,5

DEVA
| 2,3

DİĞER
| 1,4

GELECEK PARTİSİ
| 1,0

SAADET PARTİSİ
| 0,9

Kaynak: Türkiye Raporu • Oluşturan Datawrapper

Current votes of the parties[29]

Moreover, President Erdoğan now might have to compete with a stronger competitor as the joint candidate of the opposition. According to actual polls, if the Nation Alliance would choose Ankara mayor Mansur Yavaş or Istanbul mayor Ekrem İmamoğlu, it will be almost certain for the opposition to win the election. Both Yavaş and İmamoğlu outscores Erdoğan more than 10 % difference in a potential second round election while nationalist Yavaş does slightly (1.1 %) better than social democrat İmamoğlu[30]. On the other hand, İYİ Parti leader Meral Akşener also seems more advantageous against Erdoğan, while CHP leader Kemal Kılıçdaroğlu still stays behind Erdoğan in a potential second round.

---

29 *Ibid.*

30 *Türkiye Raporu* (2021), "Cumhurbaşkanlığı Seçiminde Hangi İsimler Öne Çıkıyor?", 15.05.2021, Date of Accession: 05.08.2021 from https://www.turkiyeraporu.com/arasti rma/cumhurbaskanligi-secimlerinde-hangi-isimler-one-cikiyor-4477/.

Cumhurbaşkanlığı seçimi birinci turunda sayacağım adaylardan hangisine oy verirsiniz? (%)

	Cumhur İttifakı Adayı Tayyip Erdoğan	Muhalefetin ortak adayı...	Oy kullanmam
Mansur Yavaş - Recep Tayyip Erdoğan	38,1	52,5	9,4
Ekrem İmamoğlu - Recep Tayyip Erdoğan	39,9	51,4	8,7
Meral Akşener - Recep Tayyip Erdoğan	39,1	45,4	15,5
Kemal Kılıçdaroğlu - Recep Tayyip Erdoğan	44,2	39,4	16,4
Ali Babacan - Recep Tayyip Erdoğan	43,5	36,9	19,6
Ahmet Davutoğlu - Recep Tayyip Erdoğan	44,6	32,4	23,0
Selahattin Demirtaş - Recep Tayyip Erdoğan	51,7	24,5	23,9

Kaynak: Türkiye Raporu • Oluşturan Datawrapper

Potential presidential second round votings[31]

What's Next?

According to recent polls, almost 60 % of Turkish people (57.9 %) now support an early election[32]. However, if will not be a wise decision for Erdoğan and his partner and MHP leader Devlet Bahçeli to call for an early election during an economic crisis. It seems like the governing duo needs a new success story to increase their popular support. For several years, President Erdoğan has been working on the Istanbul Canal (*Kanal Istanbul*) project to establish an artificial sea-level waterway to Bosphorus in order to accelerate the maritime trade. It is written in the Turkish press that Chinese and Qatari firms are interested in the financing of this project. Although the project does not seem risky for the continuation of Montreux Treaty or against the international law, it is known that the project also includes the establishment of new buildings and residences

---

31 *Ibid.*
32 *Türkiye Raporu* (2021), "Erken Seçim Olmalı Mı?", 16.06.2021, Date of Accession: 05.08.2021 from http://www.turkiyeraporu.com/arastirma/erken-secim-olmali-mi-3-5088/.

around Bosphorus at the expense of destroying forests. Moreover, the population density in Istanbul (Istanbul has officially 16 million residents and it is one of the biggest metropolis cities in the world) will further increase if this project will be realized. According to a poll organized by *Istanbul Ekonomi* in June 2021, the support for this project is around 40 %, whereas 60 % of Turkish people are against the *Istanbul Canal*[33]. Another poll shows that, the biggest problem of Turkish people is now -by far- the economy. 33.9 % of Turkish people think the economy is their primary problem in addition to another 19.5 % who thinks the unemployment is the major issue in the country, which makes the economy - with 53–54 %- the only decisive political factor[34]. That is why; it seems like the only chance for Erdoğan is to create an economic boom in the next two years to win the election.

However, partnership with MHP is not an easy task. MHP is a small and very ideological (Turkish nationalist) party that has never garnered even 19 % in an election during the whole republican history. MHP has rigid stances on many issues including the Kurdish Question, the Cyprus Problem, Turkey-EU relations etc. Thus, Erdoğan now faces a dilemma as he wants to make new political openings, but could not do it for not losing MHP support. Erdoğan and Bahçeli could force new hawkish policies in Cyprus and the Eastern Mediterranean by making bolder steps than the current Varosha (*Kapalı Maraş*) opening. A potential annexation of North Cyprus could be such a move; but possible diplomatic/political, economic, and even military reactions from other countries perturb Erdoğan before making this decision. Since the Republic of Cyprus (RoC) is a member of United Nations and the EU, such a move would transform Turkey into a bandit state and will destroy its relations with the international system and especially with the Western world. In case there is support coming from Russia and China, this policy could be legitimized as Turkey could leave NATO and the Western bloc in return to the recognition of TRNC and the formation of a new security alliance with Russia, China, and Iran. However, both Moscow and Beijing do not afford to support Ankara in its Cyprus policy until now. Although it has special links with Turkish Cypriots,

---

33 *Türkiye Raporu* (2021), "Kanal Istanbul Projesi'ni Destekliyor Musunuz?", June 2021, Date of Accession: 05.08.2021 from https://www.turkiyeraporu.com/arastirma/kanal-Istanbul-projesini-destekliyor-musunuz-2-5128/.

34 *Türkiye Raporu* (2020), "Türkiye'nin En Önemli Sorunu Nedir?", 26.10.2020, Date of Accession: 05.08.2021 from https://www.turkiyeraporu.com/arastirma/turkiyenin-en-onemli-sorunu-nedir-1-1918/.

it is also highly questionable whether Iran could support such a policy and recognize TRNC as well. It should not be forgotten that, so far, even Turkey's closest allies such as Azerbaijan, Qatar, Pakistan etc. did not recognize TRNC. That is why; it seems like Turkish government should find other projects to improve the economy and increase its popular support rather than the very risky Cyprus annexation move.

Among the alternatives, President Erdoğan and his team now work on Afghanistan option to improve relations with the U.S. After President Joe Biden announced his decision to withdraw American and NATO forces completely from Afghanistan by paving a way for Taliban to seize control of the country, Erdoğan and Biden agreed on a plan to make Turkey active for the management of Hamid Karzai International Airport at Kabul. It is a fact that Turkish soldiers have more legitimacy compared to American or European soldiers for Afghan people and Taliban since they are Muslims and they do not try to invade Afghan territories. However, so far Taliban did not accept Turkey's plan to operate the airport safely without interfering into Afghan domestic politics. In case Erdoğan, Biden, and Taliban could agree on such a plan, Turkey could assume important responsibilities in Afghanistan and begin to improve relations with Washington, which will certainly have positive effects over the Turkish economy. Afghanistan is an important country for certain industries; most notably the opium production, which is used extensively in the drug (pharmaceutical) business as well as lithium resources.

Conclusion

Finally, if we analyze recent political conjuncture and public polls, we can conclude that Turkey has been passing through a very difficult period similar to 1999–2001 period. In 1999, Turkey had a terrible earthquake which devastated the economy and demoralized the whole nation. In 2001, a terrible economic crisis hit the country and Turkish economy was collapsed. In 2002, AK Parti and Recep Tayyip Erdoğan were elected as saviors after these traumatic experiences. With wildfires around the country and severe economic problems, the conjuncture resembles to that period; however, we should not forget that Turkey now has a hyper-Presidential system and President Erdoğan is a strong leader who never surrenders. Thus, it will be interesting to watch Turkish Politics from now on in order to observe President Erdoğan's new moves and policies. Moreover, there will certainly be new efforts to design the opposition bloc since now it seems like they are running for a victory in the next election.

Bibliography

BBC Türkçe (2021), "Orman yangınları: Hangi iddialar ortaya atıldı, yetkililer ne yanıt verdi?", 03.08.2021, Date of Accession: 05.08.2021 from https://www. bbc.com/turkce/haberler-turkiye-58075222.

Bloomberg (2021), "Döviz Euro", Date of Accession: 05.08.2021 from https:// www.bloomberght.com/doviz/euro.

Cumhuriyet (2021), "Erdoğan: Yerleşim bölgelerindeki yangın, büyükşehir belediyelerinin sorumluluğundadır", 04.08.2021, Date of Accession: 05.08.2021 from https://www.cumhuriyet.com.tr/haber/Erdoğandan-yangin-aciklam asi-sorumluluk-buyuksehirlerin-1858027.

Cumhuriyet (2021), "Ormanlar yanarken yürürlüğe giren kanun tartışma çıkardı", 31.07.2021, Date of Accession: 05.08.2021 from https://www.cum huriyet.com.tr/haber/ormanlar-yanarken-yururluge-giren-kanun-tartisma-cikardi-1856846.

Demiralp, Selva (2021), "Enflasyon: Türkiye'de yıllık enflasyon yüzde 17'yi aştı, 'vahim tablonun' nedenleri neler?", *BBC Türkçe*, 03.05.2021, Date of Accession: 05.08.2021 from https://www.bbc.com/turkce/haberler-turkiye-56972702.

Doğruluk Payı (2019), "Türkiye'de Suriyeli Sığınmacılar", 24.06.2019, Date of Accession: 05.08.2021 from https://www.dogrulukpayi.com/bulten/turkiye-de-suriyeli-siginmacilar.

DW Türkçe (2021), "Manavgat'taki yangını 12 yaşındaki çocuğun çıkardığı belirlendi", 04.08.2021, Date of Accession: 05.08.2021 from https://www.dw.com/tr/manavgattaki-yang%C4%B1n%C4%B1-12-ya%C5%9F%C4%B1ndaki-%C3%A7ocu%C4%9Fun-%C3%A7%C4%B1k ard%C4%B1%C4%9F%C4%B1-belirlendi/a-58758463.

Haberler.com (2021), "Son Dakika: Ankara Cumhuriyet Başsavcılığı, "Help Turkey" başlığı altında yapılan paylaşımlar hakkında resen soruşturma başlattı", 05.08.2021, Date of Accession: 05.08.2021 from https://www.haber ler.com/son-dakika-ankara-cumhuriyet-bassavciligi-help-14310197-haberi/.

Haberler.com (2021), "Yangında ölen var mı? Yangında can kaybı kaç oldu?", 30.07.2021, Date of Accession: 05.08.2021 from https://www.haberler.com/ yanginda-olen-var-mi-14298184-haberi/.

Haberler.com (2021), "Yangınlar neden çıkıyor? Türkiye'de yangınların sebebi ne?", 03.08.2021, Date of Accession: 05.08.2021 from https://www.haberler. com/yanginlar-neden-cikiyor-turkiye-de-yanginlarin-14305123-haberi/.

HaberTürk (2021), "Atina'daki yangın kontrol altına alındı: 12 bin 500 dönüm alan küle döndü", 04.08.2021, Date of Accession: 05.08.2021 from https:// www.haberturk.com/yunanistan-da-dehseti-yasiyor-haberler-3152667.

HaberTürk (2021), "Türkiye yanıyor! Yangınlarda 8'inci gün", 03.08.2021, Date of Accession: 05.08.2021 from https://www.haberturk.com/turkiye-yaniyor-son-dakika-yanginlarda-7-nci-gun-iste-son-gelismeler-3151324.

Hacaloğlu, Hilmi (2021), "Türkiye'de İşsizlik Tarihi Rekora Yaklaştı", *Amerika'nın Sesi*, 10.06.2021, Date of Accession: 05.08.2021 from https://www.amerika ninsesi.com/a/resmi-issiz-sayisi-4-5-milyonu-asti-issizlik-tarihi-zirveye-yaklasti/5923524.html.

Hayatsever, Hüseyin (2021), "Türkiye, 'yangın' konusunda AB'den yardım istedi, 'uçak' tartışmaları sürüyor ", *Cumhuriyet*, 03.08.2021, Date of Accession: 05.08.2021 from https://www.cumhuriyet.com.tr/haber/turk iye-yangin-konusunda-abden-yardim-istedi-ucak-tartismalari-suruyor-1857425.

Hürriyet (2021), "Son dakika haberi: Erdoğan'dan 'Yanan alanlar turizme açılacak' iddiasına net yanıt: Söz konusu değil", 04.08.2021, Date of Accession: 05.08.2021 from https://www.hurriyet.com.tr/gundem/son-dak ika-haberi-cumhurbaskani-Erdoğandan-gundeme-dair-onemli-aciklamalar-41866342.

Hürriyet Daily News (2021), "Turkey reports 26,822 new coronavirus cases, 122 more deaths", 03.08.2021, Date of Accession: 05.08.2021 from https://www.hurriyetdailynews.com/turkey-reports-26-822-new-coronavirus-cases-122-more-deaths-153559.

Kamer, Hatice (2021), "Konya'da aynı aileden 7 kişinin öldürülmesiyle ilgili 13 kişi gözaltına alındı", *BBC Türkçe*, 30.07.2021, Date of Accession: 05.08.2021 from https://www.bbc.com/turkce/haberler-turkiye-58029461.

Karar (2021), "Türkiye'deki yangınlar neden söndürülemiyor? Türkiye'nin kaç yangın söndürme uçağı var?", 02.08.2021, Date of Accession: 05.08.2021 from https://www.karar.com/guncel-haberler/turkiyedeki-yanginlar-neden-sondurulemiyorkac-yangin-sondurme-ucagi-var-1627078.

Resmi Gazete (2021), "TURİZMİ TEŞVİK KANUNU İLE BAZI KANUNLARDA DEĞİŞİKLİK YAPILMASINA DAİR KANUN", 28.07.2021, No: 31551, Date of Accession: 05.08.2021 from https://www.resmigazete.gov.tr/eskiler/2021/07/20210728-2.htm.

SonDakika.com (2021), "Fahrettin Altun'dan sosyal medyada başlatılan "Help Turkey" kampanyasına ilginç tepki", 02.08.2021, Date of Accession: 05.08.2021 from https://www.sondakika.com/haber/haber-fahrettin-altun-dan-sosyal-medyada-baslatilan-14303123/.

Sputnik Türkiye (2021), "Fuat Oktay açıkladı: Cumhurbaşkanlığına kayıtlı 8 uçak var", 05.01.2021, Date of Accession: 05.08.2021 from https://tr.sputniknews.com/turkiye/202101051043511472-fuat-oktay-acikladi-cumhurbaskanlig ina-kayitli-8-ucak-var/.

Şençekiçer, Şükran (2021), "SosyoPolitik (77) – Prof. Dr. Levent Kurnaz: "İklim krizinde daha zor günler bizi bekliyor, hazırlıklı olmak durumundayız"", *Medyascope*, 01.08.2021, Date of Accession: 05.08.2021 from https://medyascope.tv/2021/08/01/sosyopolitik-77-prof-dr-levent-kur naz-iklim-krizinde-daha-zor-gunler-bizi-bekliyor-hazirlikli-olmak-durum undayiz/.

Türkiye Raporu (2020), "Türkiye'nin En Önemli Sorunu Nedir?", 26.10.2020, Date of Accession: 05.08.2021 from https://www.turkiyeraporu.com/arasti rma/turkiyenin-en-onemli-sorunu-nedir-1-1918/.

Türkiye Raporu (2021), "Cumhurbaşkanlığı Seçimlerinde Hangi İsimler Öne Çıkıyor?", 15.05.2021, Date of Accession: 05.08.2021 from https://www.turkiy eraporu.com/arastirma/cumhurbaskanligi-secimlerinde-hangi-isimler-one-cikiyor-4477/.

Türkiye Raporu (2021), "Erken Seçim Olmalı Mı?", 16.06.2021, Date of Accession: 05.08.2021 from http://www.turkiyeraporu.com/arastirma/erken-secim-olmali-mi-3-5088/.

Türkiye Raporu (2021), "Kanal Istanbul Projesi'ni Destekliyor Musunuz?", June 2021, Date of Accession: 05.08.2021 from https://www.turkiyeraporu.com/ arastirma/kanal-Istanbul-projesini-destekliyor-musunuz-2-5128/.

Türkiye Raporu (2021), "Salgın Yönetimi Memnuniyeti", 30.06.2021, Date of Accession: 05.08.2021 from http://www.turkiyeraporu.com/arastirma/salgin-yonetimi-memnuniyeti-2-5144/.

Türkiye Raporu (2021), "Sürekli Takip: Oy Oranları", July 2021, Date of Accession: 05.08.2021 from https://www.turkiyeraporu.com/surekli-takip/.

Ulusal Kanal (2021), "Cihat Yaycı'dan flaş açıklama: 'İhmal falan yok devlet Yunan-PKK terörüyle karşı karşıya' ", 30.07.2021, Date of Accession: 05.08.2021 from https://www.youtube.com/watch?v=QwzWf1oIsDQ.

Ozan Örmeci[*]

A New Political Star in Turkey: Ekrem Imamoğlu

Abstract This chapter is about the rising star of Turkish politics; pro-secular CHP's Istanbul Mayor Ekrem İmamoğlu.

Keywords: *Turkish Politics, 2023 Turkish elections, CHP, Ekrem İmamoğlu, Istanbul.*

Introduction

As the Republic of Turkey's 100 years anniversary approaches, the struggle on the soul of Turkey intensifies with the rising competition in politics mainly between two blocs: the governing Islamist/conservative AK Parti (Justice and Development Party) and its undisputed charismatic leader Recep Tayyip Erdoğan and the main opposition party -pro-secular and social democratic- CHP (Republican People's Party) and its Istanbul Mayor Ekrem İmamoğlu. Although he is a relatively new figure in Turkish politics, with his recent Greece visit[1], İmamoğlu has become an important international political actor recently. It should be also noted that İmamoğlu is the Mayor of Istanbul, the biggest city and the economic capital of Turkey with 16–17 million population and it is not strange for him to attract attention especially remembering the fact that President Erdoğan was also the Mayor of Istanbul (1994–1998) before becoming

---

[*] Associate Professor in the department of Political Science and International Relations (English) at Istanbul Aydın University, Istanbul, Türkiye.
Email: ozanormeci@aydin.edu.tr / ozanormeci@gmail.com.
ORCID: 0000-0001-8850-6089.

1   To read some news related to this visit, see;

- https://www.ekathimerini.com/opinion/1168221/athens-and-Istanbul-can-do-their-part/
- https://tr.euronews.com/2021/09/21/ekrem-imamoglu-yunanistan-da-atina-belediye-baskan-ile-bir-araya-geldi
- https://greekcitytimes.com/2021/09/21/imamoglu-greek-turkish-friendsip/?fbclid=IwAR0GGmNJTrvS2krXppc6mRrBrv9mswXOF3Z17lHzAVpxm5Mmn50OzCYTTqk
- https://www.ekathimerini.com/opinion/interviews/1168204/a-mayor-with-a-big-dream-for-turkey/

Prime Minister in 2003. In this piece, I am going to summarize and analyze the life story and the political rise of Ekrem İmamoğlu and I will try to analyze his worldview.

Life Story of Ekrem İmamoğlu

Born in a small village of Akçaabat, Trabzon in Karadeniz (Black Sea) region in 1970, Ekrem İmamoğlu comes from a modest Muslim Anatolian family[2]. During his childhood, İmamoğlu was raised in Cevizli and Yıldızlı villages, typical small Black Sea villages with pious Muslim population dealing with agriculture and stockbreeding as economic activities. İmamoğlu attended to Quran courses at the age of 4 and learned to read Quran in Arabic. İmamoğlu's father Hasan İmamoğlu was a tradesman and his mother Hava İmamoğlu was a farmer. Ekrem İmamoğlu's father Hasan İmamoğlu was one of the founders of center-right Motherland Party's (ANAP) Trabzon branch in the early 1980s following the September 12, 1980 military coup. The 1980s was the peak of ANAP's and its leader and former Turkish Prime Minister Turgut Özal's power and İmamoğlu family was clobse to the conservative ANAP tradition. Young İmamoğlu was graduated from the Trabzon High School and played football (soccer) and handball during his childhood. Since the city of Trabzon is famous for its football club Trabzonspor which was very successful and popular especially in the 1970s and the 1980s, as a child from Trabzon, İmamoğlu became a Trabzonspor fan. İmamoğlu took his chance for the university examination and began to study in North Cyprus at Girne American University (GAU) Management department. But when his family moved to Istanbul, İmamoğlu continued his education in Istanbul University's Management department and was graduated from here in 1994 with a BA degree in Management (English). Later he also earned MA degree in Human Resources and Management from the same university. After the university, İmamoğlu engaged in construction business. Since many of the constructors in Istanbul comes from Trabzon or other Black Sea villages and his father already had business experience, he became successful in the construction

---

2   Ekrem İmamoğlu's biography can be read from these sites:

- https://en.wikipedia.org/wiki/Ekrem_%C4%B0mamo%C4%9Flu
- https://tr.wikipedia.org/wiki/Ekrem_%C4%B0mamo%C4%9Flu
- https://www.haberler.com/ekrem-imamoglu/biyografisi/
- https://www.bbc.com/turkce/haberler-turkiye-47751170

industry and began to earn more money. In 1995, he married with Dilek İmamoğlu. İmamoğlu family has three children; two boys and a girl.

Although coming from a conservative center-right family, İmamoğlu learned the basic principles of social democracy when he was a university student in North Cyprus. He later joined CHP in 2008 during the presidency of Deniz Baykal. He was elected the head of the party's youth branch in 2009. He was also elected by the party administration the district president of Beylikdüzü in the same year. His quick political rise within the CHP was materialized on the basis of his positive energy, charismatic leadership, and hardworking personality. Young İmamoğlu reorganized the party branch in Beylikdüzü and created a young and energetic team. Before the 2014 local elections, party's new leader Kemal Kılıçdaroğlu chose İmamoğlu as the municipal candidate and with a successful electoral campaign, İmamoğlu was elected the new Mayor of Beylikdüzü with 50.44 % of the total votes. He made Beylikdüzü the fastest growing district of Istanbul and created a good image with his tolerant personality and modern family. CHP leader Kemal Kılıçdaroğlu also liked İmamoğlu's style and he chose İmamoğlu for the Istanbul municipal race in 2019 although he was almost unknown at that time by the media and most of people outside Beylikdüzü and CHP. İmamoğlu's competitor was powerful Binali Yıldırım, the former (and the last) Prime Minister and former Minister of Transportation. However, young İmamoğlu and his team organized a very good campaign and established strong links with the untraditional CHP voters such as pious people and Kurds. Thanks to these efforts, in a very surprising way, İmamoğlu won the municipal election with 14,000 votes. However, the Supreme Electoral Council (YSK) later annulled the election. This made İmamoğlu the focal point of Turkish politics and in the second election a few months later, he won this time with 800,000 votes. Since 2019, he has been serving as the Mayor of Istanbul and doing good projects despite of black propaganda and prejudices. With his France visit in 2019, he began to show his skills in diplomacy as well and tried to attract European investors and debtors to Istanbul[3]. He later visited London, participated to a conference at the Chatham House, and met with the London Mayor Sadiq Khan[4]. Lastly, this week he visited Greece and performed a successful diplomatic effort during his meetings with Athens Mayor Kostas Bakoyannis and Greek

---

3   https://www.amerikaninsesi.com/a/ekrem-imamoglu-pariste-yat%C4%B1r%C4%B1m%C4%B1-gorustu/5106417.html.

4   https://www.aa.com.tr/tr/dunya/ekrem-imamoglu-londra-belediye-baskani-sadik-hanla-gorustu/1645845.

Prime Minister Kyriakos Mitsotakis. He is often pointed out as a strong potential candidate for the opposition in the 2023 Turkish presidential election due to his high popularity and support among the youth.

Analyzing İmamoğlu's Political Style

Ekrem İmamoğlu is a pro-European social democrat. But since he comes from a center-right family, İmamoğlu is also familiar with the pious right-wing voters and their cultural world. He is a very modern individual but has a modest personality and he does not make any discrimination against any social groups. He has considerable support among Kurds and Alevis; two important different ethnic/sectarian groups in Turkey. He has also a strong support coming from people who live in Karadeniz (Black Sea) region and Karadeniz immigrants in Istanbul. "*Hemşehri*" (countryman) networks are very influential in Turkish politics and İmamoğlu represents the Black Sea tradition -similar to President Erdoğan whose family migrated to Istanbul from Rize- within this perspective. He also comes from the construction industry, which is the vanguard economic sector in Turkey in recent years. Since Turkish cities and most importantly Istanbul need urban transformation/gentrification, İmamoğlu's experience in construction business could help him as a new political leader. Another support to İmamoğlu comes from Turkish Cypriots from the North Cyprus (or the KKTC/TRNC as a de facto state that is recognized only by Turkey) since he spent a few years there and established good friendships among Turkish Cypriot community. The leader of İYİ Parti (Good Party), which is in alliance with the CHP under the banner of "*Millet İttifakı*" (People's Alliance), Meral Akşener once described him as the Mehmed the Conqueror due to his surprising victory in Istanbul in 2019[5]. There is no doubt that he is the rising star of Turkish politics since 2019. His peace messages in Greece show the worldview of İmamoğlu, which could be shortly described as European type modern social democracy. Thus, we can confidently say that İmamoğlu is in favor of Turkey's full accession to European Union (EU). He also has no prejudices or hostilities against any state; he did not make any criticism towards the United States, Russia, China, or any other state until now. But his style makes me conclude that he is more pro-European compared to other political leaders in Turkey.

---

5   https://www.ekathimerini.com/opinion/interviews/1168204/a-mayor-with-a-big-dream-for-turkey/.

İmamoğlu's success in politics is based on his calm but stubborn personality. When his first victory was unjustly annulled by the YSK, İmamoğlu never gave up. He continued to check all ballots and results and made press declarations until the morning. Since he thought he was right, İmamoğlu never thought of retreating. In the end, Istanbul voters in June made him the new political star of Turkey. Renewing the election was probably President Erdoğan's biggest mistake in his whole political career because he created a very strong and popular competitor against himself. According to the actual polls organized by *Istanbul Ekonomi*, in a potential presidential second round election, İmamoğlu would defeat Erdoğan by 51.4 % against 39.9[6]. This shows the strength of İmamoğlu. In addition, İmamoğlu's style is very calm; in order to make him angry, the voters of other parties or pro-government journalists often ask him tricky questions[7]. But İmamoğlu each time keeps himself calm and never gets angry. He responds to all questions and reactions in a civilized and gentile way. However, İmamoğlu's views on Turkey's most important problems such as the Kurdish Question or the Cyprus Problem are still unknown. Thus, in case he becomes a presidential candidate, İmamoğlu has to prepare a detailed programme for such issues in addition to Turkey's economic problems. But one thing is sure: İmamoğlu has a great potential for becoming a strong and charismatic leader. So far there are only two books written for studying the phenomenon of İmamoğlu[8]. However, these books are more of a public relations effort rather than scientific analyses.

Conclusion

Finally, I think Ekrem İmamoğlu will be the opposition bloc's joint candidate in the 2023 Turkish presidential election. That is why, we need to research and understand İmamoğlu's views better and İmamoğlu has to set up an academic

---

6   https://www.turkiyeraporu.com/arastirma/cumhurbaskanligi-secimlerinde-hangi-isimler-one-cikiyor-4477/.

7   For some examples;

- https://www.youtube.com/watch?v=lUO0sdJ1D5s
- https://www.youtube.com/watch?v=gdagOOSnH70
- https://www.youtube.com/watch?v=Zv_BkCnw4v0

8   https://www.idefix.com/ekitap/ekrem-mamoglu-nu-tanyalm – https://www.idefix.com/Kitap/Benim-Sevgili-Baskanim-Ekrem-Imamoglu/Edebiyat/Biyografi-Oto-Biyografi/urunno=0001819745001.

team to govern Turkey. Because although ruling Istanbul is almost equally difficult as ruling Turkey, for sure, to deal with national politics instead of local politics, one has to develop himself in Political Science and International Relations as well.

Ozan Örmeci[*]

Turkey in Three Blocs

Abstract This chapter is based on famous Turkish intellectual Zülfü Livaneli's analysis on the high polarization level within the Turkish society.

Keywords: *Turkish Politics, 2023 Turkish elections, Zülfü Livaneli, Political polarization in Türkiye.*

Zülfü Livaneli, famous musician and novelist, several years ago wrote that Turkey was heading towards a great polarization between Islamists, Kurds, and Turkish nationalists[1]. Livaneli later revised his views and wrote that the polarization was taking place between Islamists, Kurds, and secularists[2]. Unfortunately, Livaneli's prediction became a self-fulfilling prophecy and in recent years polarization between three major blocs in Turkey have increased considerably. In this piece, I am going to explain three different electoral blocs in Turkey.

Although on the paper Turkey is a monolithic country with 99.8 % Muslim population, in fact there are different social groups and ethnic cleavages. First of all, around 19 % of the population has Kurdish origin and identity. In addition, among the Muslim population, a considerable portion consists of Alevis, a different and secularized Muslim sect.

The biggest bloc in Turkey is the Islamist-nationalist bloc that consists of various conservative, Islamists, and nationalist groups as well as center-right voters. This group appeals to nearly 55 % of the total population and historically acts as a unified force when there is a charismatic leader. The most important common denominator for this group is the Sunni-Islam identity. This group rules Turkey since 2002 with AK Parti (Justice and Development Party) coming to power and will continue to have high chances to win elections in the future due to its population density. But the problem for this group now is that the economy

* Associate Professor in the department of Political Science and International Relations (English) at Istanbul Aydın University, Istanbul, Türkiye.
    Email: ozanormeci@aydin.edu.tr / ozanormeci@gmail.com.
    ORCID: 0000-0001-8850-6089.
1 https://www.gazetevatan.com/yazarlar/zulfu-livaneli/chp-ve-uc-kutuplu-turk iye-18454.
2 https://t24.com.tr/yazarlar/zulfu-livaneli/uc-kutuplu-turkiye-gerceklesti,11527.

of Turkey is not going very well in recent months with the rising inflation and the devaluation of Turkish lira against U.S. dollar and euro. So, the ruling bloc of AK Parti and Turkish nationalist MHP (Nationalist Action Party) under the banner of People's Alliance (*Cumhur İttifakı*) might have difficult days ahead especially if they lose the next presidential election in 2023. One other key problem for this group is that due to MHP's Turkish nationalist rhetoric and policies, Kurds and even Islamist Kurds who supported the governing bloc against the secular establishment with the hope of establishing a more democratic moderate Islamist regime in the past now support the opposition.

The second bloc consists of various segments of secularists and it is differentiated from the governing bloc on the basis of people's secular lifestyles. Of course, Kemalist-social democratic CHP (Republican People's Party) is the leading party within this bloc. CHP appeals to social democrats, democratic socialists, secular liberals, Kemalists, and secular nationalists at the same time. Good Party (İYİ Parti) on the other hand is a new right-wing political party that strengthens this bloc by stealing votes from classical Turkish nationalist party, MHP. İYİ Parti is differentiated from MHP by its strong secular identity and opposition to AK Parti and Erdoğan regime. This group reaches 30–35 % of the population and in case they might choose a charismatic candidate who could appeal to Kurds and some groups within the Islamist bloc, they might rule Turkey for a while. Istanbul mayor Ekrem İmamoğlu for the moment seems to be the ideal candidate but due to CHP's insistence on parliamentary system, Mr. İmamoğlu might not want to become a temporary President who would give up from his powers. In that case, CHP leader Kemal Kılıçdaroğlu might become the presidential candidate of the Nation Alliance (*Millet İttifakı*). On the other hand, this bloc's biggest disadvantage is the existence of strong prejudices and opposition towards the authoritarian single-party era between 1923 and 1950 among the conservative and Islamist circles.

Finally, the third bloc consists of Kurds. Kurds were able to establish their own political parties since the mid-1990s and have become an independent political actor in recent decades. Although Turkish State repeatedly closed down pro-Kurdish political parties, Kurds each time were able to establish a new and stronger political party. This bloc appeals to approximately 15 % of total population having adopted Kurdish identity and culture. They made significant electoral gains with HDP (Peoples' Democratic Party) under the leadership of young and charismatic Selahattin Demirtaş, who is now imprisoned. Many Kurds in the past supported the Erdoğan regime and voted for AK Parti since the government was implementing the peace process. However, I think Kurds will now support the opposition since the peace process was collapsed and the government is getting more nationalist.

The leader who will govern Turkey has to be embraced by different blocs and should have a mixed identity. Strong secularist rhetoric might not be enough for winning the election like Islamist and/or Turkish only rhetoric. Turkey needs a new political rhetoric appealing to all different blocs similar to early AK Parti era.

Ozan Örmeci*

Could Mansur Yavaş become a Presidential Candidate?

Abstract This chapter is on the political background of CHP's Ankara Mayor Mansur Yavaş, a rising star in Turkish politics.

Keywords: *Turkish Politics, 2023 Turkish elections, Mansur Yavaş, CHP, Ankara.*

As Turkish economy suffers from high inflation and the devaluation of Turkish lira, the opposition's hope for replacing long-term serving President Recep Tayyip Erdoğan increases. In that sense, Ankara mayor Mansur Yavaş's name recently began to be stated as an ideal candidate. In this piece, I am going to evaluate whether Yavaş could be the opposition's joint candidate for the 2023 Turkish presidential elections.

The main opposition party in Turkey, the pro-secular and social democratic CHP (Republican People's Party), under the leadership of its chair Kemal Kılıçdaroğlu, follows a different political strategy in recent years. CHP, due to its historical alienation from the conservative/Islamic masses, tries to divide the governing bloc and to expand its support among the right-wing voters by engaging in electoral cooperation with new parties. Accordingly, CHP first established strong ties with the center-right İYİ Parti (Good Parti) and took the support of the party's leader Meral Akşener. This was followed by Islamist Felicity Party (*Saadet Partisi*) and center-right Democrat Party's (*Demokrat Parti*) inclusion to the electoral bloc *Millet İttifakı* (Nation Alliance). More recently, two new right-wing parties broke off from AK Parti, Ahmet Davutoğlu's Future Party (*Gelecek Partisi*) and Ali Babacan's DEVA Party also joined the bloc of Nation Alliance against the AK Parti-MHP-BBP's People's Alliance (*Cumhur İttifakı*) bloc. Nowadays, leaders of these six parties conduct negotiations for choosing the best candidate among the alternatives. Alternatives are limited; CHP leader Kemal Kılıçdaroğlu, CHP's Istanbul mayor Ekrem İmamoğlu, İYİ Parti leader Meral Akşener, and CHP's Ankara mayor Mansur Yavaş. Recent polls suggest

* Associate Professor in the department of Political Science and International Relations (English) at Istanbul Aydın University, Istanbul, Türkiye.
Email: ozanormeci@aydin.edu.tr / ozanormeci@gmail.com.
ORCID: 0000-0001-8850-6089.

that all of these four candidates would defeat Erdoğan in a potential presidential second-round.

CHP leader Kemal Kılıçdaroğlu seems like he wants to be the candidate of the bloc due to his long struggle against Erdoğan regime. He said that he would accept the presidential candidacy in case other parties' leaders propose his name[1]. Until recently, in a potential presidential race, Kılıçdaroğlu was performing poorly against Erdoğan according to polls. However, more recent polls suggest that he could win the presidential election against Erdoğan[2].

Another potential candidate is CHP's Istanbul mayor Ekrem İmamoğlu. By making a big surprise in Istanbul in defeating AK Party candidate and former Prime Minister Binali Yıldırım in 2019, İmamoğlu became the new star of Turkish politics in recent years[3]. According to polls, he could easily defeat Erdoğan in a potential second round of presidential elections[4]. However, since the opposition wants a return to parliamentary regime and aims to choose a President who would accept symbolic and limited powers, İmamoğlu might prefer a different career path and try to become the new leader of CHP and new Prime Minister of Turkey.

İYİ Parti (Good Party) leader Meral Akşener already stated that she would not contest in the presidential election and would try to become the new PM[5]. However, polls suggest that she could be a very lucky candidate against Erdoğan.

1 https://www.cumhuriyet.com.tr/turkiye/kemal-kilicdaroglundan-cumhurbaskani-adayligi-aciklamasi-1909662.
2 https://www.indyturk.com/node/466156/siyaset/gezici-ara%C5%9Ft%C4%B1rman%C4%B1n-son-se%C3%A7im-anketi-i%CC%87kinci-turda-k%C4%B1l%C4%B1%C3%A7daro%C4%9Flu-%C5%9Fansl%C4%B1; https://turkiyeraporu.com/arastirma/cumhurbaskanligi-2-tur-secim-senaryolari-6677/.
3 For my earlier analysis on İmamoğlu, see; http://politikaakademisi.org/2021/09/22/a-new-political-star-is-rising-in-turkey-the-story-of-istanbul-mayor-ekrem-imamoglu/.
4 https://turkiyeraporu.com/arastirma/cumhurbaskanligi-2-tur-secim-senaryolari-6677/.
5 https://www.bbc.com/turkce/haberler-turkiye-58686581.

Cumhurbaşkanlığı seçimlerinde sayacağım adayların ikinci tura kalması durumunda kime oy verirsiniz? (%)
turkiyeraporu.com - Şubat 2022

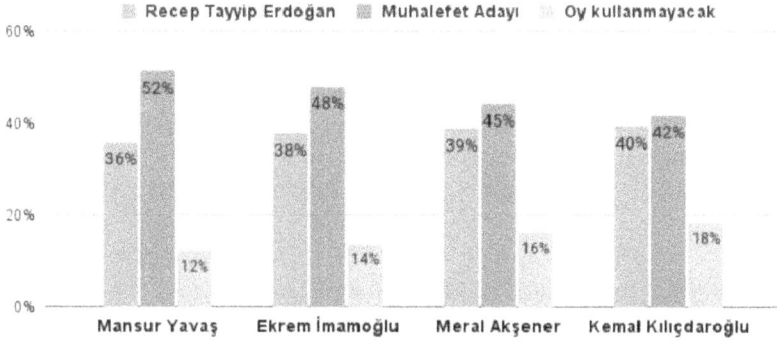

Yavaş is doing best among the alternatives according to polls[6]

According to polls, the best candidate among the alternatives is CHP's Ankara mayor Mansur Yavaş. Yavaş easily defeats Erdoğan with 52 % of the votes against Erdoğan's 36 % in a potential second-round according to *Istanbul Ekonomi*'s 2022 February research. Although Yavaş is not very mediatic and he rarely appears in tv programs, his image and reputation are very good among the public. Now let us look at the life story and political career of Mansur Yavaş.

Mansur Yavaş was born in 1955 in Ankara's Beypazarı district. He successfully graduated from Istanbul University's Law Faculty in 1983. Coming from a traditional family, he engaged in ultranationalist circles in his youth. After completing his mandatory military service as a military prosecutor, Yavaş returned to Beypazarı and began practicing law as a private attorney. Yavaş was elected a member of the municipal council of Beypazarı in 1989. He ran unsuccessfully for the office of the mayor of Beypazarı in 1994 from ultranationalist MHP (Nationalist Action Party). Yavaş continued his legal practice and council membership until 18 April 1999, when he ran again and was elected mayor from MHP with 51 % of the vote. In 2004, he increased his votes (55 %) and was reelected. He did a good job as Beypazarı municipal leader and transformed the underdeveloped district into a touristic destination. In 2009 local elections, he became MHP's candidate for Ankara municipality but stayed behind AK Parti's

---

6   https://turkiyeraporu.com/arastirma/cumhurbaskanligi-2-tur-secim-senaryolari-
      6677/.

Melih Gökçek and CHP's Murat Karayalçın with 27 % of the total votes. In 2014, this time he became candidate for Ankara municipality from CHP. Although he increased the party's votes considerably (43.8 %), he lost the election once again to Gökçek with a small margin. In 2019, he became CHP, İYİ Parti, Felicity Party, and Democrat Party's joint candidate (Nation Alliance) for Ankara for the second time and this time he defeated AK Parti's candidate Mehmet Özhaseki with 50.93 % of the votes against 47.12 %. Since 2019, he has been working as Ankara mayor and has a very good reputation for his hard work and honesty. Yavaş married Nursen Yavaş in 1986. They have two daughters: Armağan and Çağlayan.

Yavaş's name first proposed by anti-immigration and ultranationalist Victory Party (*Zafer Partisi*) leader and academic Professor Ümit Özdağ. Yavaş reacted to Özdağ by saying that he is not a candidate for the moment and the six parties' leaders will decide on the presidential candidate[7]. Although Yavaş underlines that he concentrates on his municipal projects, I think he could accept the candidacy in case six parties agree on his name. Yavaş could be an ideal President for the transitional period into parliamentary regime with his nationalist background. However, a problem might appear in case this would create disturbance among the far-left elements within the CHP as well as Kurdish voters. So far, pro-Kurdish HDP's (Peoples' Democratic Party) imprisoned leader Selahattin Demirtaş made encouraging remarks for Yavaş. He said that they will focus on principles rather than the name of the candidate[8]. However, a problem might appear if Yavaş's speeches during his youth as an ultranationalist politician might disturb and alienate classical CHP voters.

Finally, it seems like the opposition bloc will either choose Kılıçdaroğlu, Yavaş, or İmamoğlu as its joint candidate for the 2023 Presidential election. Since the 2023 election marks the 100th anniversary of the Republic of Turkey, the opposition should choose the best among the alternatives to bring competition to the election. However, I believe that President Erdoğan is still very strong among his bloc and this will not be a bird in the hand election.

---

7   https://www.indyturk.com/node/497486/haber/mansur-yava%C5%9F-%C3%BCmit-%C3%B6zda%C4%9F%C4%B1n-a%C3%A7%C4%B1klamas%C4%B1ndan-rah ats%C4%B1z-oldum.

8   https://www.cumhuriyet.com.tr/turkiye/eski-hdp-es-genel-baskani-selahattin-demir tas-kurtler-mansur-yavasa-oy-verir-mi-sorusuna-yanit-verdi-1924548.

Ozan Örmeci[*]

The Changing Status of Hagia Sophia

Abstract This chapter focuses on Turkish President Recep Tayyip Erdoğan's decision to convert Hagia Sophia Museum into a mosque after several decades and reactions coming to this move from other countries.

Keywords: *Turkish Politics, 2023 Turkish elections, AK Parti, Recep Tayyip Erdoğan, Hagia Sophia, Secularism in Türkiye.*

Introduction

After a court decision that made the 1934 Presidential decree made by Mustafa Kemal Atatürk void, Turkish President Recep Tayyip Erdoğan announced that Istanbul's famous and historical sanctuary and museum *Ayasofya* (Hagia Sophia)[1] will be used as a public mosque starting from July 24, 2020. Shortly after Turkey's Council of State (*Danıştay*) announced its long-awaited decision in favor of the possible status change, President Erdoğan immediately issued a decree and ordered the transfer of the management of the historic site from the Ministry of Culture to the Directorate of Religious Affairs *(Diyanet İşleri Başkanlığı)*, paving the way for its conversion[2].

Hagia Sophia

Built between 532 and 537 and completed in 537 in Istanbul's Fatih district, during the reign of the Eastern Roman (Byzantine) Emperor Justinian I, the

---

[*] Associate Professor in the department of Political Science and International Relations (English) at Istanbul Aydın University, Istanbul, Türkiye.
     Email: ozanormeci@aydin.edu.tr / ozanormeci@gmail.com.
     ORCID: 0000-0001-8850-6089.

1 For information about the historic building, see; https://muze.gen.tr/muze-detay/ayasofya; https://www.bbc.com/turkce/haberler/2016/03/160318_vert_tra_ayasofya; and https://en.wikipedia.org/wiki/Hagia_Sophia.

2 Isil Sariyuce & Emma Reynolds (2020), "Turkey's Erdogan orders the conversion of Hagia Sophia back into a mosque", *CNN*, 10 July 2020, Date of Accession: 14.07.2020 from https://edition.cnn.com/2020/07/10/europe/hagia-sophia-mosque-turkey-intl/index.html.

Hagia Sophia is historically a Greek Orthodox cathedral (church). During the Latin occupation of Istanbul (1204–1261), Hagia Sophia became a Roman Catholic cathedral for almost six decades, but turned into a Greek Orthodox church again in 1261. After the conquest of Istanbul in 1453 by the Ottoman Sultan Fatih Sultan Mehmet, the cathedral was turned into a mosque and served as mosque for many centuries.

However, after the establishment of modern and secular Republic of Turkey, Turkey's founder Mustafa Kemal Atatürk made a decision in 1934 to transform Hagia Sophia into a museum in order to give a peaceful message to the Christian world. A Turkish International Relations Professor Serhat Güvenç from Kadir Has University thinks that Atatürk's decision was meaningful and understandable; because Turkey was looking for international support and prestige in its early years especially after becoming a member of the League of Nations in 1932[3]. An experienced French observer of Turkish Politics Jean Marcou on the other hand claims that Atatürk's Hagia Sophia decision should be interpreted within the range of other modernization and secularization reforms including the banning of fez, the adoption of Latin alphabet, and the adoption of the equality between men and women with the Civil Law[4]. Hagia Sophia became the favorite touristic location in Istanbul over the years and has always served as a symbol for intercivilizational peace due to its historical significance both for Christians and Muslims.

The turning of Hagia Sophia into mosque again became a political controversy in Turkey first time in the 1950s with the renaissance of Islam during the time of Democrat Party and Prime Minister Adnan Menderes. In the 1960s and the 1970s, right-wing leaders including Süleyman Demirel and Necmettin Erbakan also made reference to social demands for such a move, but refrained to act due to sensitivities in the Western world. In 2016, the politicization of the issue increased with public prayers organized by Islamist groups outside of the historic building[5]. During the same year, Turkish Directorate of Religious Affairs appointed an imam to Hagia Sophia and a Friday prayer (worship) took place

3 https://www.youtube.com/watch?v=e5vXQPWLvP4.

4 Anne-Bénédicte Hoffner & Mélinée Le Priol (2020), "Sainte-Sophie, le rêve ottoman d'Erdogan", *La Croix*, 2 July 2020, Date of Accession: 14.07.2020 from https://www.la-croix.com/Monde/Moyen-Orient/Sainte-Sophie-reve-ottoman-dErdogan-2020-07-02-1201103106.

5 *CNNTürk* (2016), "Ayasofya önünde sabah namazı", 28 May 2016, Date of Accession: 14.07.2020 from https://www.cnnturk.com/turkiye/ayasofya-onunde-sabah-namazi?page=1.

after 80 years[6]. In that sense, one can claim that Hagia Sophia was already open to public prayer in certain days and in certain parts of the building.

The Decision

Before getting into a detailed political analysis, we have to carefully analyze the decision made by the Turkish Council of State[7]. The reason for doing this is that the methodology and reasoning of the law, which can be -many times- quite different from political argumentation.

First of all, the main argument of the complainant of this case (*Sürekli Vakıflar, Tarihi Eserlere ve Çevreye Hizmet Derneği*) was not about religious freedoms, but of the legality the earlier decision. The plaintiff basically claimed that:

1. 1934 decision was unconstitutional since the decree was not examined by the Council of State[8],
2. Even after the 1934 decree, 1936 registry of deeds records show that the building was licensed as a mosque, not as a museum[9], and
3. Although Hagia Sophia is presented as part of the UNESCO World Heritage, it is not stated in the official list[10].

Among these arguments, especially the third argument seems null since although it is not directly named in the list, the UNESCO World Heritage List makes reference to Hagia Sophia as part of "*Historic Areas of Istanbul*" in the 1985 decision. In fact, the list makes reference to Hagia Sophia at the entrance paragraph as follows: "*Historic Areas of Istanbul: With its strategic location on the Bosphorus peninsula between the Balkans and Anatolia, the Black Sea and*

---

6 *Sabah* (2016), "Ayasofya'da 80 yıl sonra ilk cuma namazı kılındı", 21 October 2020, Date of Accession: 14.07.2020 from https://www.sabah.com.tr/video/turkiye/ayasofyada-80-yil-sonra-ilk-cuma-namazi-kilindi.

7 The full transcript of the court decision can be read from here; http://bianet.org/bianet/diger/227263-danistay-in-ayasofya-kararinin-tam-metni.

8 Article 52 of the 1924 constitution states that the Council of State (*Şûrayı Devlet* or *Danıştay* with modern Turkish) has to examine the law draft before it turns into an act. See; "1924 Anayasası", *Türkiye Cumhuriyeti Anayasa Mahkemesi*, Date of Accession: 14.07.2020 from https://www.anayasa.gov.tr/tr/mevzuat/onceki-anayasalar/1924-anayasasi/.

9 Kenan Kıran (2020), "Ayasofya tapuda da cami", *Sabah*, 11 July 2020, Date of Accession: 14.07.2020 from https://www.sabah.com.tr/gundem/2020/07/11/ayasofya-tapuda-da-cami.

10 The list can be seen from here; https://whc.unesco.org/en/statesparties/tr.

the Mediterranean, Istanbul has been associated with major political, religious and artistic events for more than 2,000 years. Its masterpieces include the ancient Hippodrome of Constantine, the 6th-century Hagia Sophia and the 16th-century Süleymaniye Mosque, all now under threat from population pressure, industrial pollution and uncontrolled urbanization."[11]

The official 1934 decree[12]

The first argument also seems controversial since there is no proof that the Council of State did not examine the legal draft before it turns into a legal decision. Moreover, there is an official decree published by Turkish State in 1934 with the signature of Mustafa Kemal Atatürk, Turkey's then-President of the Republic.

---

11 The official page can be seen from here; https://whc.unesco.org/en/list/356.

12 Murat Bardakçı (2018), "Ayasofya Kararnamesi'nin altındaki "K. Atatürk" imzası gerçek mi?", *Habertürk*, 14 September 2018, Date of Accession: 14.07.2020 from https://www.haberturk.com/yazarlar/murat-bardakci/2141029-ayasofya-kararnamesinin-altind aki-k-ataturk-imzasi-gercek-mi.

Although there are claims about the authenticity of Atatürk's signature, since in 1934 President Atatürk was in full health, sane, and in charge of all executive affaires, I do not think there is a problem about legality of the earlier decision concerning the lawmaking technique.

Hagia Sophia's official record in the Turkish registry of deeds in 1936[13]

The most vindicating argument of the plaintiff is about the record of the registry of deeds and the court also approved this argument. 1936 record in the Turkish registry of deeds prove that Hagia Sophia was registered as a mosque, not as a museum. In that sense, the registry of deeds record paved way for the change in the status of Hagia Sophia by making 1934 decree null and void.

---

13 *Haber7.com* (2020), "İşte Ayasofya'nın Tapusu!", 11 June 2020, Date of Accession: 14.07.2020 from https://www.haber7.com/foto-galeri/63249-iste-ayasofya-nin-tapusu.

Political Analysis

Although Hagia Sophia controversy or Hagia Sophia case is primarily of a legal and technical matter, due to its political content and strong symbolism, a political science-based analysis is absolutely needed.

The first thing to be said, for sure, is about the symbolism and political message given to the world. I think President Erdoğan's immediate decision to change the status of Hagia Sophia from museum to mosque carries important political messages. These messages concentrate on Turkey's absolute sovereignty on its own soil, the strong presence of Islam as part of Turkish identity and Turkey's political system (although Turkey continues to struggle for staying as a secular state), and Turkey's increasing search for independence and multi-dimensionalism in its foreign policy. It is a fact that although Turkey has some political and economic problems, the country has boosted its self-confidence and has begun to make more unilateral steps in recent years. This is primarily caused by the reconciliation of pious masses with the state due to strong leadership of Turkish President Recep Tayyip Erdoğan, who is known as a devout Muslim and a political leader coming from a radical Islamist background. Poor Islamist masses and people coming from political Islam tradition for long decades were kept out of Turkey's state institutions due to fears of radical Islam taking the control of the secular state and decreasing individual liberties. However, as Turkey's population and economic problems increased, at one point it became impossible for the state to keep the status quo. In that sense, the peripheral elements (Islamists especially and Kurds in the early Erdoğan period) of the Republic became central political actors and the state was redesigned in accordance with this new sociological reality. The other option was unsustainable since a military coup like that of Egypt in 2013 was proven to be impossible in Turkey multiple times such as the February 28 process in 1997, the e-memorandum crisis in 2007, and the most recent failed coup attempt on July 15, 2016. So, President Erdoğan became the symbol of Turkey's Islamist transformation and established his cult leadership in the eyes of pious masses. Thus, Hagia Sophia move represents in fact the continuity in Erdoğan's political career in terms of doing things that were not done before by earlier Prime Ministers and Presidents. Erdoğan did similar bold moves in the past as well such as by resisting to military intervention attempts, defying the United States and Israel in the public (one minute crisis at World Economic Forum in Davos in 2009), conducting peace talks with the PKK, and openly criticizing Turkey's founder Mustafa Kemal Atatürk etc.

The second important thing is about President Erdoğan's success in following global political trends. While Erdoğan was once -in a world dominated by political leaders such as Barack Obama who represented change and promised peace to American people- ordering negotiations with the imprisoned PKK leader Abdullah Öcalan and was co-charing the organization of the *"Alliance of Civilizations"* with the then-Spanish Prime Minister José Luis Rodríguez Zapatero, President Erdoğan now feels like the political conjuncture is different and nationalism and unilateralism are on the rise. So, Turkey's recent political adventurism, bold military operations in Iraq, Syria, Libya, and increasing tough stance in the Eastern Mediterranean etc. show that President Erdoğan tries to unify Turkish people by creating some nationalist and Islamist causes. It is a fact that, although President Erdoğan's decision is not against international law, being part of UNESCO World Heritage List has certain requirements which might be more difficult to realize when Hagia Sophia will be open to public. So, as an important and very successful politician who senses things earlier, President Erdoğan thinks that the *zeitgeist* of the era is based on nationalism, particularism, and conservatism. In that sense, President Erdoğan is following the steps of other right-wing populist leaders such as Donald Trump (cancelling JCPOA deal, Paris Climate Accord, TTIP and TPP agreements and most recently withdrawing the U.S. from World Health Organization-WHO) and Benjamin Netanyahu (annexing Golan Heights, making plans for annexing West Bank), who are also making unilateral steps.

Thirdly, the Hagia Sophia move represents the dangerous escalation between Turkey and its Western allies in recent years due to many political disagreements. Unfortunately, Turkey has few allies left in the Western world including the United States. Moreover, it is not easy to solve problems between Ankara and Washington (U.S.) and Ankara and Brussels (European Union/ EU). While Turkey has severe disagreements with Washington in Syria (about the status and future of Syrian Kurds) and in the Middle East in general (relations with Israel, Iran policy etc.), Turkey's close relations with Russia also creates problems. Similarly, Turkey's already frozen EU membership process was recently overshadowed by rising Turkish-Greek tensions in the Aegean and the Mediterranean and Turkish-French hustles in Libya and the Eastern Mediterranean. The rise of Islamophobia and far right movements in European countries are also problematic developments in terms of Turkish accession to EU and Turkey's relations with European powers. Thus, with the Hagia Sophia move, President Erdoğan wants to show Western powers that they have to give some concessions to Ankara to keep within the right track and to sustain alliance based relationship.

Fourthly, President Erdoğan as a politician who tries to survive (read as getting reelected in politics), has to make some critical steps in domestic politics to keep his popularity and support. The emergence of two new right-wing parties in Turkey; former Prime Minister and Minister of Foreign Affairs Professor Ahmet Davutoğlu's Future Party and former Minister of Economy and Minister of Foreign Affairs Ali Babacan's Democracy and Leap (DEVA) Party are alarming signals for Erdoğan. So, as the hero of Islamist masses and a man of the people, President Erdoğan wants to reinforce his electoral support and consolidate right-wing conservative votes in the times of an economic crisis. The opening of Hagia Sophia to public prayer is a good gesture and a source of pride and joy for an average Islamist in Turkey, which would certainly increase the support of Erdoğan. It should not be forgotten that Erdoğan has always supported religious freedoms; he made the wearing of headscarf (*türban*) in public institutions and while making state (public) duties legal, removed the limitations against graduates of Prayer and Preacher Schools (*İmam Hatip Okulları*) in university exams, and restored many churches in Turkey[14].

Possible Consequences

The political consequences of the Hagia Sophia controversy are still unclear. It will certainly negatively affect Turkey's relations with the Western world (the United States[15], the EU[16], Pope Francis[17] and World Council of Churches also criticized[18]

---

14 The most famous example is the Bulgarian St. Stephen Church or the Bulgarian Iron Church in Balat, Istanbul.

15 *Ekathimerini.com* (2020), "US State Dep't 'disappointed' in Turkish government decision on Hagia Sophia", 10 July 2020, Date of Accession: 14.07.2020 from https://www.ekathimerini.com/254628/article/ekathimerini/news/us-state-dept-disappointed-in-turkish-government-decision-on-hagia-sophia.

16 Jonathan Stearns (2020), "EU Urges Turkey to 'Reverse' Hagia Sophia Reconversion Plan", *Bloomberg*, Date of Accession: 14.07.2020 from https://www.bloomberg.com/news/articles/2020-07-13/eu-urges-turkey-to-reverse-hagia-sophia-reconversion-plan.

17 *AlJazeera* (2020), "Pope 'deeply pained' over Turkey's move on Hagia Sophia", 12 July 2020, Date of Accession: 14.07.2020 from https://www.aljazeera.com/news/2020/07/pope-deeply-pained-turkey-move-hagia-sophia-200712151548612.html.

18 *BBC* (2020), "Hagia Sophia: World Council of Churches appeals to Turkey on mosque decision", 11 July 2020, Date of Accession: 14.07.2020 from https://www.bbc.com/news/world-europe-53375739.

Erdoğan's decision) and UNESCO[19], but I do not think it will create a direct political consequence. Rather, the image of Turkey as a country getting away from the Western world and secularism will be more widespread among decision-makers and also ordinary people. This might negatively affect Turkish economy as well; primarily the tourism and finance industries. Hagia Sophia controversy could also create a distance between Turkey and the Orthodox world including Russia, Turkey's both friend and enemy (frenemy) due to strong cooperation in economy, but political competition in Syria, Libya, Nagorno Karabakh etc. It would not be wrong to claim that President Erdoğan's decision could create sympathy among Muslim nations; but due to lack of democratic regimes in the Islamic world (with the exception of Tunisia), this might not turn into immediate political and economic gains for Ankara.

Conclusion

To sum up, Hagia Sophia controversy will make pious Muslims happy in Turkey for being able to pray in a historical place and also visit the place for free, but it will not help Turkey to develop better relations with the international community and especially the Christian world. It might also help President Erdoğan to keep his popularity among conservative segments; but I think the economic and political governance of the country will still be more important for average Turkish voters in the next Presidential election. So, this decision is a political move that has symbolic significance rather than severe actual political consequences.

Lastly, as an academic in favor of civilizational peace, I might suggest President Erdoğan and Turkish Directorate of Religious Affairs to make a special arrangement for this sanctuary; allowing Christians as well for Sunday prayers in order to give a peaceful message to the world. This will make Turkey a stronger country and will help Turkish government to show that they are in favor of religious freedoms, not religious hostilities.

Some cartoons depicting the changing status of the Hagia Sophia;

---

19 *SBS News* (2020), "UNESCO 'deeply regrets' Turkey's conversion of Hagia Sophia into mosque", 11 July 2020, Date of Accession: 14.07.2020 from https://www.sbs. com.au/news/unesco-deeply-regrets-turkey-s-conversion-of-hagia-sophia-into-mos que#:~:text=The%20Hagia%20Sophia%20was%20first,%22Historic%20Areas%20 of%20Istanbul.%22.

Source: https://i12.haber7.net//haber/haber7/photos/2020/28/musluman_cografyada_
ayasofya_coskusu_filistinli_karikaturistten_anlamli_mesaj_1594428459_3192.jpg

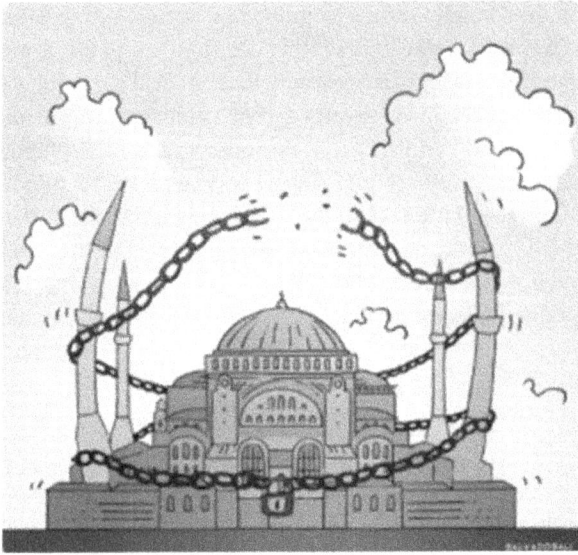

Source: https://cdn.yeniakit.com.tr/images/album/ayasofya-camii-karari-islam-dunyas
ini-sevince-bogdu-filistinli-karikaturistten-carpici-karikatur-afcdf5.jpg

Ozan Örmeci[*]

Caliphate Discussions in Turkey

Abstract This chapter is about strengthening Caliphate discussions in Turkish politics with the unstoppable success of Türkiye's Islamist President Recep Tayyip Erdoğan and his Islamist/conservative political party, the AK Parti.

Keywords: *Turkish Politics, 2023 Turkish elections, AK Parti, Recep Tayyip Erdoğan, Secularism in Türkiye, Caliphate.*

Introduction

After a court decision that made the 1934 Presidential decree void, Turkish President Recep Tayyip Erdoğan successfully converted Hagia Sophia (*Ayasofya*) into a mosque from a museum[1]. The decision was welcomed and celebrated with enthusiasm by the religious/Islamist circles in Turkey. First public prayer in Hagia Sophia was organized on July 24, 2020 and it turned into a gigantic political/religious show.

The Ceremony

The first Friday prayer at Hagia Sophia, which President Erdoğan and other top Turkish state officials participated, was broadcasted live from all Turkish tv channels. According to Turkish journals, a total of 350,000 people participated into the first prayer at Hagia Sophia[2]. However, only selected 1,000 people were taken inside the building for prayer, the rest of the population had to pray outside of the historic monument due to safety measures. In addition, a total of 21,353

---

[*]   Associate Professor in the department of Political Science and International Relations (English) at Istanbul Aydın University, Istanbul, Türkiye.
     Email: ozanormeci@aydin.edu.tr / ozanormeci@gmail.com.
     ORCID: 0000-0001-8850-6089.
1   To read my earlier analysis on the Islamization of Hagia Sophia, see; http://politikaak ademisi.org/2020/07/18/hagia-sophia-controversy-the-changing-status-of-the-histori cal-sanctuary/.
2   https://www.hurriyet.com.tr/gundem/akin-akin-ayasofyaya-350-bin-kisiyle-ilk-namaz-41572411.

policemen were on duty on that day for security reasons[3]. President Erdoğan recited Quran in Arabic himself during the ceremony[4].

The head of Turkey's Directorate (Presidency) of Religious Affairs (Diyanet İşleri Başkanlığı) Professor Ali Erbaş directed and delivered the first Friday *khutbah* (sermon). Erbaş ascended to the *minbar* (pulpit) of the mosque with a sword on in his hand, in order to revitalize the Ottoman tradition of *gaza* (conquest)[5]. Erbaş's choice of grabbing a sword and his speech took a lot of criticism from Turkey's opposition party figures including CHP (Republican People's Party) deputies Özgür Özel, Gürsel Tekin, and Mehmet Ali Çelebi[6] and İYİ Parti (Good Party) leader Meral Akşener[7]. Especially Erbaş's phrase *"Any property that is endowed is inviolable in our belief and burns whoever touches it; the charter of the endower is indispensable and whoever infringes upon it is cursed"* is largely understood as a heavy criticism towards Turkey's founder Mustafa Kemal Atatürk who gave the decision to turn the mosque into a museum in 1934[8]. Erbaş later made a public announcement and explained that his words did not target Atatürk[9].

Caliphate Discussions

The high media and public attention to the Islamization of Hagia Sophia led to the emergence of caliphate discussions in Turkey. Journalist Ruşen Çakır, who is critical of Erdoğan government's authoritarian and Islamist tendencies in recent years, said that Erdoğan's next step could be to bring back Caliphate[10]. Pro-government and Islamist journalist Abdurrahman Dilipak on the other hand

---

3 https://www.milliyet.com.tr/gundem/son-dakika-ayasofya-camiinde-tarihi-gun-86-yil-sonra-ilk-namaz-6267199.

4 https://www.duvarenglish.com/politics/2020/07/24/erdogan-recites-the-quran-at-hagia-sophia/.

5 https://www.duvarenglish.com/politics/2020/07/24/turkeys-top-religious-authority-head-delivers-friday-sermon-at-hagia-sophia-with-a-sword-in-hand/.

6 https://www.hurriyetdailynews.com/diyanet-heads-sermon-at-hagia-sophia-stirs-debate-156881.

7 https://www.sozcu.com.tr/2020/gundem/iyi-parti-genel-baskani-meral-aksener-grup-toplantisinda-41-5956448/.

8 https://www.hurriyetdailynews.com/diyanet-heads-sermon-at-hagia-sophia-stirs-debate-156881.

9 https://www.hurriyet.com.tr/yazarlar/ahmet-hakan/ali-erbas-vefat-edene-dua-edilir-beddua-degil-41572912.

10 https://www.youtube.com/watch?v=UescZSLFBPo.

supported Erdoğan and said that Muslims need and deserve to have their own spiritual leader (Caliph) similar to other faith groups[11]. In addition, Islamist magazine *Gerçek Hayat*'s (Real Life) cover stating "*Şimdi değilse ne zaman, sen değilsen kim? Hilafet için toplanın*" (If not now, when? If not you, who? Get together for Caliphate) created controversy and took a lot of criticism from pro-secular groups[12]. *Yeni Akit* tv moderator and experienced journalist Fatin Dağıstanlı also talked positively about the re-proclamation of the Caliphate[13].

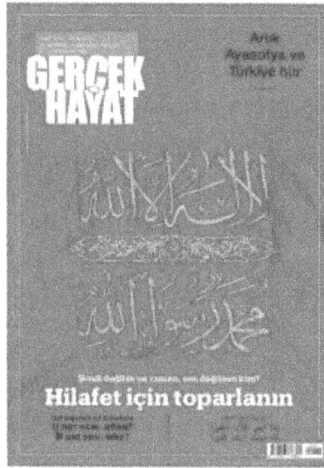

Gerçek Hayat magazine's controversial cover

President Erdoğan on the other hand denied claims about his intention to declare Caliphate and said that these malevolent discussions were created in order to overshadow the historical opening of Hagia Sophia[14]. Moreover, Communications Director of the Turkish Presidency Fahrettin Altun stated that they are against all sorts of radicalism and Caliphate discussions are

11 https://www.youtube.com/watch?v=BuA-x84gt_U.
12 https://www.haber7.com/guncel/haber/2999586-gercek-hayat-ne-yapmaya-calisiyor-provokasyona-tepkiler.
13 https://dokuz8haber.net/gundem/yeni-akit-bunun-arkasina-hilafet-gelmeli/.
14 https://www.youtube.com/watch?v=QchkMq4VS1c.

nonsense[15]. AK Parti (Justice and Development Party) deputy and Parliamentary Group Chairman Professor Naci Bostancı and party spokesman Ömer Çelik also rejected claims about their party's intention to bring Caliphate[16]. Furthermore, popular journalist Ahmet Hakan underlined that the proclamation of Caliphate would be almost impossible; since there will be other contenders from other influential Islamic countries such as Saudi Arabia, Egypt, United Arab Emirates, and Pakistan etc. as well and the Islamic world is divided into many different groups and states having different interests[17]. Erdoğan loyalist journalist and political commentator Abdülkadir Selvi also wrote that President Erdoğan is disturbed of Caliphate discussions by quoting Fahrettin Altun[18].

The History of the Islamic Caliphate

Caliphate comes from the Arabic term *"khalifah"* (*halife* in Turkish), the successor[19]. The term was used after the death of Prophet Muhammad in 632 in order to exalt his successor. After Muhammad, Abū Bakr (632–634), Prophet Muhammad's father-in-law was designated by Muslim elders as the Caliph since the Prophet did not leave any clear instruction about how to succeed him. A minority group later named as Shiites supported Prophet Muhammad's son-in-law Ali's claim to Caliphate instead of Abū Bakr, which became a turning point in the history of Islam in terms of sectarianism. Omar (634–644) replaced Abū Bakr as the second Caliph. Othman (644–656) was the third and Ali (656–661) was the fourth Islamic Caliph. However, upon the assassination of Ali, Mu'awiya (661–680) became the fifth Caliph and the Caliphate was acquired by the Umayyad dynasty in 661. The Battle of Karbala (680) during this stage further divided the Islamic world and polarized Shiites (Ali supporters) and Sunnis (Mu'awiya supporters). The Abbāsids, descendants of an uncle of Prophet Muhammad assumed the Caliphate in 749 and al-Saffāḥ (749–754) became the

---

15 https://www.trthaber.com/haber/gundem/iletisim-baskani-altundan-hilafet-tartism
    alarina-tepki-505475.html.

16 https://www.veryansintv.com/akpden-bir-hilafet-aciklamasi-daha-partinin-gundem
    ini-erdogan-belirler.

17 https://www.hurriyet.com.tr/yazarlar/ahmet-hakan/hilafet-gelse-kac-halifemiz-olur-
    41574256.

18 https://www.yurtgazetesi.com.tr/medya/selvi-erdogan-hilafet-tartismalarindan-h158
    831.html.

19 Summarized from https://www.britannica.com/place/Caliphate/The-Abbasid-caliph
    ate;   https://www.oxfordreference.com/view/10.1093/acref/9780191737275.timel
    ine.0001; and https://tr.wikipedia.org/wiki/Halifeler_listesi.

first Abbāsid Caliph. The Abbāsids dynasty lasted until 1258 when the Mongol invasion destroyed the city of Baghdad and led to the death of almost 800,000 inhabitants.

Descendants of the Abbāsids continued to keep their Caliph claim under the protection of Mamluks in Cairo, but the Islamic world stayed largely divided until 1517, when Ottoman Sultan Selim I (Selim the Grim or Selim the Resolute, Yavuz Sultan Selim in Turkish) conquered Egypt. However, until the 18th and 19th centuries, the Caliphate was not effectively used by the Ottoman Sultans politically. Starting from the 18th century, with the decline of the Ottoman statecraft, Ottoman Sultans began to use their Caliph title more often in order to increase their influence over Muslim population. Especially in the late 19th century, during the reign of Abdul Hamid II or Abdulhamid II (1876–1909), pan-Islamism became the official ideology of the Ottoman throne and the Caliphate title was tried to be used efficiently in order to survive against European imperial powers including England, France, and Russia.

The Caliphate was abolished after the emergence of modern Turkey. Mustafa Kemal Atatürk, the savior and founder of modern Turkey, saw Caliphate as an obsolete institution that is not in conformity with the global trends (the spirit of modernity, increasing nationalism, and the emergence of new nation states around the world). Atatürk also established Directorate of Religious Affairs in 1924 in order to provide religious services to people within a secular state. However, Turkish type *laicité* was based on the control of religion and religious movements by the state as opposed to American secularism that is based on complete separation of the state and religion including even the funding of religious services. Thus, opposing to strict state control, some conservative/Islamist groups in Turkey began to advocate a more libertarian state policy starting from the early days of the Republic, whereas secularists were also unhappy of the allocation of state resources to imams and religious services. Islamists gradually gained power after Turkey's transition into multi-party democracy in 1950 and in the mid-1990s, with the Welfare Party (*Refah Partisi*)-True Path Party (*Doğru Yol Partisi*) coalition government (*Refahyol*), Necmettin Erbakan became the first Islamist Prime Minister of Turkey. After Erbakan, his disciple Recep Tayyip Erdoğan took office in 2003 and so far continued to rule Turkey as the leader of AK Parti. Erdoğan was able to create a larger space for Islam and Islamists people within the system by removing the headscarf ban in universities and public institutions and by allowing the graduates of Prayer and Preacher Schools (*İmam Hatip Okulları*) to be employed everywhere. Hagia Sophia move was the last big step of Islamization for Erdoğan. However, for many, it was just a symbolic move and was made for domestic political purposes (more public support).

The efforts of reestablishing Caliphate in the Islamic world persisted although Turkey was able to stay away from these discussions thanks to its strong secular tradition. Political Islamist movements such as the Muslim Brotherhood (*Ikhwan*) in Egypt proposed ideas for the proclamation of Caliphate. In Iran, Shiites were able to establish their religious leadership (called the Supreme Leader) after the Islamic Revolution of 1979. After Ruhollah Khomeini (1979–1989), Ali Khamenei (1989–) is Iran's current Supreme Leader. Starting from the early 2000s, some of the leaders of radical Islamic terrorist organizations such as Al-Qaeda and ISIS (IS, ISIL or DAESH) also declared their Caliphate. Abu Bakr al-Baghdadi, the leader of ISIS, who was killed by American military forces in 2019 for instance, was a self-declared Caliph in the Islamic world. The success of anti-American and radical terrorist groups in using the Caliphate issue in gathering and recruiting terrorists around the world by brainwashing them, led to the popular discussions in the Islamic world about whether the Caliphate should be reestablished by intellectual people who defend peaceful methods and peaceful coexistence with people from other religions.

The Abolition of Caliphate in Turkey

Under the leadership of Mustafa Kemal Atatürk, Turkey successfully conducted its Independence War (1919–1922) against the invading Greek Army in Anatolia. The first constitution adopted by Atatürk and his parliament (Turkish Grand National Assembly), the 1921 constitution (*Teşkilât-ı Esasiye Kanunu*)[20] underlined the importance of popular with its first Article stating; "*Sovereignty is vested in the nation without condition*". However, there was not any regulation concerning the Caliphate within the short (composed of only 23 Articles) constitution. In fact, with the revision made in the constitution in 1923, the official religion of the state was stated as Islam[21]. However, on October 30, 1922, Atatürk and his parliament legislated a bill named "*Türkiye Büyük Millet Meclisi'nin, hukuku hâkimiyet ve hükümraninin mümessili hakikisi olduğuna dair*" (law no 308) that allowed the separation of the Sultanate from the Caliphate. The next day, the Ottoman Crown Prince Abdulmejid II (II. Abdülmecid) was

---

20 https://anayasa.tbmm.gov.tr/docs/1921/1921ilkmetin/1921-ilkhali.pdf.
21 https://anayasa.tbmm.gov.tr/docs/1921/1921-2/1921-2.pdf.

elected the last Ottoman Caliph by the parliament instead of his deposed cousin Mehmed VI Vahideddin (Sultan Vahdettin).

After Atatürk's declaration of a Republic on October 29, 1923, a new constitution was prepared and accepted by the TGNA. The 1924 Constitution[22] repeated in the Article 2 that *"the official religion of the state is Islam"* and did not contain any specific Article about the Caliphate or secularism. However, with a law (no 481) legislated by the parliament in 1924, the Caliphate was abolished[23]. The first Article of the law stated that *"The Caliph is deposed and the Caliphate is abolished since it is already present within the meaning and concept of the government and the Republic"* (Halife haledilmiştir. Hilâfet, Hükümet ve Cumhuriyet mâna ve mefhumunda esasen mündemiç olduğundan hilâfet makamı mülgadır). This was a bit controversial and vague statement that allowed Political Islamists to claim that the Parliament has right to claim Caliphate. However, in 1928, a revision was made within the Article 2 of the 1924 Constitution and *"Islam is the official religion of the state"* statement was removed[24]. Moreover, in 1937, secularism (*laiklik*) was added to the Article 1 of the constitution as part of the *"Six Principles"* of Atatürk (*Türkiye Devleti, cumhuriyetçi, milliyetçi, halkçı, Devletçi, lâik ve inkılâbçıdır*)[25]. So, Turkey constitutionally outlawed the post of the Caliphate and Turkey's subsequent constitutions (1961 and 1982 constitutions) also kept secularism as a safeguard against radical Islamist movements with the Article 2 within the constitution. In fact, the 1982 constitution made secularism even an unchangeable principle with the Article 4 stating that *"The provision of Article 1 regarding the form of the State being a Republic, the characteristics of the Republic in Article 2, and the provisions of Article 3 shall not be amended, nor shall their amendment be proposed."*[26] Thus, defending Caliphate in Turkey is unconstitutional and unlawful.

---

22 For the original constitution; https://anayasa.tbmm.gov.tr/docs/1924/1924-ilkhali/1924-ilkhali.pdf.

23 Full name of the law was "Hilafetin ilgasına ve Hanedanı Osmaninin Türkiye Cumhuriyeti nıemaliki haricine çıkarılmasına dair kanun". To read the bill; https://www.tbmm.gov.tr/tutanaklar/KANUNLAR_KARARLAR/kanuntbmmc002/kanuntbmmc002/kanuntbmmc00200431.pdf.

24 https://anayasa.tbmm.gov.tr/docs/1924/1924-1/1924-1.pdf.

25 https://anayasa.tbmm.gov.tr/docs/1924/1924-4/4-degisiklik.pdf.

26 https://global.tbmm.gov.tr/docs/constitution_en.pdf.

Caliphate in the Modern World: Absurd or Necessary?

We can categorize the views stated for the caliphate discussions into two main categories. Those who are in favor of the Caliphate point out the lack of leadership in the Islamic world, which leads to radical groups such as Al-Qaeda and ISIS to grasp power and negatively direct and represent Muslims around the world. It is a fact that people who are following these radical groups and their extremist leaders are often poor and uneducated young Muslims who are deprived of modern life conditions and adequate education. These people claim that, with a good spiritual leadership, Muslims could be better directed and radicalism can be curbed. However, this view is still largely seen in the Western world including Turkey as dangerous and radical.

The second view is the secular approach that asserts that the post of Caliphate does not belong to modern world and even discussing it is absurd. Supporters of this view claim that, similar to the emergence of Protestantism and the gradual secularization of European nations afterwards, Islamic world needs more individualism and secularism rather than religious authorities and indoctrination. Moreover, these people also underline that the religious leadership battles between influential Muslim states such as Turkey, Saudi Arabia, and Egypt could lead to further problems in the Islamic world. For instance, Mustafa Akyol, a young political commentator who tries to develop a secular and liberal interpretation of Political Islam claims that, "*Caliphate is not a 'requirement of Islam', but a 'historical experience of Muslims'*" and "*Today, it can't bring any good. Instead, it can bring more intra-Muslim conflict on who 'the real Caliph' is.*"[27]

A third view which I want to discuss here is the establishment of a modern scientific body within the Islamic Cooperation Organization (former Organization of Islamic Conference) that could be used as a new platform to discuss Islamic theocratic matters within the light of science, modernity, rationalism, and contemporary political, economic, and sociological necessities. With the participation of all Muslim countries' most sophisticated experts, an organization of this sort could be used as a mechanism to prevent the spread of radicalism in the Islamic world and to stop hatred ideology towards Christians, Jews, Hindus, non-believers etc. I state this view because although I share the secular view that Caliphate is not a solution, it is also a fact that there are widespread radical groups and organizations that use this gap for their own

---

27 https://twitter.com/AkyolinEnglish/status/1288493992393560064.

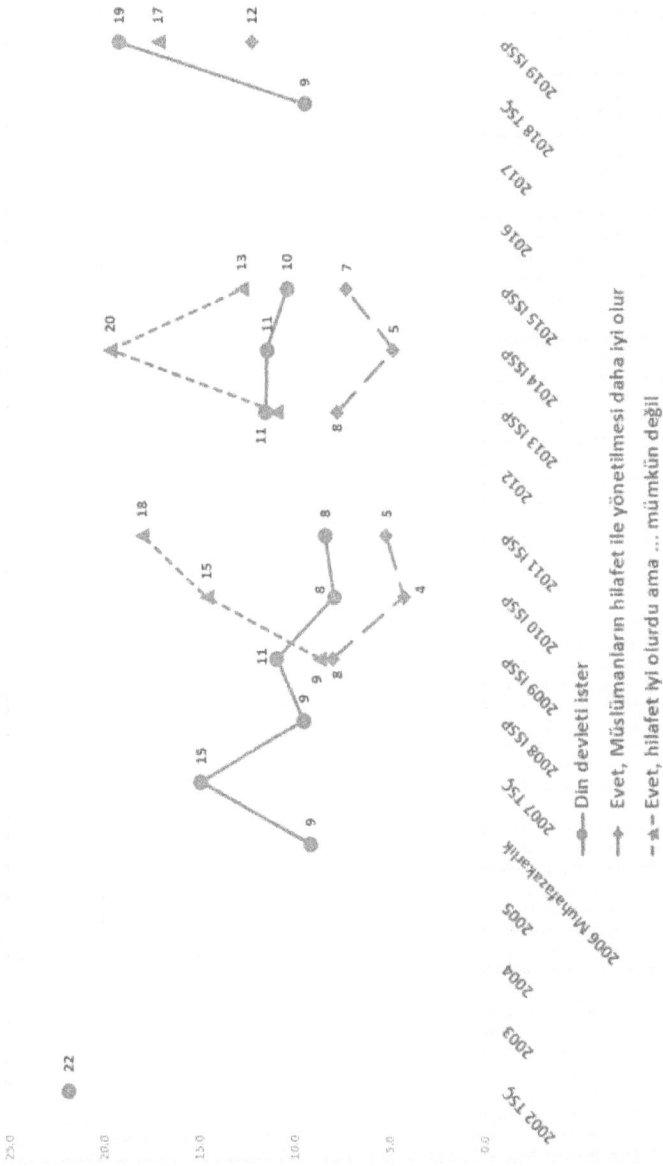

Din Devleti ve Hilafete Kamuoyu Desteği, 2002-2019

— Din devleti ister

↑ Evet, Müslümanların hilafet ile yönetilmesi daha iyi olur

⟋ Evet, hilafet iyi olurdu ama … mümkün değil

The graph for ISSP surveys that show support in Turkey for Sharia and the Caliphate[28]

28 https://yetkinreport.com/2020/07/20/ayasofya-seriat-hilafet-ve-kamuoyu/.

purposes. So, a scientific institution within the Islamic Cooperation Organization that will deliver good messages to Muslims in terms of individual faith, similar to the contemporary mission of the many other religious leaders, could be an alternative model.

In terms of Turkey, we should also mention that the Turkish society is largely secularized and the support for the reinstatement of Caliphate is still low. According to Murat Yetkin, an experienced Turkish journalist, who makes a reference to Ali Çarkoğlu and Ersin Kalaycıoğlu's regular International Social Survey Programme (ISSP) surveys[29], the support for a Sharia-based state do not exceed 20 % in contemporary Turkey[30]. However, Yetkin underlines that support for Caliphate has been constantly raised in the last decade. So, although few people want Sharia rules, the idea of Turkey leading the Sunni Islamic world has become a more popular view in the last years due to neo-Ottomanism discussions and the success of President Erdoğan's Islamist policies. Thus, we should not underestimate the Islamization of Turkey and the attractiveness of the *grandeur* feelings that pioneering the Islamic world spreads to right-wing (Islamists, conservatives, and Turkish nationalists) people. Another problematic issue that is on the agenda in Turkey on the other hand is the violence against women and problems related to male-female equality which seem to be increasing simultaneously with the rise of Political Islam.

Conclusion

Finally, I think, Turkey and all other Muslim/Islamic countries have to focus on the democratic quality and life standards of their citizens before Caliphate claims. It is a fact that there are injustices against Muslims, no Muslim dominated state is represented in the United Nations Security Council, and Muslim countries are more backward and less democratic compared to Western states, but the solution to these problems is not about Caliphate. The real aim should be to establish somehow democratic regimes that are supported by people and to create better conditions for people so that there could be peace and stability. The mechanism I mentioned earlier within the Islamic Cooperation Organization can also be an alternative view to solve radicalism problem among Muslim nations.

---

29 http://w.issp.org/menu-top/home/.
30 https://yetkinreport.com/2020/07/20/ayasofya-seriat-hilafet-ve-kamuoyu/.

Ozan Örmeci[*]

Turkish Politics in Critical Conjuncture

Abstract This chapter contains an earlier analysis about the 2023 Turkish elections. The article takes a glance on contemporary political developments taking place within the country with a particular focus on negative trends in Turkish economy.

Keywords: *Turkish Politics, 2023 Turkish elections, AK Parti, CHP, Recep Tayyip Erdoğan, Kemal Kılıçdaroğlu.*

The Republic of Turkey is heading for double elections on June 18, 2023 on its 100th anniversary; presidential election and parliamentary election. This means that there is almost a year left until the elections and political parties and candidates should start making necessary preparations. In this critical conjuncture, Turkish politics is very active and exciting these days with alternative views and programmes. Although Turkey has begun to be considered as a "*not-free*" country in recent years by the Freedom House[1], in fact the existence of different political parties, leaders, and programmes show that democracy might still prevail in this country. In this piece, I am going to summarize most recent political developments in Turkey.

The most spoken issue in Turkey in recent months is of course the economic crisis. Turkey's annual inflation is announced as 70 % recently[2], which might tell us how the loss of purchasing power of people decreased significantly in recent months. Of course, coupled with the depreciation of Turkish lira against U.S. Dollar and Euro in recent years[3], this has a terrible effect on people and it might distance average voter from the current government and Recep Tayyip Erdoğan

---

[*] Associate Professor in the department of Political Science and International Relations (English) at Istanbul Aydın University, Istanbul, Türkiye.
Email: ozanormeci@aydin.edu.tr / ozanormeci@gmail.com.
ORCID: 0000-0001-8850-6089.

1 See; https://freedomhouse.org/country/turkey/freedom-world/2022.
2 https://edition.cnn.com/2022/05/05/economy/turkey-inflation-soars/index.html#:~:text=Istanbul%20Turkey's%20annual%20inflation%20jumped,last%20year's%20lira%20crash.
3 https://www.reuters.com/markets/europe/turkish-lira-declines-weakest-since-december-over-ukraine-concerns-2022-03-09/#:~:text=The%20lira%20is%20now%20down,points%20to%2014%25%20since%20September.

regime. Although Turkish President Recep Tayyip Erdoğan still shows and performs his immense skills of populism[4], this might not be enough this time due to the ongoing economic crisis. In the meantime, Erdoğan continues to keep his electoral coalition People's Alliance (*Cumhur İttifakı*) with ultranationalist parties MHP (Nationalist Action Party) and BBP (Great Unity Party).

Another popular theme in Turkish politics is the situation of Syrian migrants. Recently, an anti-immigration party was established in Turkey by Professor of Political Science and nationalist academic Ümit Özdağ (1961–): Victory Party (*Zafer Partisi*)[5]. Son of the leading putschist of the 27 May 1960 military intervention staff captain Muzaffer Özdağ, Ümit Özdağ was a popular nationalist academic from Gazi University and a well-known figure within the Turkish nationalist MHP. However, after challenging party leader Devlet Bahçeli, he resigned from party and joined Meral Akşener's Good Party (İYİ Parti). Özdağ also resigned from İYİ Parti recently and established Victory Party. Although not much chance is given to him for elections, it is for sure that his anti-immigration policies appeal to ordinary people who are upset due to economic conditions within the country in recent years. Özdağ blames Syrian migrants of theft and abuse and claims that they would send all migrants to Syria forcefully[6]. Özdağ also engaged in a battle words with Turkey's Minister of Interior Süleyman Soylu recently[7]. Özdağ represents far-right tradition and Turkish Trumpism in this critical conjuncture. What is surprising is that, Özdağ's policies also find support among the secular social-democratic CHP (Republican People's Party). For instance, CHP's Bolu mayor Tanju Özcan began to implement ten times more expensive prices for water to Syrian migrants[8] and CHP leader Kemal Kılıçdaroğlu announced a plan to send all Syrian migrants in two years[9]. Of course, huge immigration in short time span is a major problem for all countries. However, we must be careful not to blame victims of the war (in this case, people

---

4   For an academic study on this, see; https://dergi.bilgi.edu.tr/index.php/reflektif/arti cle/view/97/78.

5   For its website, see; https://zaferpartisi.org.tr/.

6   https://www.amerikaninsesi.com/a/turkiye-suriyeliler-i-geri-gonderecek-mi/6535 858.html.

7   https://www.dailysabah.com/politics/battle-of-words-between-soylu-ozdag-turns-into-standoff/news.

8   https://www.gazeteduvar.com.tr/bolu-belediye-baskanindan-irkci-uygulama-multecil ere-10-kat-fazla-su-faturasi-haber-1529631.

9   https://www.sozcu.com.tr/2021/gundem/kilicdaroglu-suriyelileri-ulkelerine-nasil-gonderecekklerini-4-maddede-acikladi-6724917/.

who escaped from the brutality of the Syrian regime and ISIS terrorism) and as international public, we should do our best to help Syrian migrants. It must not be forgotten that Turks also migrated to Anatolia from different geographies and they are not one of the autochthon peoples of Anatolia.

Another dynamic party of Turkish politics is CHP. CHP won many municipalities of metropolitan cities in 2019 local elections and consolidated its power. CHP's Istanbul Mayor Ekrem İmamoğlu and Ankara Mayor Mansur Yavaş became two new political stars within the country. İmamoğlu recently organized a trip to his hometown Karadeniz region (Artvin, Rize, and Trabzon) as he was the declared official candidate of the opposition. This trip took both positive and negative reactions from the media; especially İmamoğlu's choice of inviting pro-Erdoğan journalist Nagehan Alçı took harsh criticism from opposition circles[10]. At the same time, CHP leader Kemal Kılıçdaroğlu announced that he wants to become the presidential candidate of the Nation's Alliance (*Millet İttifakı*). Kılıçdaroğlu even said that "*either support me or clear the way*"[11]. Since the opposition bloc insists on a transition (return) to parliamentary system, they should carefully choose their Presidential and Prime Minister candidates in this critical conjuncture. CHP's biggest advantage before the elections is the continuation of the bloc of 6 parties; CHP, İYİ Parti, Felicity Party (*Saadet Partisi*), Democrat Party (DP), Future Party (*Gelecek Partisi*), and DEVA Party. However, a few days before, CHP's provincial head in Istanbul, Canan Kaftancıoğlu was sentenced to prison[12]. Kaftancıoğlu is often praised for her organizational capacity to avoid electoral fraud in Istanbul and pointed out as the architect of İmamoğlu's stunning victory back in 2019.

Finally, I think we should expect more moves on the side of the government and opposition in the coming months. President Erdoğan might try to use the card of nationalism and take advantage of the closure of the pro-Kurdish HDP (Peoples' Democratic Party). Erdoğan might also use classical tactics of cultural war between Islamism and secularism to consolidate the conservative bloc. The opposition bloc on the other hand might choose the appropriate candidate and begin working on a new and liberal programme in order to avoid ideological side slip.

---

10 https://www.bbc.com/turkce/61388936.

11 https://www.cumhuriyet.com.tr/turkiye/kemal-kilicdaroglundan-adaylik-aciklamasi-1931561.

12 https://www.dailysabah.com/politics/supreme-court-upholds-prison-sentence-for-chp-Istanbul-head-kaftancioglu/news.

Ozan Örmeci*

Key Issues for 2023 Turkish Elections

Abstract This chapter contains an earlier analysis about the 2023 Turkish elections. The article deals with contemporary political issues in Türkiye as well as electoral blocs created by two major parties; AK Parti and CHP.

Keywords: *Turkish Politics, 2023 Turkish elections, AK Parti, CHP, Recep Tayyip Erdoğan, Kemal Kılıçdaroğlu.*

Turkey will organize two elections simultaneously in June 2023: presidential and parliamentary elections. These elections will not only determine the governing body of the country, but somehow the future of the country as well at its 100th year anniversary. At one side, there is the governing People's Alliance (*Cumhur İttifakı*) electoral bloc composed of President Erdoğan's Islamist originated right-wing AK Parti (Justice and Development Party), Turkish nationalist MHP (Nationalist Action Party) led by Devlet Bahçeli, and Turkish nationalist-Islamist BBP (Great Unity Party) led by Mustafa Destici. This bloc defends an authoritarian presidentialism and a more nationalist and Islamist country. On the other hand, there is the opposition bloc of Nation Alliance (*Millet İttifakı*) which includes 6 parties: pro-secular CHP (Republican People's Party) led by Kemal Kılıçdaroğlu, center-right Good Party (İYİ Parti) led by Meral Akşener – a party split from MHP and began to take steps towards center-right, center-right DP (*Demokrat Parti*) – a small party led by Gültekin Uysal, Islamist Felicity Party (*Saadet Partisi*/SP) – a party following Necmettin Erbakan's National View (*Milli Görüş*) tradition and chaired by Temel Karamollaoğlu, and two other right-wing parties that were split from the AK Parti: Ali Babacan's DEVA Party and Ahmet Davutoğlu's Future Party (*Gelecek Partisi*). This bloc defends a return to parliamentary system as well as the restoring of the classical Turkish Foreign Policy principles. In that sense, these elections will be battle of two opposing camps/blocs. However, there are some key issues to be known before the elections.

---

*   Associate Professor in the department of Political Science and International Relations (English) at Istanbul Aydın University, Istanbul, Türkiye.
Email: ozanormeci@aydin.edu.tr / ozanormeci@gmail.com.
ORCID: 0000-0001-8850-6089.

First of all, in 2023 elections, the electoral threshold would be 7 % instead of 10 %. After the 12 September 1980 military coup, in order to stop the strengthening of Islamist and pro-Kurdish political parties, the architects of the system decided to implement 10 % electoral threshold. However, both Islamist and Kurdish movements gained power in time and now they could easily pass 10 %. On the contrary, Turkish nationalist MHP might have a problem with the 10 % electoral threshold according to polls. That is why, in March 2022, Turkish parliament adopted a new law to reduce the electoral threshold to 7 %. The reduced electoral threshold might not change the general picture, but it is still a novelty for Turkish Politics. In the meantime, I should add that the electoral threshold is still too high and it should be reduced to 5 % in the coming years.

Secondly, a new political debate started in Turkey recently about the constitutional guarantees for Islamic dressed women which might heavily affect the outcome of the 2023 elections. The debate came into surface with CHP leader Kemal Kılıçdaroğlu's unexpected statement and CHP's draft on the legal guarantee for turban (Islamic veil). President Recep Tayyip Erdoğan saw this as an opportunity and proposed a constitutional change to provide constitutional guarantees for Islamic dressing. However, AK Parti and MHP votes in the parliament reach only 334. In that sense, to organize a referendum (360 votes needed) or to amend the constitution (400 votes needed) AK Parti needs CHP deputies' support. The amendment is arranged in a way that it could open the door for hijab and burka for female public officers in Turkey, which would not be an ideal scenario for the 100th anniversary of the secular republic[1]. In addition, in case CHP refuses to support the amendment, President Erdoğan might use this issue to weaken the opposition during his electoral campaign and take advantage of the already existing cleavages (fault lines) in Turkish Politics.

Thirdly, the Kurdish vote and pro-Kurdish party HDP's (Peoples' Democratic Party) choice for the election will be crucial for the outcome. Journalist İsmail Saymaz claims that since its leader Selahattin Demirtaş is jailed, HDP will choose its former Siirt deputy and Diyarbakır mayor Gültan Kışanak as its presidential candidate. In the first round, it is obvious that HDP will contest itself. However, in the second round, HDP will probably support the opposition bloc Nation Alliance's candidate. In that sense, President Erdoğan's biggest disadvantage for these elections is his weakness in terms of Kurdish support. However, Erdoğan

---

1 The phrase used in the proposed amendment is: "*dressings that women prefer in relation to their religious beliefs*" (*kadınların dini inancı nedeniyle tercih ettiği kıyafetler*) which can clearly be interpreted as the allowing of the use of hijab and burqa.

might use some tactics before the elections to increase his popularity among the Kurds.

Fourthly and most importantly, the opposition bloc's choice of presidential candidate will be a crucial factor for the result of the elections. CHP leader Kemal Kılıçdaroğlu wants to become a candidate himself and it seems like thanks to economic problems of the country and Erdoğan's growing unpopularity, he might have high chances to win the presidential race. However, polls suggest that CHP's Ankara Mayor Mansur Yavaş and Istanbul's Mayor Ekrem İmamoğlu are more popular and they have higher chances against Erdoğan compared to Kılıçdaroğlu. Most recently, İmamoğlu is sentenced to more than two years in prison and banned him from politics for calling members of Turkey's supreme election council *"fools"* in a press release three years ago after the annulation of the local elections he won it with a slight difference. İmamoğlu won the repeated election with a much larger majority and became a champion of democracy in Turkey. Since then, he has been organizing political events and he has become the new rising star of Turkish Politics. In that sense, this unconfirmed court decision might make İmamoğlu a kind of *"new Erdoğan"*, an unwanted man of the people taking the control of the system. In fact, many observers in Turkey consider the verdict as an effort to prevent İmamoğlu's presidency. That is why, after the decision, İYİ Parti leader Meral Akşener came to Istanbul to support İmamoğlu and the duo organized meetings to denounce the unjust court decision. İmamoğlu will appeal to this decision and will do his best to prevent a political ban. However, İmamoğlu's decision might be confirmed prior to election date. In that sense, the opposition's choice of the presidential candidate will be the most important decision they must take before the election. Six parties will decide who will be the candidate, but I think the final decision will be taken between Kılıçdaroğlu and Akşener. Mansur Yavaş could also be an ideal candidate; but his ultranationalist past and MHP background might alienate leftist and Kurdish voters some analysts claim. Another choice would be to pick up a different candidate like Ekmeleddin İhsanoğlu in the 2014 presidential election. If such a decision is made, former President of the Republic Abdullah Gül and CHP's Eskişehir mayor Yılmaz Büyükerşen could be surprise alternatives.

Lastly, we might talk about the decision of small parties before the elections. These parties might contest in the elections independently or as part of another bloc or they might support one of these two big blocs. In that sense, Ümit Özdağ's Victory Party (*Zafer Partisi*), Muharrem İnce's Homeland Party (*Memleket Partisi*), Mustafa Sarıgül's Party for Change in Turkey (*Türkiye Değişim Partisi*), and Erbakan's son Fatih Erbakan's New Welfare Party (*Yeniden Refah Partisi*) are political parties having some real potential in terms of votes.

Ozan Örmeci[*]

Could Turkish Elections Be Postponed?

Abstract This chapter contains an in-depth analysis on the 2023 Turkish elections with a special attention given to the effect of the 2023 Turkish earthquakes, which caused a major damage to the country's economy. The paper also discusses whether the elections should be postponed to be organized in a free and fair manner.

Keywords: *Turkish Politics, 2023 Turkish elections, AK Parti, CHP, Recep Tayyip Erdoğan, Kemal Kılıçdaroğlu, 2023 Turkish earthquakes.*

Introduction

Türkiye (Turkey) as a nation has been suffering since 6 February 2023, when two devastating earthquakes hit the country's southeastern cities. Centered in Kahramanmaraş, the disasters demolished 10 Turkish cities including Kahramanmaraş, Hatay (Antakya), Osmaniye, Adıyaman, Gaziantep, Kilis, Şanlıurfa, Diyarbakır, Malatya, and Adana. According to official statistics, approximately 41,000 people lost their lives due to the disaster. However, the death toll could reach 50,000 to 100,000 in the coming days considering the fact that many people's bodies are not yet discovered in ruins. In this article, I am going to summarize the outcomes of the devastating *"twin earthquakes"* in Türkiye and Syria and discuss whether it could lead to a postponement of the 2023 elections.

Outcomes of the Tragedy

This great tragedy not only disrupted the normalcy of life in Türkiye, but also terribly affected the general psychology of the nation. State of emergency was declared for 3 months in these 10 cities. Turkish people initiated aid campaigns and ten thousands of volunteers went to these cities to help rescue efforts. As a normal reaction, Turkish media began to cover almost only earthquake stories and all other issues are forgotten. Miraculous rescues from wreckages after long

---

[*] Associate Professor in the department of Political Science and International Relations (English) at Istanbul Aydın University, Istanbul, Türkiye.
 Email: ozanormeci@aydin.edu.tr / ozanormeci@gmail.com.
 ORCID: 0000-0001-8850-6089.

hours created bliss, whereas pictures of death bodies and demolished cities caused despair. Famous Geology and Geophysics Professors (Celal Şengör, Şener Üşümezsoy, Ahmet Ercan, Naci Görür, Cenk Yaltırak etc.) began to appear on Turkish tv channels similar to 1999 Gölcük (Izmit) earthquake. The country's risks due to earthquakes, especially the situation of Istanbul where almost 20 million people reside and the country's economy is based, is largely spoken on tv channels. Some of these Professors focused on an imminent threat, whereas some others underlined that there is no real risk of collapse for Istanbul in the short or medium run.

The negative economic effects of the disaster on the other hand will be better understood in the coming years since the state will allocate millions of dollars for the reconstruction of these cities as well as the caring of earthquake victims. Turkish President Recep Tayyip Erdoğan promised to rebuild all residences and resettle people into their homes in a year. However, realistically speaking, fulfilling this promise could be impossible since Turkish economy was already in crisis before the earthquake and Turkish people's purchasing power has been falling constantly in the last few years. With the twin earthquakes, the recovery could be even harder for Turkish economy, if not impossible. So, Türkiye needs more time to relieve and dress the wounds.

The only positive outcome of the disaster was the incredible solidarity shown by Turkish people and many other countries who contributed to rescue efforts and aid campaigns. Countries who helped Türkiye during this process are: Albania, Algeria, Argentina, Armenia, Australia, Azerbaijan, Bangladesh, Belarus, Bosnia Herzegovina, Brazil, Bulgaria, Croatia, Czechia (Czech Republic), El Salvador, Estonia, Finland, France, Germany, Georgia, Greece, Hong Kong, Hungary, India, Iraq, Islamic Republic of Iran, Israel, Italy, Japan, Jordan, Kazakhstan, Kosovo, Kuwait, Kyrgyzstan, Lebanon, Libya, Lithuania, Malaysia, Malta, Mexico, Moldova, Mongolia, Montenegro, Netherlands, Pakistan, Palestine, People's Republic of China, Poland, Portugal, Qatar, Romania, Russian Federation, Saudi Arabia, Serbia, Slovakia, South Korea, Spain, Sweden, Switzerland, Tajikistan, Taiwan, TRNC (Turkish Republic of Northern Cyprus), Tunisia, Turkmenistan, Ukraine, United Arab Emirates (UAE), United Kingdom, United States of America (USA), Uzbekistan, and Venezuela. Especially Israeli, Greek, and Armenian help during this process were largely covered by Turkish and international media since Türkiye has some traditional political-diplomatic problems with these countries. This process proved that there is still chance for a rules-based and solidarity-oriented international order especially in times of crises and countries are not existential threats to each other.

2023 Turkish Elections: Could There Be a Postponement?

The terrible disaster hit Türkiye just a few months before the critical elections; Türkiye was normally heading towards a joint presidential and parliamentary elections on June 18, 2023. Turkish President Recep Tayyip Erdoğan previously declared his wish to hold the elections on May 14, 2023, the historic date/anniversary of Turkish transition into multiparty democracy back in 1950. However, due to negative effects of this unexpected disaster, which led to the relocation of millions of people into different cities in addition to infrastructural problems, now there are talks in Turkish mainstream politics whether these elections should be postponed or not.

For instance, very recently, one of the top figures of the ruling AK Parti (Justice and Development Party) and former speaker of the Turkish Parliament Bülent Arınç demanded the postponement of the elections. This was largely understood by the Turkish people as an effort of kite flying to observe the reactions of the opposition. It is a fact that terrible twin earthquakes changed the demographics of Türkiye considerably and many people should be re-registered to electoral roll in different cities in the coming months. In fact, even the number of parliamentarian seats allocated to cities on the basis of population could be changed due to large resident mobility. However, due to ongoing polarization in domestic politics, the opposition could perceive this as an effort to steal the election. That is why, although I admit the fact that a disaster of this size would normally result in the postponement of the election in a regular democratic country, due to Türkiye's extremely high polarization in domestic politics and leaning towards authoritarianism in recent years, it might be a wiser decision to make the elections on time. The opposition by the way already rejected a possible postponement.

Moreover, there could be problems related to the constitutionality of the postponement decision. Turkish constitution does not allow any delay for the elections unless the country is engaged in a war. Article 78 of the constitution clarifies the issue as follows: "*If holding new elections is deemed impossible because of war, the Grand National Assembly of Türkiye may decide to defer elections for a year. If the grounds do not disappear, the deferment may be repeated in compliance with the procedure for deferment.*" Mr. Arınç responded to this fact by simply saying that "*constitutions are not sacred texts*". Many legal experts on the other hand claim that delaying the election would not be constitutional and Türkiye's Supreme Electoral Council or Supreme Election Committee (*Yüksek Seçim Kurulu*-YSK) does not possess such a right/privilege.

Honestly speaking, what I smell out in the street is that, President Erdoğan might try to postpone the election for several months by using a YSK decision stating that voter rolls are not ready yet and the institution in charge needs more time to organize new registrations. This happened once in Turkish political history before and in 1966, YSK decided on the postponement of the mukhtar election in Varto district of Muş. However, the earlier decision was about the mukhtar election, now this is about the whole country. Osman Can, a prominent Professor on Constitutional Law, states that *"YSK could track the voters if they relocate since we have a very modern system of registry that could be updated, and most importantly we have more than three months until the elections, we have time"* and underlines the unconstitutionality of the postponement decision. Professor Hasret Çomak from Istanbul Kent University also underlines that YSK does not have any right to delay the election. But as President Erdoğan is the only wirepuller in the country since the failed coup attempt in 2016, I think he might prefer the postponement of the election in order to gain more time and to focus on rebuilding efforts as well as the recovery of the economy.

The Candidate of the Opposition: Kılıçdaroğlu Makes Important Gains

In addition to these developments, with his increasing activism in recent months, pro-secular CHP's (Republican People's Party) leader Kemal Kılıçdaroğlu gains popularity among people. Kılıçdaroğlu immediately went to demolished cities after the earthquake and tried to articulate the feelings of victims. He showed a good leadership skill during the disaster although his harsh criticism towards President Erdoğan and to the government was perceived *"untimely"* by some. Belonging to Alevi faith and coming from Kurdish/Zaza background, Kılıçdaroğlu's chance to win the election is often considered very low until now in a Sunni-Turkish dominated conservative/nationalist society. However, due to terrible economic situation of the country, the unsuccess of the crisis management of the government during the disaster and his rising performance, in my opinion, Kılıçdaroğlu could now defeat Erdoğan in a presidential race.

Kılıçdaroğlu's candidacy could be announced in the coming weeks if the election is not postponed. Kılıçdaroğlu has already the support of his party (CHP) and many other small parties (center right Democrat Party-DP, Ahmet Davutoğlu's Future Party/*Gelecek Partisi*, Ali Babacan's DEVA, and Islamist Felicity Party/*Saadet Partisi*). The only missing support given is Good Party (İYİ Parti) leader Meral Akşener's. If Kılıçdaroğlu could convince Akşener as well, he will be the next Presidential candidate of the opposition bloc. I think he has very high chances now to win the election although before six months, he was not such a strong candidate. That is because -as Soner Çağaptay mentions– the government showed a real slow and uncoordinated response to the earthquake disaster and Kılıçdaroğlu gives strong promises to end the corruption in the country.

But Istanbul mayor Ekrem İmamoğlu and Ankara mayor Mansur Yavaş also still have chances to become the presidential candidate of the opposition. İmamoğlu was recently tried to be temporarily banned from active politics by a court decision, but the appeal process continues. İmamoğlu is a rising star of Turkish politics, but since his candidature could be risky in legal terms, he could wait for his time for CHP leadership and Prime Ministry in the coming years after Türkiye returns to parliamentary system. Yavaş on the other hand comes from Turkish nationalist MHP (Nationalist Action Party) background, a fact that might alienate traditional CHP voters and Kurds from the opposition. Moreover, these two municipal leaders are very successful in their jobs and Türkiye definitely needs successful administrators to develop and protect itself from natural disasters such as the earthquake.

Conclusion

Finally, 2023 Turkey-Syria earthquakes was one of the biggest disasters recorded in modern history. However, as a very strong country, Türkiye already began to recuperate and it will continue to develop in the coming years to become a regional power. In that sense, Türkiye's rise is unstoppable due to its young and dynamic population and developed status in many industries.

In the coming days, President Erdoğan and his team might try to postpone the elections due to earthquakes. Although there are very justifiable arguments for such a decision, as far as I am concerned, that would not be wise and it will further increase the polarization within the country. However, in case YSK and the government convince the opposition for a short term delay only for arranging the electoral facilities and voter rolls, there could be a few months postponement.

Lastly, in my opinion, Türkiye has to celebrate its 100th year anniversary with a democratic presidential and parliamentary election in 2023 and it should start setting a new course for the future.

Ozan Örmeci*

Growing Polarization in Türkiye after the Earthquakes

Abstract This chapter contains an in-depth analysis on the 2023 Turkish elections with a special attention given to the effect of the 2023 Turkish earthquakes, which caused a major damage to the country's economy. The paper also focuses on the recent political polarization caused by the government's mismanagement during the crisis.

Keywords: *Turkish Politics, 2023 Turkish elections, AK Parti, CHP, Recep Tayyip Erdoğan, Kemal Kılıçdaroğlu, 2023 Turkish earthquakes.*

Introduction

Turkish people still suffer psychologically and economically due to the terrible earthquakes that occurred on February 6, 2023 in the south-eastern villages of the country. Centered in Kahramanmaraş, two sequenced earthquakes almost destroyed 10 Turkish cities and led to the death of 45,000 Turkish citizens. The death toll could be even higher in the coming days with the discovery of missing dead bodies.

As a political consequence of the disaster, the state's lack of coordination during the crisis led to growing criticism and anger towards the ruling AK Parti government (2002–) and its undisputed leader Turkish President Recep Tayyip Erdoğan (2014–). In this piece, I am going to analyze increasing political polarization in Türkiye and whether it is an advantageous situation for the government and opposition.

Political Agenda after the Earthquakes

Devastating outcomes of the earthquakes caused the opposition's growing reaction to the government because of its lack of preparation before the disaster as well as its lack of coordination after the disaster and during the ongoing crisis.

* Associate Professor in the department of Political Science and International Relations (English) at Istanbul Aydın University, Istanbul, Türkiye.
Email: ozanormeci@aydin.edu.tr / ozanormeci@gmail.com.
ORCID: 0000-0001-8850-6089.

The government (President Erdoğan himself) on the other hand responded to these claims by simply saying that *"the earthquake is a matter of destiny"*[1] and *"it's not a noble-minded behavior to make politics when the nation mourns"*[2]. One of the founding members of the AK Parti, former Parliament speaker Bülent Arınç proposed the postponement of the election[3], but so far no decision is taken about the delay of the elections. Although there is no regulation within the constitution on that matter, many political observers close to the government claim that in case Türkiye's Supreme Election Committee (YSK) asks for a delay due to problems in the voters lists in these 10 cities affected from the earthquakes, the President might try to postpone the elections, a decision which would certainly increase the polarization in the country even further.

The opposition on the other hand wants Presidential and parliamentary elections to take place either in May or June this year. However, the opposition also has its own problems related to the choice of the Presidential candidate. While the main opposition party CHP's leader Kemal Kılıçdaroğlu wants to become a candidate himself with the support of 5 other parties within the Nation Alliance (*Millet İttifakı*) electoral coalition that includes Meral Akşener's Good Party/İYİ Parti, Gültekin Uysal's DP/Democrat Party, Ahmet Davutoğlu's Future Party/*Gelecek Partisi*, Ali Babacan's DEVA Party, and Temel Karamollaoğlu's SP/Felicity Party, the leader of the second biggest party within this bloc -Meral Akşener- obviously shows her hesitation and negative attitude towards him. Akşener speaks of *"a candidate who could win the election"*[4] by implying Kılıçdaroğlu's Alevi faith and lower chance to become President in a Sunni-dominated country. Akşener also clearly endorsed Istanbul mayor Ekrem İmamoğlu as the opposition's Presidential candidate[5] when he was tried to be temporarily banned from politics in an unjust manner via a court decision a few weeks ago. It seems like there will be a tough negotiation process between Kılıçdaroğlu and Akşener in the coming days and the opposition's Presidential candidate will be either Kılıçdaroğlu or İmamoğlu.

On the other hand, Turkish people began to organize protests in crowded places. For instance, during this week's football matches in the *Süper Lig* (Türkiye's Premier football division), many club's fans protested the government by calling

---

1   See; https://www.youtube.com/watch?v=75hF5IobMFA.
2   See; https://www.youtube.com/watch?v=VbYnHWPIeaA.
3   http://politikaakademisi.org/2023/02/19/could-turkish-elections-be-postponed/.
4   See; https://www.youtube.com/watch?v=OqmuIntpQ5k.
5   See; https://www.youtube.com/watch?v=L0tRzpJyzTQ.

President Erdoğan and his government to resignation. The protests started with Fenerbahçe fans[6] and continued with Beşiktaş fans[7]. It seems like these protests could continue in the coming days especially in crowded places like stadiums and universities etc. The government tries to convince people that the disaster was not their fault and keeps the People Alliance (*Cumhur İttifakı*) electoral bloc with two nationalist parties Devlet Bahçeli's MHP (Nationalist Action Party) and Mustafa Destici's BBP (Grand Unity Party). President Erdoğan also promised to construct new buildings for victims in a year with the help of TOKİ (Housing Development Administration of the Republic of Türkiye), whose buildings were not demolished during the terrible disaster. President Erdoğan's job is really difficult this time since Türkiye was already in an economic crisis and earthquakes further deteriorated the situation.

Political Polarization: Is It Helpful to Government More Than the Opposition?

While the political polarization in the country increases, it might be a good decision to scientifically discuss the effects of political polarization in Türkiye. As a close witness of Turkish political life since 2002, I remember that in all elections in recent years[8] when the opposition tried to demonize Erdoğan and AK Parti due to their Islamist identity or poor performance in governing, Turkish people and especially the right-wing voters showed a resistance and defended Erdoğan as a reaction to secular establishment. For instance, before the 2007 parliamentary election, although there were huge demonstrations organized by the opposition, called as the Republican Rallies (*Cumhuriyet Mitingleri*), these protest movements served as a catalyst to reunite the right-wing bloc and kept Erdoğan and AK Parti at the government. That is why, as far as I'm concerned, the opposition should be careful in playing the card of polarization, which has always resulted in the victory of Erdoğan and the bigger right-wing/Islamist-nationalist bloc in Türkiye so far. That is because the AK Parti has more than 11 million members[9], more than 8 times higher than the number of members of CHP -the second most popular party both in votes and in membership size- a fact proving that uniting the electorate of this party would not be a good idea

6   See; https://www.youtube.com/watch?v=gjCJJQNN0PM.
7   See; https://www.youtube.com/watch?v=_OHfqrPiQ-Y.
8   2007, 2011, 2015 (June), and 2015 (November) parliamentary elections as well as 2014 and 2018 Presidential elections.
9   https://www.yargitaycb.gov.tr/kategori/109/siyasi-parti-genel-bilgileri.

for winning the election. Another reason is that, due to his eventual win in his fight against the secular establishment, Erdoğan is the sacred right-wing leader who was able to remove the ban on headscarf (*türban*) in public offices, to solve the problem of Prayer and Preacher (*İmam Hatip*) Schools' graduates to enter into universities without limitation, and the one who survived a bloody military coup attempt in 2016. In that sense, Erdoğan's cult leadership for the Islamist/nationalist bloc is still very strong.

On that matter, there are several good publications/studies made earlier by various Political Scientists. For instance, *"Dimensions of Polarization in Turkey 2020 Survey"*[10] conducted by the German Marshall Fund of the United States and Istanbul Bilgi University Migration Research Center proved that Turkish citizens mostly live in echo-chambers in which existing views are reconfirmed and other voices are shut out. In that sense, looking at the results, Özgür Ünlühisarcıklı concluded that the polarization could work in favor of the government if the government implements *"policies that would strengthen social security, provide high-quality public education for all citizens, and visibly decrease social inequality"*[11]. So, one can claim that, if the government shows a good reaction to disaster in a way to help victims and to decrease social inequalities, they could still have a chance to win the election. However, since there is very short time (only 2.5 or 3.5 months) left before the election, a postponement decision seems necessary for the government to convince its electorate about its success.

Hakan Yavuzyılmaz on the other hand discusses the features of competitive authoritarian regimes and concludes that[12] this type of regimes could have two main problems: (1) elite-level defection/rivalry and (2) and mass-level/oppositional counter-mobilization. The AK Parti elite still seems very solid and there are no signs of large-scale elite-level defection. However, the second problem might appear for the government as the opposition could organize mass-level oppositional mobilization in stadiums, universities, and/or mass demonstrations. In the past, as I provided the example of Republican Rallies earlier, this mobilization was not very helpful to the opposition. However, during this process Turkish economy was still in very good shape. Now, it seems like Turkish economy is in ruins and the rising inflation and terrible effects of the earthquakes might not produce same results. Moreover, the unjust political decisions made by the government also could result in the success of

10 https://www.turkuazlab.org/wp-content/uploads/2020/12/Survey_Key_Findings.pdf.
11 https://www.gmfus.org/news/importance-mitigating-polarization-turkey.
12 https://www.tandfonline.com/doi/pdf/10.1080/19448953.2021.1888600.

the opposition even though there is growing polarization within the country. Journalist Güney Yıldız for instance claims that Erdoğan's polarization tactic was not successful in the 2019 Istanbul local election as the decision for the cancellation of the first election was not justified[13].

In addition, Halil Karaveli earlier pointed out[14] the dominant conservative nature of Turkish society by referring to a 2021 survey organized by Kadir Has University[15]. This study showed that the two-thirds of the Turkish population identified themselves as conservative, nationalist, and Islamist, whereas only 13 % as social democrat and socialist. In that sense, the opposition might be very careful not to mobilize only groups associated with the left and should be open to right-wing/conservative groups in these demonstrations.

Conclusion

Finally, it seems like although there is no black and white difference on that matter, earlier data shows that strong political polarization generally works in favor of the right-wing bloc since it is larger. However, in case there is a serious injustice made (for example, the cancellation of 2019 Istanbul local election) and/or growing economic problems, the polarization might help the secular opposition as well. That is why; the key issue will be the performance of the government from now on.

Lastly, since there is only 3 months left for the election, which might not be long enough to convince voters about the good performance of the government, the government's only chance seems to me is to postpone the election. That is why, I'm afraid President Erdoğan might use a YSK decision to postpone the election for a few months. However, this decision should be justified and well-explained to people in order to prevent the arise of victimized opposition perception.

---

13 https://www.forbes.com/sites/guneyyildiz/2019/06/24/Istanbul-elections-failure-of-political-polarisation-in-turkey/?sh=dde361366be2.

14 https://www.socialeurope.eu/turkey-from-polarisation-to-pluralism.

15 https://www.khas.edu.tr/wp-content/uploads/2022/05/turkeytrends2021-web-press.pdf.

Ozan Örmeci[*]

Crack in the Opposition Might Secure Victory for Erdoğan

Abstract This chapter focuses on the opposition's strategy of establishing a large electoral bloc against President Recep Tayyip Erdoğan's increasingly authoritarian leaning presidency in Türkiye. The paper discusses İYİ Parti leader Meral Akşener's decision to oppose to Kılıçdaroğlu's candidacy.

Keywords: *Turkish Politics, 2023 Turkish elections, AK Parti, CHP, Recep Tayyip Erdoğan, Kemal Kılıçdaroğlu, İYİ Parti, Meral Akşener.*

Introduction

Türkiye (Turkey) is heading towards presidential and parliamentary elections on the 100th year anniversary of the foundation of the Republic with a lot of question marks. In this piece, I am going to analyze most recent domestic political issues in Türkiye and comment on whether the opposition can win the election or not.

Elections at a Time of Many Uncertainties

First of all, unfortunately, Turkish elections are approaching at a time of great uncertainties. To begin with, the date of the elections is not determined yet. Before the terrible earthquake on February 6, 2023, President Erdoğan declared his intention to hold the elections on May 14 in order to pay respect to Türkiye's transition into multiparty democracy via the first free and fair parliamentary elections on 14 May 1950. On the other hand, elections (presidential + parliamentary election) are normally scheduled for 18 June. Until now, the opposition bloc has always wanted elections to be held as soon as possible.

Second uncertainty is about whether President Recep Tayyip Erdoğan could become a candidate or not. Normally, a politician has a limit of only two mandates for Presidency according to the Article 101 of the Turkish constitution.

---

[*] Associate Professor in the department of Political Science and International Relations (English) at Istanbul Aydın University, Istanbul, Türkiye.
Email: ozanormeci@aydin.edu.tr / ozanormeci@gmail.com.
ORCID: 0000-0001-8850-6089.

Erdoğan was elected President of the Republic first in 2014 and later in 2018 and already served two terms. Here, some legal experts and political scientists claim that since the political regime of Türkiye changed from parliamentary system to presidential system via the controversial referendum in 2017, Erdoğan legally should have right to contend one more time. Some others however do not support this view and assert that Erdoğan could not become a presidential candidate normally. If we legally accept this approach, the only solution for Erdoğan to become a candidate once again is a parliamentary decision for the renewal of the elections. Article 116 of the Turkish constitution clearly states that a President who already served twice can become a presidential candidate again in case the parliament takes a decision to renew the elections. The parliament can make such a decision with the 3/5 majority. Since there are 600 seats in the Turkish Grand National Assembly (TGNA), Erdoğan needs 360 votes for the renewal of the elections. However, the ruling AK Parti (Justice and Development Party) has only 285 seats in the parliament. Since -ruled by Devlet Bahçeli- the Turkish nationalist MHP (Nationalist Action Party) is a member of People Alliance (*Cumhur İttifakı*) and supports AK Parti in all issues, we can count 48 MHP deputies on the side of Erdoğan as well, which makes 333 seats in total. Thus, Erdoğan still needs the support of 27 parliamentarians within the TGNA to secure his candidacy. In that sense, having problems with the chosen candidate of the opposition bloc (Nation Alliance-*Millet İttifakı*) İYİ Parti (Good Party) could help Erdoğan with its 37 deputies to renew the elections.

The third important uncertainty on the other hand is about the allocation of seats for cities. Since the recent devastating earthquake killed more than 50,000 people in Türkiye and forced millions of people to migrate and settle into different cities than their original place of residence, normally there should be a considerable change in the number of seats for cities who are negatively affected from the disaster and became deserted. In that sense, Türkiye's YSK (Supreme Election Board/Supreme Election Committee) announced the number of parliamentary seats for each city just a few days ago but did not make any changes considering the earthquake. That is why, there can be great injustice about the value of votes given by people in different cities.

The fourth and the last uncertainty is about the number of candidates that will be racing in the presidential election. It is now certain that both AK Parti chair Recep Tayyip Erdoğan and pro-secular CHP (Republican People's Party) chair Kemal Kılıçdaroğlu are officially presidential candidates. However, with the recent crack in the opposition (I will elaborate it in the next section), İYİ Parti also could declare a presidential candidate for itself now, making it three. Pro-Kurdish HDP (People's Democratic Party) will also declare its own presidential candidate soon, which makes it four. Muharrem İnce's Homeland Party (*Memleket Partisi*) could also declare a presidential candidate either by themselves alone or with the support of Ümit Özdağ's anti-immigrant Victory Party (*Zafer Partisi*). Far left parties such as Turkish Labour Party (*Türkiye İşçia Partisi*-TİP), Left Party (*Sol Parti*), and EMEP also could present a joint presidential candidate this time instead of supporting HDP or CHP. With his Patriotic Party (*Vatan Partisi*), veteran left-wing politician Doğu Perinçek could also become a candidate once again by collecting 100,000 signatures from citizens. Thus, we still do not know exactly the number of presidential candidates.

Crack in the Opposition: Why Now?

Although the opposition bloc called Nation Alliance (*Millet İttifakı*) seems to have very high chance this time against President Erdoğan due to Türkiye's decline in democracy in recent years as well as the poor economic performance of the country and the terrible crisis management of the government during the earthquake, a new and unexpected political development has changed the whole picture and caused despair for the opposition. Composed of 6 different political parties (Kemal Kılıçdaroğlu's CHP, Meral Akşener's İYİ Parti, Ali Babacan's DEVA Party, Ahmet Davutoğlu's Future Party, Temel Karamollaoğlu's Felicity Party, and Gültekin Uysal's Democratic Party), the Nation Alliance or the so-called "*sextet chair*" (*altılı masa*) had a recent political crisis about the joint candidate. While 5 political party leaders reconciled on the choice of CHP leader Kemal Kılıçdaroğlu as their common presidential candidate, İYİ Parti Meral Akşener did not accept this and left the opposition bloc.

İYİ Parti is a secular right-wing political party established by people coming from Turkish nationalist MHP background, which might have directed them not to support Kılıçdaroğlu, a Zaza and Alevi politician from Tunceli (Dersim). İYİ Parti officials however do not accept this accusation and they reveal that a candidate who has higher chance to win the presidential election such as Istanbul mayor Ekrem İmamoğlu or Ankara mayor Mansur Yavaş could be chosen instead of Kılıçdaroğlu. Akşener made a very harsh statement recently, accusing Kılıçdaroğlu and other political parties of forcing İYİ Parti to bend the knee to Kılıçdaroğlu. If İYİ Parti and Akşener could not be convinced, the opposition might have serious damage just a few weeks before the elections, which might change the whole picture.

Although Akşener's opposition to the choice of Kılıçdaroğlu has some valid points such as the results of previously made opinion polls that show Yavaş and İmamoğlu very much ahead of Kılıçdaroğlu, for me, this was not enough to destroy the sextet chair. Thus, Akşener and her party might now have another plan such as joining the People's Alliance (*Cumhur İttifakı*) or playing to the next election after 5 more years of Erdoğan and AK Parti rule by not supporting CHP and Kılıçdaroğlu at this election. Their new strategy will soon be understood. However, looking at the harshness of her speech, I am now convinced that Akşener would not return to the sextet chair.

Who Could Win?

With Akşener and İYİ Parti gone, all calculations before the elections are changed now. In this part, I will try to present you some number by using the average of previous opinion polls. AK Parti has still around 30 to 35 % votes, but we are not sure what will be the effect of the earthquake and poor performance of the government during this disaster. MHP could still get 5 to 10 % votes in addition to Mustafa Destici and BBP's 1 %, which makes People's Alliance votes 36 to 46 %. Thus, it is very much likely that President Erdoğan this time could not be elected in the first round.

CHP and its bloc on the other hand also stays short of % 50+1 majority. CHP could get 25 to 30 % of the votes by itself. However, without İYİ Parti's 12 to 18 %, the rest of the opposition bloc could make only around 4 to 7 %. That will make the vote for Kılıçdaroğlu 30 to 37 %. However, Kılıçdaroğlu still has a chance since the pro-Kurdish HDP could support him in the second round. By leaning on Kurdish identity, HDP could get 10 to 15 % and could be the decisive factor in the second round of the elections.

So, what we should expect from a potential second round between Kılıçdaroğlu and Erdoğan? Recently made polls suggest that Kılıçdaroğlu could defeat Erdoğan with a slight difference, but it will not be an easy election. Moreover, Erdoğan might try to alienate voters from Kılıçdaroğlu by underlining his different ethnic and sectarian identity. Although this is a very inappropriate behavior, unfortunately, in some democratic countries where class-based voting is weak, such as the United States and Türkiye, this could be used by right-wing and especially far-right politicians and -the worst of all- it could work. Moreover, the opposition's failure to present a joint candidate will be definitely used by President Erdoğan as an example of incompetence. Thus, I think, unless Akşener is convinced, now the presidential election is open to two possibilities almost equally; I would guess 60 % Erdoğan and 40 % Kılıçdaroğlu will win.

Conclusion

Finally, in my opinion, 2023 elections will be a very difficult challenge for Turkish democracy, but the country will soon get over it and will celebrate its 100th year anniversary with a new government and a refreshed parliament democratically elected by Turkish people.

Most recent news show that Akşener and İYİ Parti could return to the table for a joint candidate. It is written in the Turkish press that Yavaş and İmamoğlu could become Vice Presidents to strengthen Kılıçdaroğlu's presidency. Next few days will be critical for the opposition and if Akşener stays within the bloc, the opposition could win the election in a relatively easier manner.

Note: As expected, Akşener returned to table and the Nation Alliance entered into elections as a whole. However, this problematic event cost some votes to the alliance due to the lack of confidence given to voters.

Ozan Örmeci[*]

Explaining the Rise of Erdoğan from Huntington's Perspective

Abstract This chapter tries to analyze the rise of Islamist politics in Türkiye and Turkish President Recep Tayyip Erdoğan on the scene by following the writings and projections of famous American political scientist Samuel Huntington.

Keywords: *Turkish Politics, AK Parti, Recep Tayyip Erdoğan, Islamism, Political Islam, Samuel Huntington, Clash of Civilizations.*

Introduction

Samuel P. Huntington (1927–2008)[1] was a prominent American political scientist and academic. Huntington spent more than half a century at Harvard University and worked as the White House Coordinator of Security Planning for the National Security Council during the Carter administration. He is best known for his 1993 theory, *"The Clash of Civilizations"*[2] which he first asserted in his article *"The Clash of Civilizations?"*[3] in Summer 1993 edition of the *Foreign Affairs* magazine in response to his former student Francis Fukuyama's 1992 book, *The End of History and the Last Man.* Huntington later developed his views and published his chef d'oeuvre *The Clash of Civilizations and the Remaking of World Order in 1996* as a book[4].

---

* Associate Professor in the department of Political Science and International Relations (English) at Istanbul Aydın University, Istanbul, Türkiye.
 Email: ozanormeci@aydin.edu.tr / ozanormeci@gmail.com.
 ORCID: 0000-0001-8850-6089.
1 For information; https://en.wikipedia.org/wiki/Samuel_P._Huntington.
2 For details about his theory see; http://politikaakademisi.org/2015/12/21/the-clash-of-civilizations-by-samuel-huntington/.
3 The article is here; https://www.foreignaffairs.com/articles/united-states/1993-06-01/clash-civilizations.
4 The book is available at Amazon.com; https://www.amazon.com/Clash-Civilizations-Remaking-World-Order/dp/B004U522OS/.

Essence of the Theory

With his theory, Huntington rejected classical Marxist and liberal approaches and revitalized the Weberian tradition of superstructure by focusing on the civilizational aspects of nations and states. He thought that people's cultural and religious identities (the civilization that they belong) will be the primary source of conflict in the post-Cold War world. He divided nations on earth into 9 main civilizational categories: Western (European and North American)[5], Orthodox (mainly Russia), Islamic, African, Latin American, Sinic, Hindu, Buddhist and Japanese. He claimed that a civilization is a cultural entity and the highest level of grouping that distances people from other people. In his view, civilization is defined both by common objective elements, such as language, history, religion, customs, institutions, and by the subjective self-identification of people. Civilizations obviously blend and overlap, and may include subcivilizations as well. Western civilization has two major variants, European and North American, and Islam has its Arab, Turkic and Malay subdivisions.

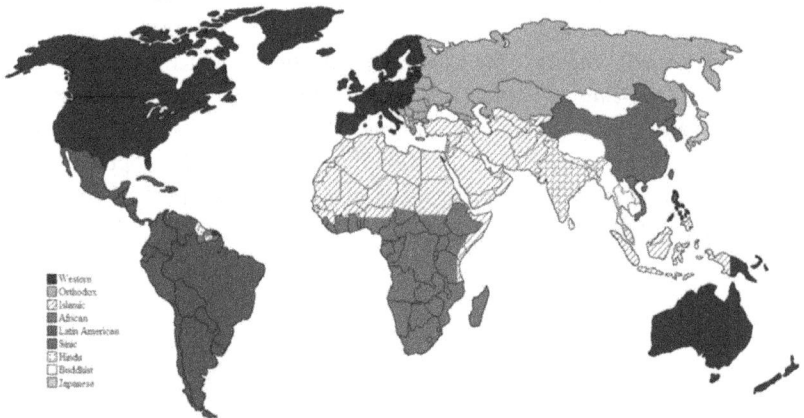

Major civilizations according to Huntington

---

5   Huntington does not make any reference to Catholic-Protestant and secular-religious cleavages in Western countries which might be a major source of criticism against his theory.

Five Types of Countries

Samuel Huntington also categorized countries in terms of their attitude towards their own and other civilizations. There are some countries that are fully identified with one culture and civilization. These countries are called as *"member states"* by Huntington. For instance, Egypt is with Arab-Islamic civilization and Italy is with European-Western civilization and they are member states of their civilizations.

Some countries historically and culturally represent on the other hand the origin of one specific civilization. This is not the same as belonging strictly to a particular civilization, but rather representing the birth and origin of that civilization. These states are called as *"core states"*. Arab states for instance represent the origin of Islamic civilization although Pakistan or even Turkey might only be member states in Islamic civilization.

A *"lone country"* or a *"lone state"* on the other hand lacks cultural commonality with other societies. Ethiopia for example, is culturally isolated by its predominant language, Amharic, written in the Ethiopie script; its predominant religion, Coptic Orthodoxy; its imperial history; and its religious differentiation from the largely Muslim surrounding peoples. While Haiti's elite has traditionally relished its cultural ties to France, Haiti's Creole language, Voodoo religion, revolutionary slave origins, and brutal history combine to make it a lone country as well. Japan is also a *"lone country"* although it has strong political and military ties with Washington. Japanese culture is particularistic and does not have a universal religious or political aspect.

In addition, there are some *"cleft countries"* that include large groups of people from different civilizations. *"Cleft countries"* often have problems about their unity. In Sudan for instance, civil war has gone on for decades between the Muslim north and the largely Christian south. Huntington wrote that the same civilizational division has bedeviled Nigerian politics for a similar length of time and stimulated one major war of secession plus coups, rioting, and other violence. Other examples can be listed as India (Hindus and Muslims), Sri Lanka (Sinhalese Buddhists and Tamil Hindus), Malaysia and Singapore (Chinese and Malay Muslims), China (Han Chinese, Tibetan Buddhists, and Uyghur Muslim Turks) and Indonesia (Muslims and Timorese Christians).

The last category is *"torn countries"* and it includes states such as Turkey, Russia, Australia, and Mexico[6]. Torn country concept refers to states and nations

---

6   Ukraine is also often added to this list.

that had a strong cultural change in their history (often Westernization) due their political elite's preferences. Peter the Great and Catherine the Great of Russia and obviously Mustafa Kemal Atatürk from Turkey are great examples of leaders that implemented a cultural change. However, their legacy is often mixed and controversial[7].

Mustafa Kemal Atatürk

Turkish Example

Turkey is the country that in fact gives its true meaning to Huntington's concept and theory of "*torn country*". Turkey for long centuries during the Ottoman Empire represented the Islamic civilization and Ottoman Sultans carried the title of Caliphate. However, after the collapse of the Ottoman State following the First World War, Mustafa Kemal Atatürk established modern Republic of Turkey and began to implement his shocking reforms that aim to make Turkey a part of the Western civilization. Rejecting the idea of a multinational empire, Kemal aimed to produce a homogeneous nation state. Huntington wrote:

---

7   Huntington wrote that for a "torn country" to successfully to redefine its civilizational identity, at least three requirements must be met. First, the political and economic elite of the country has to be generally supportive of and enthusiastic about this move. Second, the public has to be at least willing to acquiesce in the redefinition of identity. Third, the dominant elements in the host civilization, in most cases the West, have to be willing to embrace the convert.

He (Atatürk) abolished the caliphate, the central source of religious authority, ended the traditional education and religious ministries, abolished the separate religious schools and colleges, established a unified secular system of public education, and did away with the religious courts that applied Islamic law, replacing them with a new legal system based on the Swiss civil code. He also replaced the traditional calendar with the Gregorian calendar and formally disestablished Islam as the state religion. Emulating Peter the Great, he prohibited use of the fez because it was a symbol of religious traditionalism, encouraged people to wear hats, and decreed that Turkish would be written in Roman rather than Arabic script. This latter reform was of fundamental importance. "It made it virtually impossible for the new generations educated in the Roman script to acquire access to the vast bulk of traditional literature; it encouraged the learning of European languages; and it greatly eased the problem of increasing literacy." Having redefined the national, political, religious, and cultural identity of the Turkish people, Kemal in the 1930s vigorously attempted to promote Turkish economic development. Westernization went hand-in-hand with and was to be the means of modernization.

Atatürk's model of Westernization worked successfully during the Cold War since Turkey was a very important country for the Western world in terms of security. However, the end of Cold War brought some problems to Turkish model as well as Turkey's relations with the Western world. Turkey's geopolitical and military importance was no longer present according to some Western analysts since Soviet threat ended. The end of Cold War also dragged Turkey into a new search for identity. Islamic and Turkic identities became much more apparent and stronger in this new era. Especially the resurgence of Islam was unstoppable in Turkey and led to fundamental changes in Turkish state structure and Turkish foreign policy. Although Turkey was once hopeful about becoming a member of the European Union (EU), the idea seems rather absurd right now looking both from Brussels and Ankara. Huntington thinks that Turkish people unlike Turkish state elite began to reject the idea of Westernization and the process caused even stronger anti-Western sentiments. This is the true reason of Turkey's Islamization process. However, Turkey's situation is still open to discussion.

Explaining the Rise of Erdoğan

Huntington also wrote that Turkey could have another transformation in the years to come since it is now in the situation of a beggar pleading for membership in the West. Moreover, its historical heritage makes Turkey a perfect candidate for transforming into a *"core state"* for representing the Islamic civilization. Although Turks have a long pre-Islamic history as well, Huntington believes that the strong legacy of the Ottoman Empire make this country potentially a stronger core country than Saudi Arabia, the original home of Islam. He further states that Turkey has the history, population, middle level of economic development, national coherence, and military tradition and competence to be the core state of Islam. However, Atatürk's legacy still prevents Turkey to make such a radical shift and fully embrace its Islamic identity. In that sense, Huntington finally concluded that Atatürk's reforms are still strong and Turkey needs a strong Islamic leader who would be of Atatürk's caliber (a kind of second Atatürk who will be more Islamic and will reverse his reforms) and who would transform Turkey into an Islamic core state without any hesitations. He even wrote that Turkey will have to reject Atatürk as Russians rejected Lenin after the collapse of USSR in order to fully embrace this new identity.

Huntington's this last comment in fact describe the coming of Recep Tayyip Erdoğan, an Islamist politician whose rise started in the mid-1990s as the municipal leader of Istanbul. Erdoğan is now the undisputed chef and the President of Turkey and he is a great example of *"from zero to hero"* model. Erdoğan is a man of the people with his aggressive, anti-Western and Islamic rhetoric and he openly opposes to Atatürk's reforms and secularism. His electoral success shows that Erdoğan fits into Huntington's description perfectly well, but he still represents only the half of the country. The other half of Turkey on the other hand still seems closer to Atatürk's model.

How Turkey will manage this bipolar social and political structure will of course be a million dollar question in the 21st century and a major research subject for political scientists and sociologists. But Huntington's prophecy is interesting since he wrote this book when political Islam in Turkey (Erbakan tradition) was weak and did not have high approval (only 20–21 %) in the mid-1990s.

Ozan Örmeci*

Türkiye Will Hold Its Elections on May 14, 2023

Abstract This chapter is about 2023 Turkish elections by assessing the strengths and weaknesses of the government and the opposition bloc.

Keywords: *Turkish Politics, 2023 Turkish elections, AK Parti, CHP, Recep Tayyip Erdoğan, Kemal Kılıçdaroğlu, 2023 Turkish earthquakes.*

Introduction

Now the date is set; Türkiye (Turkey) will hold its presidential and parliamentary elections on May 14, 2023. As a country that has always been struggling to embrace full democracy in the last 70 years, the elections will be decisive in terms of choosing a future for the country. At one side, Turkish President Recep Tayyip Erdoğan and his right-wing conservative party coming from Islamist origins AK Parti (Justice and Development Party) leads the People Alliance (*Cumhur İttifakı*) bloc, on the other hand, pro-secular CHP (Republican People's Party) and its leader Kemal Kılıçdaroğlu leads the Nation Alliance (*Millet İttifakı*) bloc. Erdoğan and Kılıçdaroğlu are both presidential candidates and it is certain that the presidential election will be a race between these two. While Erdoğan's bloc represents hyper-presidentialism and a more authoritarian country leaning towards becoming a regional power, the opposition bloc defends parliamentary democratic regime and a return to Türkiye's classical Western-oriented foreign policy. In this piece, I am going to analyze 2023 Turkish elections and summarize recent political developments within the country.

---

*   Associate Professor in the department of Political Science and International Relations (English) at Istanbul Aydın University, Istanbul, Türkiye.
     Email: ozanormeci@aydin.edu.tr / ozanormeci@gmail.com.
     ORCID: 0000-0001-8850-6089.

Opposition Finally Chooses a Presidential Candidate: Kemal Kılıçdaroğlu

Turkey's main opposition bloc, the Nation Alliance is a loose electoral coalition between six parties. The bloc is led by CHP, the political party that has established the Republic of Türkiye in 1923 under the leadership of its first chair and the heroic founding father of the country, Mustafa Kemal Atatürk. Although CHP was a revolutionary republican and a radical modernist party in the 1920s and the 1930s, it had eventually transformed into an authoritarian state party afterwards and lost its popular support especially among the pious (Islamist) and Kurdish voters. The party lost the first free and fair election in the country in 1950, on May 14 and stayed away from the government for a decade, but began to make a new political opening in the 1960s and 1970s under İsmet İnönü and Bülent Ecevit's leaderships by transforming itself into a populist leftist party appealing to working population and especially to workers and urban poor.

CHP was closed down in 1980 by the military regime, but was reestablished in 1992. This new CHP was more bourgeois-centered; defending free-market and especially focusing on protecting the secular regime and the unitary state structure against rising Islamist and Kurdish movements. The party could not become very successful in the elections during Deniz Baykal's leadership, but eventually has become the second biggest and the main opposition party in Türkiye since 2002. In 2010, Kemal Kılıçdaroğlu was elected the party's new chair following a sex tape scandal. Coming from Alevi faith, Kılıçdaroğlu has tried to open the party to different groups within the Turkish society by bringing center-right, Islamist, and liberal figures to the old party structure and cadre. Although Kılıçdaroğlu increased the party's votes by 5 % compared to Baykal period, he still seemed to have no chance to defeat Erdoğan until recently.

However, starting from his Justice March (*Adalet Yürüyüşü*) in 2017, Kemal Kılıçdaroğlu has showed his strength of purpose to defeat Erdoğan and began to implement a new strategy. By using cleavages within the governing bloc and the pro-government MHP (Nationalist Action Party), he helped the flourishing of new right-wing parties that embraced anti-Erdoğanism. So, first the Good Party (İYİ Parti) was established by Meral Akşener and his friends, by splitting from MHP, with the help and active support of CHP. Later, Gültekin Uysal's center-right Democrat Party (DP) and Temel Karamollaoğlu's Islamist but anti-government Felicity Party (*Saadet Partisi*-SP) began to support Kılıçdaroğlu and his newly established bloc, the Nation Alliance. However, this was not enough for the opposition to defeat Erdoğan in 2018 when Muharrem İnce lost the presidential election against Erdoğan in the first round. Kılıçdaroğlu did not give up and continued to develop this new strategy. In the end, he saw the joining of two new right-wing parties to his electoral bloc; Ali Babacan's DEVA and Ahmet Davutoğlu's Future Party (*Gelecek Partisi*-GP), both splitting from the governing AK Parti. Kılıçdaroğlu also maintained his friendly relations with the pro-Kurdish HDP (Peoples' Democratic Party) and tried to embrace everyone without making any discrimination. Moreover, he was successful in managing the "*sextet chair*" (*altılı masa*) and solved a recent crisis with Akşener to confirm his candidacy in a way that showed his strong leadership abilities. Now, Kılıçdaroğlu seems to have a real chance to win the presidential election and almost all polls show that he could win the election with 55–56 % votes to Erdoğan's 44–45 % in a potential head-to-head second round. Especially if HDP decides to support Kılıçdaroğlu in the first or at least in the second round, his chance would be extremely high for winning the presidential race.

Alarm for Erdoğan and Efforts to Bring New Actors to the Governing Coalition

Erdoğan is still the leader of AK Parti and People Alliance and his strategy is to expand the governing bloc. Erdoğan has already the support of Devlet Bahçeli's Turkish nationalist MHP (Nationalist Action Party) and Mustafa Destici's Islamist-Turkish nationalist BBP (Great Unity Party) parties on his ranks. However, seeing the increasing performance of the opposition, Erdoğan now wants to expand his bloc. For instance, he recently convinced Hüda-Par (Free Cause Party) to join the People Alliance. However, led by Zekeriya Yapıcıoğlu and supported by former Kurdish Hezbollah members and supporters, this party is a very radical political organization both in its approach to secular regime and to the Kurdish Question. Although not defending openly autonomy or independence, the party is very much pro-Kurdish and calls for the constitutional recognition of Kurdish language and identity in addition to the mother tongue education. Although these are in fact basic democratic rights, in semi-democratic regimes like Türkiye, this could create problems in politics. Moreover, the party also openly advocates a Sunni Islamic regime by criminalizing adultery and recognizing religious (Islamic) marriages. It is a fact that Hüda-Par could bring some votes from Kurds, but the real and the main pro-Kurdish political actor in the country will continue to be the HDP.

In addition, Erdoğan and AK Parti are recently in talks with two small parties; the Democratic Left Party (*Demokratik Sol Parti*-DSP) – former political party of Bülent Ecevit which is not an important political actor anymore and the Motherland Party (ANAP) – a reestablished political party named after Turgut Özal and Mesut Yılmaz's famous party who ruled Türkiye in the 1980s and 1990s. These two political parties would not bring many votes to Erdoğan, but could improve the psychological situation of the governing bloc. However, if Erdoğan and his team achieve to convince the New Welfare Party (*Yeniden Refah Partisi*), an Islamist and anti-Western political party led by famous Islamist politician Necmettin Erbakan's son Fatih Erbakan, this could be a real game-changing factor. Although not spoken openly in the media, this party has already 270,000 members and is one of the biggest parties in Türkiye in terms of membership size. The party has also approximately 2 % electoral support according to most recent polls. This shows that it might not change the overall picture, but having the New Welfare Party on his ranks could bring Erdoğan more votes. However, Fatih Erbakan could become a presidential candidate independently as well. Lastly, having this party with him or not, Erdoğan needs a small miracle to win this election.

Other Presidential Candidates

There will be some other candidates contending in the 2023 Türkiye presidential elections. For instance, recently, former MHP deputy and a Turkish nationalist politician having strong ties with Azerbaijan, Sinan Oğan was announced to be the candidate of 7 right-wing and Turkish nationalist parties. Oğan is an influential public figure who has been appearing on televised debates very frequently, but he does not have high chance. Among the political parties who support Oğan -it is called as the "*Ata İttifakı*" (Patriarch Alliance)-, the only influential political actor is Professor Ümit Özdağ's Victory Party (*Zafer Partisi*). Having an anti-immigrant and ultranationalist rhetoric, this party has a real potential among Turkish far-right voters. There are already some opinion polls that suggest that this party could get 1.6–2 % votes in the coming parliamentary elections.

Former CHP deputy and the leader of Homeland Party (*Memleket Partisi*) Muharrem İnce will become a presidential candidate as well. İnce is an excellent orator, but having lost the presidential election to Erdoğan in 2018 and not supported by his party CHP anymore, İnce and his party could get maximum 2–3 %. Moreover, in order to confirm his candidacy from outside the parliament, İnce needs the signature of 100,000 Turkish citizens.

Veteran left-wing politician and the leader of the Patriotic Party (*Vatan Partisi*) Doğu Perinçek could become a presidential candidate as well with the support and the signature of 100,000 Turkish citizens. Perinçek does not have any real chance to win the election.

Turkish far-left might also declare its presidential candidate soon. Composed of socialist/communist political parties including TİP (Turkish Labor Party), EMEP, and the Left Party (*Sol Parti*), this bloc is named as the Labor and Freedom Alliance (*Emek ve Özgürlük İttifakı*). This bloc might eventually decide to endorse Kılıçdaroğlu as well especially in case HDP follows this path.

Conclusion

To conclude, I can say that, 2023 Türkiye elections will be very interesting for political scientists and international observers. It seems like we could witness a democratic transition of power although it is almost unimaginable to think mighty Erdoğan to give his seat to his main rival Kılıçdaroğlu. Polls show that Kılıçdaroğlu could win the election even with a large (5 to 8 %) points difference, but I am sure that Erdoğan will try everything and show an amazing performance before the elections. Let us hope that Turkish people will make the right decision.

Ozan Örmeci[*]

Turkey's Boss: Recep Tayyip Erdoğan

Abstract This chapter is about the life story and the political style of Turkish President Recep Tayyip Erdoğan.

Keywords: *Turkish Politics, AK Parti, Recep Tayyip Erdoğan, Islamism, Political Islam.*

Recep Tayyip Erdoğan working in his office

For those who will examine Turkish political life decades and centuries from now, Recep Tayyip Erdoğan will undoubtedly be the most important, interesting and controversial figure in Turkish politics in the 2000s. In this article, I will examine the life story and leadership characteristics of Recep Tayyip Erdoğan, who has been serving as the Prime Minister and the President of the Republic of Turkey for about 20 years.

[*]   Associate Professor in the department of Political Science and International Relations
     (English) at Istanbul Aydın University, Istanbul, Türkiye.
       Email: ozanormeci@aydin.edu.tr / ozanormeci@gmail.com.
       ORCID: 0000-0001-8850-6089.

The son of a Black Sea family, Recep Tayyip Erdogan was born in Istanbul in 1954. He completed his primary education in Kasımpaşa Piyale Primary School. He was not a very bright student, and in the year he graduated, he only got "*Very Good – 5*" in 4 courses; Turkish, Writing, Physical Education, and State and Departure. The Religious Studies course was 4 (Good). When the school principal asked "*who will pray*" in the classroom one day, only that finger was raised. The principal had placed a newspaper in front of the board as a prayer rug and invited his student to prayer. However, little Tayyip immediately objected; "*There is a picture on this newspaper, prayers cannot be performed*". From that day on, his friends began to call Recep Tayyip "hodja". He continued his education at Istanbul İmam Hatip High School with the guidance of his school principal. His father, who was an extremely authoritarian and religious person, was also pleased that his son wanted to attend İmam Hatip High School. His father, Reis Kaptan, who was very influential in the formation of Tayyip Erdoğan's personality, was really a strict person. It was as if he had carried the maritime rules into his home; for example, even the penalties were according to the rules of the sea. Little Tayyip tried to keep his father's word, but when he upset him, he would resort to an interesting way; he would bend over and kiss his shoes. Seeing this, Reis Kaptan calmed down, tears were flowing from his eyes. One day, the next-door neighbor Müşerref Abla, who knew that Recep Tayyip had a bad mouth, made him swear again, laughed out loud, and then punished him by hitting his butt. Hearing this, Reis Kaptan had punished his five-six-year-old son by hanging them from the ceiling. 15–20 minutes later, his uncle took down little Tayyip.

Recep Tayyip, who started the Secondary school of İmam Hatip High School in 1965, had an average appearance in his classes, while he was extremely active socially. He also played on the school football team. However, young Tayyip, afraid of his father's anger, had to play football in secret. When he was transferred to Camialtıspor, one of the amateur teams of Kasımpaşa, at the age of 15, his father would have to learn that he played football. At such a young age, Tayyip Erdoğan, like many conservative young people like himself, started to attend the meetings of the National Turkish Students' Union (MTTB). In this period when nationalist-conservative youth were encouraged to become politicized by the state during the anti-communist struggle in Turkey, MTTB was the institution where Erdogan and similar right-wing anti-communist youth made their first political socialization. Recep Tayyip, who has been fond of literature, especially poetry, since his youth; he participated in various debates within the MTTB and recited the lines of his beloved poet Necip Fazıl Kısakürek aloud in front of his friends. Although he was not very successful in his classes, he always stood out among his friends with his leader personality. In 1972, Recep

Tayyip Erdoğan was one of the people who formed the three-person team that brought the Istanbul İmam Hatip High School the first place in the High School Debate Competition. He also took part in the *Mehter* team of the school and was carrying a banner in front of the team due to his tall stature. At the same time, he continued to play on the school football team. Despite his belief, he wore short shorts while playing on the football team, as per the rules, and he could accept it. Years later, he would make a statement saying "*I know I am a sinner*" because of this. Erdoğan graduated from Istanbul İmam Hatip High School in 1973 with a good grade. His grades weren't very bright, as he only got 10 out of 10 in Physical Education course. Quran and Arabic lessons were interestingly poor.

Having graduated from Istanbul İmam Hatip High School, Recep Tayyip wanted to study at Mülkiye, but since Mülkiye only accepted high school graduates, he could not enroll. For this reason, he took the exam at Eyüp High School in 1974 and graduated from a regular high school by giving difference courses. However, the points he received were still not enough for Mülkiye. He entered Marmara University Istanbul Academy of Economics and Commercial Sciences. In the same year, he was transferred to İETT, one of the 1st amateur cluster teams of Istanbul. He appeared on the staff of workers and received a regular salary. In this way, he could continue his education and earn a living thanks to his hobby, football. Starting from those years, Necmettin Erbakan became his idol in politics. At the invitation of his friend Nuri Avcı, he attended a meeting of the Beyoğlu district organization of Erbakan's National Salvation Party (MSP) in 1975 and became a member of the party. However, he had to keep his membership secret because he was afraid of his authoritarian father, who was a supporter of Süleyman Demirel's Justice Party (AP). Admiring Erbakan so much that he named his first son Necmettin, he immediately stood out among the MSP youth and was elected as the Head of the MSP District Youth Branch and also a Member of the General Administrative Board of the Youth Branch. These duties continued until 1980. Starting from his youth, due to his ambition in politics and his charismatic personality, it was spoken among his friends and party members that he could become a leader in the future, and he was called the "*President*". In 1977, he took the stage at the National Pride Night, organized by the MSP Youth Branch and attended by Necmettin Erbakan, and enthusiastically recited poems and enthralled the audience. One of those who watched and affected the young Erdoğan was Emine Gülbaran, the daughter of a family from Siirt who would become his future wife, and a member of the Idealist Women's Association. Erdoğan was also impressed by this young lady, who was veiled by the force of her brother. With the intervention of the seers, the young couple got married in 1978 without meeting in person within 6 months. They had two children within 2 years. Years later, Tayyip Erdoğan would interpret the relationship that Emine Erdoğan described as *"lightning love"* as *"I have never been in love in my life"*. Continuing his political activities as well, Erdoğan was still against anarchy, which was very common on the right and left at that time, and according to journalist Ruşen Çakır, he managed to keep his friends away from the conflict environment. While leftists and nationalists were killing each other, Islamists were preparing themselves for the new era away from the events.

Erdoğan, who was uncomfortable with the management of the commando colonel who came to İETT after September 12, left here. His political duties were also automatically terminated. After graduating from university in 1981, Erdoğan completed his military service as a reserve officer in 1982. After September 12, while many of his colleagues were running towards Turgut Özal and ANAP, Erdoğan remained loyal to Necmettin Erbakan and joined the Welfare Party (*Refah Partisi*-RP). In return for this loyalty, he rose immediately and became the head of the Welfare Party Beyoğlu district and then the provincial head of Istanbul. At the age of 31, he became the provincial chairman of a rapidly rising party in Turkey's most important city. Now the winds were blowing fast behind him. During this period, one of the important names of the Islamic world and Afghan Prime Minister and commander Gulbeddin Hikmetyar, who was supported by the United States against the Soviet occupation for a while, had young politician Tayyip Erdoğan sitting at his knee during his visit to Turkey, and there was a lot of controversy when this square came to the fore in the future. Erdoğan was a parliamentary candidate from Istanbul in the 1986 midterm elections, but was not elected. In the 1989 local elections, he became the Beyoğlu mayoral candidate. He drew attention with the new methods he followed in the election campaign. Erdoğan was trying to establish a dialogue with people from all walks of life, even the most marginalized sections. However, he did not win the election and was sentenced to 10 months in prison for insulting the incumbent judge on the grounds of electoral fraud, but his sentence was commuted to a fine. Finally, in the 1991 general elections, he ran as the first candidate of the Welfare Party in Fatih and won the elections. However, due to the preferential voting system, the dream of being a member of the parliament was destroyed. During these years, he drew attention with his radical Islamic discourse. The phrase *"one cannot be both secular and Muslim"* was uttered in those days and was a phrase that would follow Erdoğan throughout his political career. Promising that he will close the brothels, he will make Pierre Cardin's chador show, he will open Hagia Sophia to worship, and that he will build a large mosque in Taksim, in the 1994 local elections, he was elected as the Mayor of Istanbul Metropolitan Municipality from the Welfare Party. Erdoğan, who came to the agenda with the fugitive shantytown that *Hürriyet* newspaper announced with the headline "*Wow Tayyip Ağa Wow*" before the election, was a new hope, one of their own, for millions of voters living in the slums, fed up with prohibitions, corruption, and poverty. At the age of 40, the son of Reis Kaptan from Rize became the mayor of Istanbul. As journalist Ruşen Çakır has stated, Erdoğan and his friends, who are among the innovative names of the Islamist movement, were actually not less Islamist than the classical MSP line, but even more strictly Islamist. They only adopted modern methods and wanted to spread Islamism to the public with these methods. As a first step, Erdoğan banned alcohol in Istanbul Metropolitan Municipality establishments. However, despite this prohibitive attitude, the increase in quality and hard work in municipal services created satisfaction in the electorate.

The Welfare Party, which won many municipalities, especially Istanbul and Ankara, in the 1994 local elections, emerged as the first party in the 1995 general elections. Refahyol (Refah Partisi-DYP coalition) was established under Erbakan's Prime Ministry. Erdoğan's rapid rise attracted attention, and according to some, it even bothered Erbakan. Erdoğan opposed to Erbakan's attitude during the 28 February process within the Welfare Party, which was shaken by the 28 February process. However, Erbakan would reply to Erdoğan, "*These things are not child's play*". While Erbakan, who had to forcefully sign the resolutions of the MGK (National Security Council), started to fall out of favor with the National Outlook (*Milli Görüş*) electorate, Erdoğan, who had a more radical and harsh rhetoric, was rising rapidly. Erdoğan, who made a speech in Siirt, his wife's hometown on December 12, 1997, was now greeted with "*Prime Minister Tayyip*" banners. The speech he delivered and the poem he recited that day would carry Erdoğan first to prison and then to the top. Everything was designed to take him to the top. Erdoğan, who was stripped of his mayorship and sent to prison, was now the leading figure for the Islamic section. Erdoğan, who was imprisoned for 4 months with a convoy of hundreds of vehicles saying "*This song will not end here*". While Erdoğan was in prison, the successor of RP, Virtue Party (*Fazilet Partisi*) received only 15 % of the votes in the 1999 general elections, under the leadership of Recai Kutan, causing great disappointment. Moreover, it would not be long before the Virtue Party was closed by the Constitutional Court after the Welfare Party. After the closure of the Virtue Party, instead of joining the Felicity Party, which Erbakan pointed out, Erdoğan worked with younger National Outlook figures (Abdullatif Şener, Abdullah Gül, Mehmet Ali Şahin, Bülent Arınç, Melih Gökçek, Kadir Topbaş etc.) and founded the Justice and Development Party (AK Parti) in 2001 and became its first leader. Now, he was making hundreds of thousands excited with the song

"*Everything reminds me of you*" in the squares. Erdoğan, who also paid a visit to the United States at the beginning of 2002, had contacts with senior officials. The Americans, who knew Turkey very well, had noticed Erdoğan's power and popularity in the grassroots long ago, as *Aydınlık* magazine announced many years ago. While his old radical speeches were broadcast in Turkey, Erdogan was answering questions on this subject as "*I have changed*" and "*We took off the National Outlook shirt*".

Erdoğan brought his party to the top with 34 % of the votes in the 2002 general elections. However, he could not become a member of parliament or Prime Minister due to his political ban. With the constitutional amendment and the renewed Siirt elections, which were organized with the support of the CHP, he finally entered the Parliament as a deputy and became the Prime Minister of the Republic of Turkey by taking the job from Abdullah Gül, whom he had entrusted for a short time, and establishing the 59th government in 2003. The Justice and Development Party, which also won the 2004 local elections and its charismatic leader Erdoğan were on the top of Turkish politics. In this period, Turkey-European Union full membership negotiations started, giving hope to those who were skeptical from the very beginning. However, the government's Islamist rhetoric was on the rise before long, and there was a great polarization in the country due to the harsh opposition developed by the CHP. It is claimed that as Erdoğan's self-confidence increased, his authoritarian tendencies increased, and the Presidential elections in 2007 were turning into a major crisis in a short time. Erdoğan wanted to choose the President himself based on his majority in the parliament, although there was very little time left until the end of his term of office. CHP leader Deniz Baykal and the secular establishment opposed to this. In the end, despite the increasing opposition towards him and the reservations of the military -even the April 27 e-memorandum- after the general elections, the AK Parti, which had a 47 % increase in the votes in the 22 July 2007 elections, ensured that Abdullah Gül became the 11th President. Erdoğan was now a mighty Prime Minister who was the sole ruler of the system. Erdoğan no longer had to conform to the system, the system had to adapt to him. Relying on his success at the ballot box, Erdoğan virtually restructured Turkey in line with his own ideology.

Over the years, the importance given to relations with the EU has decreased, an active regional foreign policy vision, called neo-Ottomanism by some, has been put forward, and Turkey has now looked more to the East. Erdoğan, who frequently makes statements and practices that anger sensitive segments about secularism in the country, still maintains his position as the sole ruler of the system. Erdoğan, in fact, in time has become one of the most important portraits of 21st century world politics with his harsh criticisms of Israeli President Shimon Peres at the Davos Economic Forum, his popularity at a second level of Gamal Abdel Nasser in the Arab world, and his controversial practices within the country. We will see how Erdoğan's political career will be shaped in the future, but now let's focus on some of Erdoğan's personal and ideological characteristics and leadership methods.

Recep Tayyip Erdoğan, -I think everyone will accept- has become an authoritarian political leader in the last years, probably influenced by his father's authoritarian personality and the hierarchical and harsh relations in the family, and, like many other charismatic leaders, succeeded in making his authority accepted by the public. Erdoğan, who was observed to have a harsh and authoritarian approach towards the opposition from time to time, did not allow his authority to be questioned in the internal party functioning. The fact that the AK Parti, which can be said to attach importance to democratic principles in many other areas at least in appearance, fell short in terms of the bylaws governing the functioning of the party can also be explained by the fact that Erdoğan's leadership is indisputable. Similar to the indisputability of Erdoğan's leadership, the postponement of the AK Parti's provincial elections in case of a second candidate created various debates in the opposition media about the party's understanding of democracy. Another important point to be said about Erdoğan's character is; Erdoğan is an incredibly ambitious and combative person. Erdoğan, who was brought up from a family belonging to the lower-middle section of society, -despite the various difficulties he faced throughout his life- never gave up and managed to get up and fight again in every defeat. Many negative events, such as the failures he experienced in his first political attempts and candidacy, and his imprisonment, could have never stopped Erdoğan, on the contrary, has made him even more ambitious. The excessive ambition and self-confidence seen in many important politicians are also seen in Erdoğan. Undoubtedly, Erdoğan's involvement in politics from a young age and his leadership personality may have been influential in the development of these characteristics. Erdoğan also has a very charismatic physiognomy for Eastern societies and the people of Turkey, although not by Western standards. With his tall stature, bully (külhanbeyi) gait, mustache, and an image that can be interpreted as an Islamic derivative of actor Nejat İşler, who is claimed to be Erdoğan's relative, Erdoğan has more than the charismatic qualities found in leaders and is almost the young brother of the neighborhood in terms of conservative voters. Despite Erdoğan's occasional excesses, obvious mistakes, and his words that he realized and changed within a few days, he is still loved by some of the people. From my point of view, it made me think that he has an element of sympathy and luck, just like the characters portrayed by famous Turkish comedian and actor Kemal Sunal in Natuk Baytan films.

Undoubtedly, Erdoğan's most important feature is his *"man of the people"* nature. Although Erdoğan was the representative of a political movement that was considered excessive in the past, with his personal characteristics and unique character, he established an incredible bond with the public and made himself popular and respected. With his shouldering the coffin before everyone else during the funeral prayers he attended, his shouting and use of folk sayings and some rude words, his fatherly attitudes and words towards the children he was handing out toys to, Erdoğan was perhaps the leader who succeeded the most in becoming a man of the people in Turkish political history and was the most distant from elitism. The unplanned urbanization and industrialization process in Turkey, the migration from the village to the city, and the hybrid culture Turkey has created in this environment can actually be seen in Erdoğan's life codes. Erdoğan, who grew up in a neighborhood environment in Kasımpaşa, learned the neighborhood culture from a young age, and in his political life, he preferred simple public discourse and excited the masses. At this point, it should be emphasized that Erdoğan is a really good orator. As an observer who had the opportunity to listen to him live in the squares several times, I can say that Erdogan fascinated the audience in his public speeches and deeply impressed people with his loud voice and interesting intonations and accents. Erdoğan's rhetoric lessons at İmam Hatip High School and the fact that he was a good debater and poetry reader from an early age were certainly very influential in the development of this feature.

If we need to evaluate Erdoğan's ideological tendencies, the first thing to emphasize is; Erdoğan is an Islamist leader who grew up in the conditions of the Cold War in Turkey. The main factor in Erdoğan's perception of the world, especially until recent years, has been the religion of Islam and the ideology of Islamism (Political Islam). Admiring Erbakan since his youth, Erdoğan is a politician of the National Outlook by the core. However, according to many observers, this feature of Erdoğan, which can be considered as radical for democratic life, weakened over time and Erdoğan made a natural synthesis of his own worldview with ideologies such as liberalism, Turkish nationalism, and democracy. Indeed, Erdoğan may not be considered a classical National Outlook member in terms of the importance he attaches to the market economy and his love of wealth. Throughout his rule, Erdoğan has been a politician who insisted on privatization and made an effort to stay closer to the capital circles. However, Erdoğan also gave priority to conservative-Islamic circles close to him in the issue of capital, and he sometimes approached the capital circles

(TÜSİAD circle) known for their secular stance (when there were discussions on secularism and foreign policy) more coldly. It is necessary to look for the basis of Erdoğan's ideological characteristics, which can be considered excessive, in the anti-communist struggle during the Cold War, which turned into frenzy in Turkey. Erdoğan's contemptuous and exclusionary attitudes towards students, opposition student movements, trade union movements, different faith groups, and left-socialist parties are a reflection of the spirit created in our country during the Cold War. In addition, Erdoğan is a leader with a pragmatic approach despite these basic ideological characteristics and Islamist romanticism. On the basis of Erdoğan's approach to the EU; it can be argued that rather than admiration for Western civilization or the ideal of being a member of the EU, the idea of weakening the military-bureaucratic tutelage, which is thought to prevent the rise of the Islamist section in Turkey, lies in this process.

Another important feature of Erdoğan is his successful application of polarizing leadership in terms of ballot box results. Erdoğan adopted a harsh and divisive rhetoric on various issues such as secularism, Kemalism, military position, Alevism, contemporary life at the expense of polarizing the society, and in Turkey, where the right predominates, he always managed to surpass his left rival CHP in Deniz Baykal's era, thanks to polarizing politics. In this sense, it can be argued that Erdoğan uses the extreme rhetoric he sometimes uses deliberately, perhaps in a very planned and rational way, rather than ideological blindness or fanaticism. However, the sudden and extreme reactions he gave from time to time, especially the Davos Economic Forum; confirms that Erdoğan still has some sharp ideological points besides this rationalist-based polarizing leadership. His hypersensitivity on Palestine, his persistent refusal to see some facts (Omar al-Bashir incident, Hamas' activities, etc.) and his courage beyond real politics arouse foreign observers to think that Erdoğan is still basically an Islamist. It paves the way for him to see himself as a hero.

Erdoğan has been one of the powerful and authoritarian leaders to re-emerge in non-Western societies in the 21st century. Along with his counterparts such as Vladimir Putin in Russia and Hugo Chavez in Venezuela, Erdoğan has been a leader loved by a significant portion of the public but with authoritarian tendencies. While Chavez made populist economic choices despite his authoritarianism with the policies he implemented at this point, Putin and Erdoğan became leaders who stood close to the capital segments. It is possible to see the authoritarian tendencies of Erdoğan, Putin and Chavez, especially in their attitudes towards the media and opposition movements, and draw similarities between them.

Recep Tayyip Erdoğan is undoubtedly one of the most controversial and important leaders in the political history of the Republic of Turkey. Frankly, since Mustafa Kemal Atatürk, no other leader has had such an impact on Turkey and left his own traces. In fact, he still has the chance to provide a great service to this country in order to make a synthesis of the modern values brought by the Turkish Revolution with top-down methods with traditional values and to ensure social peace in Turkey. However, Erdoğan perhaps prefers polarization and sometimes underestimating or marginalizing his political opponents rather than social peace, considering the ballot box success. Undoubtedly, the exclusionary attitudes towards the religious-Islamic segment, which was widely practiced in Turkey for a period of time, also had an impact on the formation of this situation, and since then, the revanchist approach has become very common in conservative circles in Turkey.

Bibliography

Biyografi.net, http://www.biyografi.net/kisiayrinti.asp?kisiid=1074.

Can Dündar, "Lider Recep Tayyip Erdoğan Belgeseli", http://www.belgeselizle. org/belgeseller/Recep-Tayyip-Erdogan-Belgeseli-692.html.

"Erdogan: 'Two Things Will Be Voted on Here'", *The Wall Street Journal*, http:// online.wsj.com/article/SB10001424052748703453804575479651464540 536.html.

Heper, Metin, "A Democratic-Conservative Government by Pious People: the Justice and Development Party in Turkey", *Blackwell Companion for Contemporary Political Thought*, ed. by Ibrahim M. Abu-Rabi, New York: Blackwell.

Kim Kimdir, http://www.kimkimdir.gen.tr/kimkimdir.php?id=1590.

Odatv.com "Başbakanı Ayağından Tavana Kim Astı", http://www.odatv.com/ n.php?n=basbakani-ayagindan-tavana-kim-asti-0311101200.

Ozan Örmeci*

Kemal Kılıçdaroğlu: The Opposition's Candidate

Abstract This chapter is about the life story and political style of Turkish opposition's leader Kemal Kılıçdaroğlu.

Keywords: *Turkish Politics, CHP, Kemal Kılıçdaroğlu, Kemalism, Social Democracy, Turkish Left.*

Kemal Kılıçdaroğlu

* Associate Professor in the department of Political Science and International Relations (English) at Istanbul Aydın University, Istanbul, Türkiye.
Email: ozanormeci@aydin.edu.tr / ozanormeci@gmail.com.
ORCID: 0000-0001-8850-6089.

Introduction

While the state and all people have been trying to heal the wounds of the destruction caused by the great earthquakes in Türkiye (Turkey), conscious people, who think that this unfortunate situation that the country fell into could only be solved by making some changes in the state mechanism and political system, have started to attach more importance to politics in this process. In that sense, the presidential and parliamentary elections Türkiye will hold on May 14, 2023 will determine the future of the country in its 100th year anniversary.

In this article, I will present you the opposition's presidential candidate and pro-secular CHP (Republican People's Party) leader Kemal Kılıçdaroğlu and discuss his political style and personality from the perspective of Political Science.

Kemal Kılıçdaroğlu: An Anatolian Child Rising to the Top

Now, let us review the life story of Kemal Kılıçdaroğlu, who is now the opposition's official presidential candidate. Before moving on to Kemal Kılıçdaroğlu's political messages and personality, let us first take a closer look at his biography.

Kemal Karabulut, who was born on December 17, 1948 in the Nazimiye district of Tunceli as the fourth child of the land registry officer Kamer Bey and the housewife Yemuş Hanım, took the name Kemal Kılıçdaroğlu with his surname change in 1950, when his family took the surname *"Kılıçdaroğlu"*, which refers to the identity of his great-grandfathers. Being a successful student, Kılıçdaroğlu attended the Ankara Academy of Economics and Commercial Sciences after graduating from Elazığ Commerce High School as the most successful student. Kılıçdaroğlu, who attracted attention with his hard work and high grades throughout his school life, took part in the Science Board of the Federation of Social Democracy Associations as a 1968 generation left-wing university student, but did not show a very prominent and activist tendency. This can also be considered as an indication of Kılıçdaroğlu's cautious and democratic personality. During these years, the young Kılıçdaroğlu was the President of the Association for Social and Cultural Actions and participated in many political actions. However, Kılıçdaroğlu, who had a humanist political line starting from his youth, never participated in physical political conflicts and always adopted democratic methods of struggle. During this period, Kılıçdaroğlu also became classmates with the nationalist activist Devlet Bahçeli, who would become the chairman of the MHP in the following years, and did not have any problems with him.

Kılıçdaroğlu graduated from school in 1971 and started his career in the Ministry of Finance by passing the account specialist exam. Kılıçdaroğlu, who later became an accountant, stayed in France for a year and learned French at an intermediate level during this period. Kılıçdaroğlu, who continued his accounting expertise until 1983, was appointed to the General Directorate of Revenues in the same year. Here, he first served as the Head of the Department, and later served as the Deputy General Manager of the same institution. Kemal Kılıçdaroğlu was appointed to Bağ-Kur in 1991. Kılıçdaroğlu, who served as the General Manager here, moved to the General Directorate of the Social Insurance Institution (SSK) in 1992. Kılıçdaroğlu later served as the Deputy Undersecretary at the Ministry of Labor and Social Security for a short time, was selected as the "*Bureaucrat of the Year*" by the *Economic Trend* magazine in 1994, thanks to his outstanding performance.

Kemal Kılıçdaroğlu, who held many important positions for the Turkish State in his professional life and left a clean record behind him, voluntarily resigned from the Social Insurance Institution (SSK) in January 1999, in the hope of entering politics from the DSP (Democratic Left Party), a social democratic party led by Bülent Ecevit, a charismatic left-wing leader whom he had admired since his youth. However, Kılıçdaroğlu had to postpone his entry into politics when Ecevit did not nominate him at that time. Thus, instead of politics, for a while, he presided over the Informal Economy Specialization Commission during the studies of the 8th Five-Year Development Plan, and also lectured at Hacettepe University in Ankara for a while. In this process, Kılıçdaroğlu also served as the President of the Citizens' Tax Protection Association. Kılıçdaroğlu, who later served as a member of the Board of Directors of Türkiye İş Bankası, was also invited to the Republican People's Party's (CHP) Science Culture Platform with the then-party chair Deniz Baykal's suggestion during these years and carried out some studies there. Kılıçdaroğlu entered the parliament for the first time as CHP Istanbul deputy in the general elections of 3 November 2002 and was reelected Istanbul deputy in the 22 July 2007 elections.

While Kemal Kılıçdaroğlu was not widely known in the Turkish public until 2007, in this year, he started to draw attention with his labor-friendly statements and concrete criticisms of the government's policies in journalist Tuncay Mollaveisoğlu's "*Poverty and Corruption*" program on *Kanaltürk TV*, then-owned by famous journalist Tuncay Özkan, and became a hope especially for leftists. While there was great anxiety and despair on the left after the great success of the AK Parti in the 22 July 2007 elections, Kılıçdaroğlu gained public support with his documented opposition in the debates he had with AK Parti Deputy Chairman Şaban Dişli and Dengir Mir Mehmet Fırat and forced these names to resign from their positions as Vice Presidents. Kılıçdaroğlu, who became known as a *"dualist"* and *"gladiator"* with his outstanding performance in these debates, also put the popular Ankara Metropolitan Mayor Melih Gökçek in a difficult situation before the 29 March 2009 local elections in a televised debate.

Kılıçdaroğlu, who was selected as the Istanbul Mayor candidate by the CHP chairman Deniz Baykal at that time due to his outstanding performance, reached wide audiences and became well-known throughout the country during his mayoral campaign, which he carried out together with the CHP Istanbul Provincial President Gürsel Tekin. Kılıçdaroğlu, who reinforced his popular image and conveyed his messages to large masses, especially with his walking on muddy roads in shantytowns with hole shoes and renting a house in a middle-class neighborhood, was also appreciated by the public for his modest personality and honesty. Even though Kılıçdaroğlu was not elected Istanbul Mayor during this period, he aroused great love and respect in the society and in the media by his ability to establish a warm dialogue with people from many different segments of the society and to respond in a civilized manner to the taunts of his interlocutors without getting angry. During the election campaign, Kılıçdaroğlu was nicknamed *"Gandhi Kemal"*, inspired by the legendary leader of India, Mahatma Gandhi on the basis of his physical resemblance to him. In the same period, the nickname of *"Second Ecevit"* was also used for Kılıçdaroğlu. Kılıçdaroğlu received 2,566,000 votes as the candidate of CHP in Istanbul in the 29 March 2009 local elections (the party increased its votes by 25 % compared to the previous elections and brought it to 37 % in the elections), and despite not winning the election, according to many, achieved great success. If it is taken into account that the CHP received 2,323,000 votes in the same elections in the Istanbul Provincial General Assembly, with his personal charisma and leadership, he managed to get the votes of 243,000 people who did not vote for the party. In addition, the song *"Kılıçdaroğlu"*, prepared by the folk music artist Onur Akın for the election campaign, created a great sensation and helped Kılıçdaroğlu's name to be heard everywhere, even in the most remote villages. This success did not remain only within the borders of Istanbul; the votes of AK Parti Ankara Mayor Melih Gökçek, who was worn out by Kılıçdaroğlu before the election, decreased from 55 % to 38 % in this election.

Although it is claimed that his image has eroded after the election defeat, Kılıçdaroğlu, who continued to frequently appear in television programs as the Deputy Chairman of the CHP Group, visited nearly 50 cities in a 1,5 year period and held conferences and public sessions. In the same period, Kılıçdaroğlu, who invited the sharp-tongued name of the AK Parti, Bülent Arınç, to a duel in an open session, received a response from him as *"not my equal"*. Kılıçdaroğlu announced his candidacy for the Chairman of the CHP on May 6, 2010, after the conspiracy against CHP leader Deniz Baykal following a sex tape scandal due to intense pressure from the media and the public. So, he was elected at the 33rd Ordinary CHP Congress on 22 May 2010 the 7th Chairman of the party after Mustafa Kemal Atatürk, İsmet İnönü, Bülent Ecevit, Deniz Baykal, Hikmet Çetin, and Altan Öymen. In his speech at the congress, Kılıçdaroğlu first promised to lower down the election threshold of 10 %, which prevents the true manifestation of the national will. In addition, he stated that the intra-party democracy will be ensured by changing the law on political parties. He also stated that investments will be encouraged in the Southeastern Anatolian Region, where the population of Kurdish origin is densely populated, and the economic causes of terrorism will be eliminated. He also said that the state will give unemployment benefits to all unemployed families with the family insurance system, and most importantly, ethnic and sectarian-based identity politics would not be followed. Moreover, he promised to lift the parliamentary immunity and to take concrete steps to reduce the unemployment in the country. Not a specialist in foreign policy at those years, Kılıçdaroğlu only criticized the European Union's double standard practices towards Türkiye. Kılıçdaroğlu, who received positive points in the public opinion with his address *"Recep Bey"* to then-Prime Minister Recep Tayyip Erdoğan, made criticisms about the glorious life behind the Prime Minister's victim image and announced his modest assets published on his personal website. Kılıçdaroğlu, who has created great excitement among the youth, women, and the social democratic base with his honest image and popular discourse, was now seen as the leader who will carry the CHP to power.

However, the political leadership process of Kılıçdaroğlu, which will extend perhaps to the presidency soon, did not start as successfully as expected. Kılıçdaroğlu, who made important democratic initiatives on behalf of the CHP on issues such as the freedom of headscarf in universities and public institutions and the absence of restrictions in university entrance exams for Imam Hatip Schools' graduates, was not able to defeat AK Parti and Erdoğan in many elections. Despite the increase in vote rates of the party, CHP was still not a serious contender for AK Parti until recently. In fact, CHP, which received 19.39 % of the votes in the 2007 general elections under the leadership of Deniz Baykal, took 20.87 % in the 2011 general elections, 25.98 % in the 2015 June general elections, 24.95 % in the 2015 November general elections, and 25.32 % in the 2018 general elections under the leadership of Kılıçdaroğlu. In that sense, Kılıçdaroğlu's vote increase remained at the level of 5 % compared to the Baykal period. Likewise, in the presidential elections, Kılıçdaroğlu could not show a superior performance that would meet the great expectations. In the 2014 presidential election, together with the MHP, CHP leader chose Ekmeleddin İhsanoğlu a candidate, but could not prevent Erdoğan from being elected in the first round with 51.79 %. Kılıçdaroğlu, who made Muharrem İnce a presidential candidate this time in the 2018 election, had to watch his candidate losing the election against Erdoğan in the first round again, this time with an even bigger difference in votes.

However, Kemal Kılıçdaroğlu, a stubborn politician who does not give up easily, has started to follow a different strategy from this date on against the seemingly undefeatable AK Parti and its mighty leader, Recep Tayyip Erdoğan. First of all, he organized a long walk called "Justice March" to show everyone how convinced and dedicated he is to defeat Erdoğan and to become Prime Minister or President. In this process, Kılıçdaroğlu, who managed to maintain his seat as chairman of CHP against Muharrem İnce during the party congress, drew a stronger profile with some restrictions on intra-party democracy. In addition, Kılıçdaroğlu succeeded in gaining serious gains in the context of his policy of recruiting opposition elements within the ruling bloc by supporting them. So, Kılıçdaroğlu, who first attracted the İYİ Parti (Good Party) and Meral Akşener from the MHP, later took the Felicity Party (*Saadet Partisi*) and the Democrat Party (DP), which were close to the government, with him, and finally, pulled the Future Party (*Gelecek Partisi*) and DEVA Party (*Demokrasi ve Atılım Partisi*), which emerged from the AK Parti recently, to his bloc. By doing this, he became the mastermind and the leader of the Nation Alliance (*Millet İttifakı*) or the "*sextet chair*" (*altılı masa*). In this way, Kılıçdaroğlu, who learned *realpolitik* over time, ensured that his party and bloc settled in a wide electoral base that could defeat the AK Parti, and he succeeded in opening his party/bloc not only to leftist voters, but to wider masses of the center and the center-right. In this way, Gandhi Kemal paved the way for his victory, probably in the 2023 elections.

Kılıçdaroğlu's Identity, Ideology, and Political Style from the Perspective of Political Science

In addition to these biographical and personal characteristics of Kemal Kılıçdaroğlu, another important feature for me is that, before he became a well-known name in the media, I had chance to meet and talk to him on a few occasions. Starting from 2008, I had the chance to meet with Kılıçdaroğlu, whom we visited at the Grand National Assembly of Turkey for the first time on the day he became the Deputy Chairman of the Group, and to listen to his ideas closely. In these meetings, Kemal Bey deeply impressed me and my friends with his moderate style, social democratic economic preferences, special attention to the youth, and his honest image that gave us confidence as well as the public, and gave the impression that he would fill the populist left leader's seat that was vacated after Ecevit.

If I need to make a brief reminder about these meetings, Kılıçdaroğlu stated that he did not find the polarization environment in the 2007 Republican Meetings correct and he publicly expressed his social democratic views to us by expressing that no segment of the society should be excluded. Likewise, Kılıçdaroğlu, despite criticizing some of the double standards practices of the EU towards Turkey, underlined the importance of the EU membership process for Turkey's democratization and drew a Westernist profile. In addition, Kılıçdaroğlu stated in our correspondence that we should not despair about the course of the country and invited everyone, including me, to the democratic struggle. With these views and style, Kılıçdaroğlu has succeeded in creating the ideal candidate image for me in difficult times since then. Nowadays, I am very happy to see that my prediction years ago that Kılıçdaroğlu was the ideal candidate to govern Turkey turned out to be true. Moreover, I think that Kılıçdaroğlu's approach is correct and necessary in order to solve the economic, political, and social problems facing Turkey by raising the bar for democracy. Because, in an environment of desperation and economic hardship in nowadays Türkiye, riveted by the earthquake disaster, Kılıçdaroğlu stands out from many other politicians with his honesty, modesty, determination, and superior morals despite all these years.

Apart from these, Kılıçdaroğlu's identity, personality, and ideas are almost like a chance for Türkiye, a country which has a strong national identity and a non-sectarian belief structure based on secularism, unlike countries such as Syria, Iraq, and Libya, which are dragged into civil wars and turmoil in the Middle East. For me, the election of a politician from Tunceli and of Alevi and Zaza origin as the President of Türkiye, just like the election of an African American Barack Obama as the President in the United States of America several years ago, will be a very positive development that will prove that the political system in Turkey is not based on racist and sectarian foundations. This will both increase the loyalty of our citizens from different identities (Kurd, Alevi, Zaza, Eastern, leftist, etc.) to the Republican regime and to the state, and will show the whole world the level of development of Turkish democracy and the level of civilization of the Turkish people. However, at this point, Kemal Bey and his team need to stay away from compatriotism, sectarianism, and class-based politics by making politics on a line that covers all identities and groups. The way to do this is to adopt a transparent and democratic management approach based on merit.

If it is necessary to analyze Kemal Kılıçdaroğlu's ideological line, it can be said that he is a social democrat with a predominant Westernism. However, this stance is not against Mustafa Kemal Atatürk and Kemalism, but an inclusive social democratic line that includes the line of the great leader. Kılıçdaroğlu, who sincerely wants Turkey's EU membership, is not a politician who would easily make concessions to Brussels. Despite his humanist and progressive ideas, Kılıçdaroğlu also developed his realism aspect over time. In addition, Kılıçdaroğlu, who does not want to give very harsh messages on the Syrian and Afghan refugees, does not ignore the reactions from the grassroots and also tries to deal with this issue peacefully.

Although Kemal Kılıçdaroğlu comes from the left and always defends the rights of the working classes, he should not be considered as a politician who thinks in a Marxist political plane. Because Kılıçdaroğlu's worldview is inclined to Mustafa Kemal Atatürk's line of solidarism rather than a Marxist understanding based on social classes. In that sense, similar to Atatürk, he tends to see the Turkish society on the basis of different professions, not different classes. Thus, Kılıçdaroğlu will be a leader who acts and decides according to the national interest rather than the class interest. In this context, if Kılıçdaroğlu is elected, he will want to play the role of conciliator between the capital owners and the working classes.

Kılıçdaroğlu's most distinctive and angular political attitude is that he is an honest leader who fights against corruption. Therefore, those who want to work with Kılıçdaroğlu should be very meticulous and careful in ethical/moral issues. Likewise, in the state, Kılıçdaroğlu will not defend people whose corruption has been proven, regardless of their view or party. This attitude is the line needed by Türkiye, which is in the swamp of economic crisis and corruption. Kılıçdaroğlu's this attitude brings to my mind the Chinese President Xi Jinping as well. In this sense, Kılıçdaroğlu may adopt a more modest style reminiscent of Ecevit in the state and have the protocol amended accordingly.

As Kılıçdaroğlu has repeatedly said, if he comes to power, he will struggle against the advantageous positions of Islamic groups in Türkiye. The way to do this is to build dormitories for all students and not to force any student to stay in Islamic brotherhoods' dormitories. Similarly, unjust staffing in the state will be prevented and people who are pro-secular and of different faiths will be employed in state jobs as well. However, at this point, Kılıçdaroğlu should take a careful position and not activate fault lines that might increase social polarization. This, in my opinion, will be successful if it manifests itself as not being exclusionary against Islamic groups, but only eliminating their unfair competitive situation.

Kılıçdaroğlu's foreign policy, on the other hand, will most likely be on a multidimensional line with a Western orientation. To open this; Kılıçdaroğlu will put Turkey back on the route of EU membership, but will not take a concessive position against Brussels, will try to improve relations with the United States, but will not risk Turkey's independence, will not break relations with other great powers, especially Russia and China, due to national interests, but the West will prioritize. He will also want to improve relations with neighboring countries, but will not act dreamily in this regard. Kılıçdaroğlu will receive advice and support from experienced names within his party such as Faruk Logoğlu, Ünal Çeviköz, and Osman Korutürk. Ahmet Davutoğlu, a component of the Nation Alliance, will undoubtedly be a great opportunity for Kılıçdaroğlu as well with his previous experiences and immense knowledge.

Kılıçdaroğlu will also take action to return the country to the parliamentary system without losing much time in domestic politics and will try to make the Grand National Assembly of Turkey the most fundamental institution of the country's politics. For this reason, Kılıçdaroğlu, whose modest style prevails, may turn the Presidential Palace into a public library, educational institution or community center and may impose restrictions on some issues in the state budget. In this context, his Presidency will mark a period in which Kılıçdaroğlu will temporarily direct the country's politics directly, but eventually will leave a significant part of his powers to someone else after returning to the democratic system. This person could most likely be Istanbul Mayor Ekrem İmamoğlu, and under Kılıçdaroğlu's Presidency, he could become the main person running the country as Prime Minister and CHP chairman.

If Kılıçdaroğlu is elected, he should not hold grudges and should do everything in accordance with the law on the basis of justice. Because in Turkey and in many other non-institutionalized political systems, power changes can often turn into blood feuds and revenge processes. In order to prevent this, Kılıçdaroğlu must act carefully and in coordination with state institutions.

Conclusion

Finally, it should be said that the negative view of Kemal Kılıçdaroğlu's presidential candidacy because of his Alevi faith or his hometown being Tunceli is a shame not only for those who express this, but also for Türkiye. A person's choice of ethnicity or religious/sectarian belief is often not even in his own power. To engage in discrimination and exclusion for such a reason would be an openly racist attitude. In this context, I remind you that the state, the political elite, and the media organs in Türkiye should publish responsibly in this regard. Lastly, I wish that the 2023 presidential and parliamentary elections to be beneficial for our country. I would also like to add that as a Turkish patriot, we are ready to serve at every level of Turkey, no matter who is elected, and our sole purpose is to serve the public. Good luck to our nation…

Ozan Örmeci[*]

2023 Turkish Elections: 46 Days Left

Abstract This chapter contains an in-depth analysis on the 2023 Turkish elections on the eve of the elections. The paper focuses on the strategies of the government and the opposition and discusses which side could be more advantageous.

Keywords: *Turkish Politics, 2023 Turkish elections, AK Parti, CHP, Recep Tayyip Erdoğan, Kemal Kılıçdaroğlu, Muharrem İnce, Sinan Oğan.*

Introduction

In Türkiye (Turkey), presidential and parliamentary elections are scheduled for May 14, 2023. So, this means only 46 days left for the country to choose its new President and form a new parliament. However, due to the electoral system, in case none of presidential candidates gets more than half of the votes in the first round, there will be a second round two weeks after, on May 28, 2023.

In this article, I am going to first present presidential candidates and their blocs in Türkiye, later analyze recent opinion polls about the elections, and lastly focus on some crucial factors which might affect the results of the presidential and parliamentary elections.

Four Candidates Set for Presidency

Now it is official and only four presidential candidates will contend on May 14, 2023, for becoming Turkish President. Let us focus on these candidates, their backers, and their ideological preferences.

The joint candidate of the People Alliance's (*Cumhur İttifakı*) is Türkiye's 12th and current President (2014–) Recep Tayyip Erdoğan. This bloc is consisted of Islamist/conservative AK Parti (Justice and Development Party), Turkish nationalist/far-right MHP (Nationalist Action Party) whose chair is veteran politician Devlet Bahçeli, and Turkish nationalist/far-right/Islamist BBP (Great Unity Party) whose leader is Mustafa Destici. However, after witnessing the

---

[*]   Associate Professor in the department of Political Science and International Relations (English) at Istanbul Aydın University, Istanbul, Türkiye.
     Email: ozanormeci@aydin.edu.tr / ozanormeci@gmail.com.
     ORCID: 0000-0001-8850-6089.

rise of the opposition by bringing together different political parties and actors, President Erdoğan also adopted the same strategy and added two new political parties to his bloc very recently. These two new political parties are New Welfare Party (*Yeniden Refah Partisi*/YRP) and Free Cause Party (*Hür Dava Partisi*/ Hüda Par).

The New Welfare was established by Türkiye's former Islamist Prime Minister Necmettin Erbakan's son Fatih Erbakan in late 2018. The party represents a classical version of Turkish political Islam with anti-Occidentalist (anti-Western) ideas and connotations and puts forward a more radical Islamist agenda compared to AK Parti. The party adopts a hardliner positioning especially about women rights, adultery, Cyprus Dispute, and relations with the United States (U.S.) and the European Union (EU). However, due to the passiveness of the other pro-Erbakan National View/National Outlook (*Milli Görüş*) political organization Felicity Party (Saadet Partisi/SP), this party is on the rise recently. Albeit founded recently, the party has approximately 270,000 members and according to recent polls 1–3 % potential votes. In fact, the party founder and leader Fatih Erbakan was running for presidency independently and already collected 70,000 signatures, but later upon the proposal of Erdoğan, he decided to join the People's Alliance and withdrew from the presidential race on behalf of Erdoğan. The New Welfare Party will surely bring new votes to AK Parti and Erdoğan, but their misogynist rhetoric and appeals could disturb female voters and lead to loss of some votes as well.

The Free Cause Party (Hüda Par) on the other hand was established in late 2012 by former members and supporters of Kurdish Hezbollah (also known as *Sofik*), a very radical Islamist (Sunni) and Kurdish terrorist organization who conducted serious crimes against the state (such as the killing of former police captain Gaffar Okan) and against more liberal Islamist figures (such as Gonca Kuriş) in the past. The party openly advocates a federal state system and cultural rights for Kurds. The party's leader is Zekeriya Yapıcıoğlu, a former Hezbollah militant. Hüda Par does not possess a very high vote potential, but their challenge to PKK and HDP (Peoples' Democratic Party) is an asset for Erdoğan and the Turkish State to resist against the secular leftist appeals of these groups (PKK/ HDP).

The joint candidate of the People's Alliance, President Recep Tayyip Erdoğan (1954–) has been ruling Türkiye since 2003; first as Prime Minister (2003–2014), later as President of the Republic in the parliamentary system (2014–2018), and lastly as Türkiye's President (2018–) within a system of Turkish type of presidentialism. Erdoğan became an influential political figure in 1994 as being shockingly elected Istanbul Mayor from Necmettin Erbakan's Welfare Party

(*Refah Partisi*/RP) against the secular establishment. Coming from a traditional Sunni Turkish family from Rize, Erdoğan was raised in Istanbul's Kasımpaşa neighborhood and attended to an İmam Hatip School. Erdoğan was graduated from Marmara University's Faculty of Economics and Administrative Sciences, but some critics claim that his university diploma is not genuine. Coming from an Islamist background, Erdoğan has always been a controversial figure in the secular establishment. However, his charisma and strong bonds with the Islamist masses made him an undisputed and undefeated leader. In fact, since 2002, Erdoğan never lost an election himself, but his party's defeat at 2019 local elections in Istanbul and Ankara is considered as his only loss. Moreover, this time Erdoğan's job is tougher because recent polls show that he could get around maximum 44–45 % of the votes in the first round of the presidential elections.

Recep Tayyip Erdoğan

The joint candidate of the Nation Alliance (*Millet İttifakı*) is Kemal Kılıçdaroğlu. Born in 1948 in Tunceli (formerly known as Dersim), Kılıçdaroğlu comes from an Alevi-Zaza family. He was educated in Economics at the Ankara Academy of Economics and Commercial Sciences (now Gazi University), from which he graduated in 1971. Having worked long years in important state institutions including the Social Insurance Institution (SSK), Kılıçdaroğlu has been a member of the parliament from pro-secular CHP (Republican People's

Party) since 2002. After making a rapid rise in petty politics with his anti-corruption campaigns and clean record, he was elected pro-secular CHP's new chair in 2010 with great support from media and party members, following a sex scandal that forced former chair Deniz Baykal to resignation. He also served as the Vice President of the Socialist International between 2012 and 2014.

Kemal Kılıçdaroğlu represents the classical secular/Kemalist heritage of the Turkish State, but he was able to bring new votes and supporter groups to his party by following a new strategy. So, starting from 2017, beginning with his famous Justice March (*Adalet Yürüyüşü*), he was able to convince new right-wing groups to support his leadership against Erdoğan's authoritarian-leaning rule. Accordingly, -separated from MHP- Meral Akşener's Good Party (İYİ Parti) and two other right-wing parties; Gültekin Uysal's center-right Democrat Party (DP) and Temel Karamollaoğlu's Islamist Felicity Party (*Saadet Partisi/ SP*) began to support him. More recently, two new parties founded by former AK Parti cadres; Ali Babacan's DEVA (Democracy and Leap Party) and Ahmet Davutoğlu's Future Party (*Gelecek Partisi*) also began to endorse him and joined the Nation Alliance now called as the "*sextet chair*" (*altılı masa*). Another recent success of Kemal Kılıçdaroğlu was to convince pro-Kurdish HDP not to contend in this presidential election with their own candidate. In that sense, Kılıçdaroğlu secured 11–13 % additional votes from secular Kurdish groups and Turkish far-left before this election.

Kılıçdaroğlu followed a very clever strategy to secure his presidential candidacy as well. He forced all political parties within his bloc to focus first on the Nation Alliance's programme rather than the presidential candidate and slowly began to convince all political parties by making his candidacy the only viable option in time. So, by underlining the strength of AK Parti in municipal councils, he convinced many people that Ankara Mayor Mansur Yavaş or Istanbul Mayor Ekrem İmamoğlu should not be presidential candidates. In the end, when his candidacy became a political reality, he also managed a good leadership skill to convince İYİ Parti leader Meral Akşener after a short-term political crisis. Akşener was normally endorsing İmamoğlu and/or Yavaş for presidency, but upon social pressures, he gave green light to Kılıçdaroğlu's candidacy.

Kılıçdaroğlu is the leader of CHP, the oldest political party in the country. CHP was closed by the military regime following the 1980 military coup but was reestablished by Deniz Baykal and İsmail Cem in 1992. That is why, Kılıçdaroğlu is not a lonely man and he represents a very strong political tradition in Türkiye. Although established as a modernist, Kemalist, statist, and Turkish nationalist political party a century ago, the new CHP is much more a European-type social democratic/socialist party, trying to catch everyone and become a centered political actor. I think Kılıçdaroğlu has a great chance in winning the presidential election in the first round. If we make a simple calculation according to previous opinion polls, Kılıçdaroğlu's chance will be better understood by everyone: CHP (25 %) + İYİ Parti (13 %) + Other components of Nation Alliance (3 %) + HDP (11 %): 52 %.

Kemal Kılıçdaroğlu

The only potential problem for Kılıçdaroğlu and the Nation Alliance seems to be the situation of Muharrem İnce. Born in 1964 in Yalova, İnce had been a CHP partisan since his youth. He eventually became a member of the parliament from CHP in 2002 and served within the Turkish Grand National Assembly until 2018. He was a very influential and popular figure with his brilliant speeches in media and in the parliament and served as CHP's parliamentary deputy group leader between 2010 and 2014. He was also chosen the presidential candidate of his party in 2018, but lost the election to Erdoğan. After this defeat, he was heavily criticized and disfavored by CHP circles. He tried to challenge Kılıçdaroğlu to become the new leader of CHP but failed two times. Resigned from CHP, he established the Homeland Party (Memleket Partisi) in 2021 to take his chance in politics independently from his former party. İnce represents a more nationalist and classical Kemalist version of CHP and he criticizes Kılıçdaroğlu especially based on his moderate approach towards HDP and pro-Kurdish groups having links with the PKK. İnce's party is very weak in organization and the only figure known from his party is Professor İpek Özkal Sayan from Ankara University.

However, İnce is an excellent orator and he has considerable popularity and support among young and apolitical voters due to his word games, jokes, and effective use of social media. In that sense, in case İnce could reach 7–8 % votes in the first round of the presidential election by convincing many voters among the classical CHP and İYİ Parti supporters, he could create a chance for Erdoğan to beat Kılıçdaroğlu in the second round.

Muharrem İnce

The fourth and the last presidential candidate is Sinan Oğan. Born in 1967 in Iğdır, Oğan is a classical Turkish nationalist politician. He coordinates a Turkish think-tank called TÜRKSAM for many years. Graduated from the department of Management at Marmara University in 1989, Oğan obtained a PhD in International Relations and Political Science from the Moscow State Institute of International Relations in 2009. He has close links with Azerbaijan and the Azeri political elite. He was a MHP deputy within the Turkish parliament between 2011 and 2015, but later resigned from his party due to disagreements with the party leader Devlet Bahçeli. Oğan is endorsed by Ancestral Alliance (*ATA İttifakı*), a new political bloc composed of four right-wing nationalist parties: Professor Ümit Özdağ's Victory Party (*Zafer Partisi*), Justice Party (*Adalet Partisi*), My Country Party (*Ülkem Partisi*), and Turkey Alliance Party (*Türkiye İttifakı Partisi*). Among these, the only noticeable party in the opinion polls is Özdağ's Victory Party. With its ultranationalist and anti-immigrant rhetoric, the party became visible and popular recently among the far-right voters.

Sinan Oğan

Recent Opinion Polls

If we analyze the recent opinion polls for the presidential race, we see that Nation Alliance candidate and CHP leader Kemal Kılıçdaroğlu leads all polls. However, the results are very different; whereas some polls suggest that Kılıçdaroğlu could be easily elected in the first round of the election with 51–53 % of the votes, some others claim that he could not take more than 45–46 % in the first round. In my opinion, unless Muharrem İnce makes a big progress, Kılıçdaroğlu will win the presidential election in the first round. However, in case the election goes to the second round, of course Erdoğan could still have a chance to win slightly by creating a political polarization based on Kılıçdaroğlu's Alevi and Kurdish (Zaza) identity.

If we look at Erdoğan's support in the presidential race on the other hand, we see that it changes between 40 and 47 %, but none of the polls suggest that Erdoğan could win the election in the first round anymore. Among the other candidates, Muharrem İnce seems more pretentious as some polls already suggest that he could get around 7 % of the total votes in the first round. However, many other polls show İnce somewhere between 3 and 5 %, which might not be enough to secure a second round. Lastly, Sinan Oğan has 1 to 3 % potential mostly with the votes coming from anti-immigrant Zafer Partisi.

If we look at the recent opinion polls about parliamentary elections, we still see that AK Parti is the leading party of the country despite of all problems. AK Parti's vote ranges from 31 to 37 %, but most of the people are sure that AK Parti could still become the largest bloc within the parliament. CHP's votes on the other hand are pointed as somewhere between 25 and 28 %. Of course, many things could change in 46 days and CHP could still make a progress during the presidential campaign. For instance, the effect of the terrible earthquakes in Türkiye in February 2023 diminished AK Parti's votes and had a positive effect on the opposition. İYİ Parti is expected to get 10 to 13 % of the votes in the parliamentary elections. Recent polls show that pro-Kurdish HDP could get 10 to 12 % of the votes. MHP on the other hand is shown somewhere between 5 to 7 %. Muharrem İnce's *Memleket Partisi*'s presence is also felt in parliamentary election polls, as his party is expected to take 3 to 6 % of the total votes for the moment. Ali Babacan's DEVA party is important as well since the party could get 1 to 3 % of the votes according to recent polls. Lastly, the New Welfare Party could get 1 to 2 % of the total votes in a parliamentary election.

Factors That Might Change the Results

First of all, especially in terms of presidential election, the most important parameter would be the performance of Muharrem İnce. We already know that İnce is an excellent speaker who could agitate masses. So, if he would be able to increase his votes considerably by organizing large demonstrations and appearing in tv channels more frequently, by getting high votes in the first round, he could secure the second round and thus, could create another chance for Erdoğan. However, it is also possible that İnce and Kılıçdaroğlu could get into contact and make an agreement for the second round. Kılıçdaroğlu could try to convince him by offering him a position in the new cabinet as well. So, it seems to me like the "*İnce affair*" will be important for the outcome of the presidential election.

Secondly, since Turkish political parties take help from public relations (pr) experts in recent years, the success of the electoral campaigns could change the preferences of the voters. Until now, AK Parti has been very successful in organizing such campaigns in the Turkish context. However, recently, CHP has also begun to use more modern techniques and increase its popularity by modern social science methods. In that sense, we will be able to see soon two mega political campaigns organized by AK Parti and CHP, which would be influential in directing in the indecisive and apolitical voters.

Thirdly, there is an unspoken important dimension of the elections. If the presidential election goes to the second round, the composition of the parliament could direct voters to vote for Erdoğan or Kılıçdaroğlu. In other words, in case AK Parti or CHP gets more seats in the parliament on May 14, 2023, but the presidential election goes to second round, votes at the center might be headed to the leader of the majority bloc. Since almost all polls show AK Parti ahead in the parliamentary elections, I think it might be a wise decision for Kılıçdaroğlu to convince Muharrem İnce to withdraw from the presidential race and endorse him. Because otherwise, in a scenario based on AK Parti majority in the parliament after 14 May, Kılıçdaroğlu's whole *"return to parliamentary system"* rhetoric could be nonsense and it might direct voters at the center to give one last chance to Erdoğan.

Conclusion

To conclude, Türkiye's 2023 presidential and parliamentary elections will be very interesting for international observers. Personally, I would prefer a democratic country having good relations both with the West and the East and I am hopeful about Turkish people's ability to make a good choice. In that sense, I am sure that the elections will take place in a secure and democratic environment and Türkiye will return to normalcy following the elections.

Ozan Örmeci*

2023 Turkish Elections: Erdoğan Victory Is Expected

Abstract This chapter is about the analysis of the first round results of the 2023 Turkish elections. The chapter predicts Erdoğan's victory in the second round of the presidential elections.

Keywords: *Turkish Politics, 2023 Turkish elections, AK Parti, CHP, Recep Tayyip Erdoğan, Kemal Kılıçdaroğlu.*

Introduction

Turkish people went to ballot boxes yesterday during a sunny Sunday on May 14, 2023 to determine the future of the country in a democratic way. Elections took place in a calm and safe environment and no violence-based events took place throughout the country. Although finalized election results are not officially announced, it seems like there will be a second round for the presidential election between the current Turkish President and AK Parti leader Recep Tayyip Erdoğan and the opposition's candidate and CHP leader Kemal Kılıçdaroğlu two weeks later on May 28, 2023. On the other hand, Erdoğan's bloc (People's Alliance-*Cumhur İttifakı*) achieved to secure a large parliamentary majority against the opposition's Nation Alliance (*Millet İttifakı*) bloc. These results could be defined as Erdoğan's another victory since he has very high chance to win the presidential election in addition to a clear parliamentary majority.

Presidential Election: Erdoğan Almost Won in the First Round!

2023 Presidential election in Türkiye is often pointed out as the most important election in 2023 by the international media since two competing leaders have offered very different perspectives for the future of Türkiye during the 100th year anniversary of the Republic. Incumbent President Erdoğan offered a status

---

*   Associate Professor in the department of Political Science and International Relations (English) at Istanbul Aydın University, Istanbul, Türkiye.
      Email: ozanormeci@aydin.edu.tr / ozanormeci@gmail.com.
      ORCID: 0000-0001-8850-6089.

quo based on hyperpresidentialism, a more Islamic and nationalist vision for Türkiye to become a regional power based on its developing defense industries, and better relations with the Russian Federation. The opposition leader Kemal Kılıçdaroğlu on the other hand promised a return to classical Westminster parliamentary system, better relations with Western countries (the United States and the European Union), dialogue and negotiation methods for all political and diplomatic problems, and a more secular vision for the new generations.

RECEP TAYYİP ERDOĞAN	KEMAL KILIÇDAROĞLU	SİNAN OĞAN	MUHARREM İNCE
%49.36	%44.99	%5.21	%0.43
26.714.954 OY	24.348.806 OY	2.820.548 OY	233.358 OY

Unofficial results of the first round of presidential election (**Source:** *NTV*)

Unofficial results show that, after 20 years in power, Turkish President Recep Tayyip Erdoğan is still very powerful and popular in the country as he slightly lost his chance to win the election in the first round with approximately 49.4 % of the total votes (around 27.1 million votes). On the other hand, the opposition leader Kemal Kılıçdaroğlu, who was declared to be the favorite candidate by almost all public opinion poll companies, had a record vote (for the opposition) around 45 % (approximately 24.6 million). Ultranationalist candidate Sinan Oğan had got 5.2 % % (around 2.9 million), whereas the pro-secular Kemalist candidate Muharrem İnce, who was withdrawn from the race a few days before the election upon social pressures, reached 0.4 % (240.000 votes) since his name was written in the ballot.

Results show that Erdoğan is ahead of Kılıçdaroğlu with a 2.5 million votes difference, which seems very unlikely to be narrowed down in the second round. Ultranationalist candidate Sinan Oğan has around 3 million supporters, but Kılıçdaroğlu has to take almost all votes of Oğan to win over Erdoğan in the second round. For me this option is out of the question since most of Oğan's

Turkish nationalist and far-right voters will vote for Erdoğan due to pro-Kurdish HDP's support to Kılıçdaroğlu. Moreover, I think the parliamentary election results will provide an extra motivation for the pro-government voters. That is why; I guess Erdoğan will win the election in the second round easily with 54–58 % of the total votes.

Erdoğan's victory will be a huge defeat for the opposition as the opposition supporters were very motivated and convinced for victory this time. The election will probably lead to a leader change in CHP, making Istanbul mayor Ekrem İmamoğlu the new leader of the pro-secular party. Erdoğan on the other hand will shape the future of the country without any barriers for another 5 years term and will strive to make Türkiye a more Islamic, nationalist, and militaristic regional power. However, Erdoğan might have to work with new names in his cabinet since he decided to put all his deputies into parliamentary positions before the elections. A refreshed cabinet with fresh names and new faces could create a space for Erdoğan to establish better relations with the West, but the general trend gives me the idea that Türkiye might have even more problematic relations with Washington and Brussels in the near future and it would have to develop closer ties with Putin's Russia and China instead.

Parliamentary Elections: People's Alliance Domination

Parliamentary elections were a big victory for the government as the pro-Erdoğan bloc secured around 322 seats (267 for AK Parti, 50 for MHP, and 5 for New Welfare Party-YRP), a clear majority in the parliament. Similar to Erdoğan's votes in the presidential election, pro-government bloc had got around 49.4 %. The opposition on the other hand stayed around 35 %, which led to 169 seats for CHP (around 37 of these seats will go right-wing parties within the bloc) and 44 for Good Party-İYİ Parti. With a vote around 10–11 %, pro-Kurdish and leftist bloc (Labour and Freedom Alliance-Emek ve Özgürlük İttifakı) also secured 65 seats in the Turkish Grand National Assembly (TBMM); 61 for HDP and 4 for Turkish Labour Party (TİP). Although HDP's performance was found low in general, it must be stated that due to the party closure case at the Constitutional Court, HDP entered into the election under the banner of Green Left Party (YSP), a new left-wing and environmentalist party, which might have been influential in the decrease of party's traditional votes.

İttifak Adı	Oy Oranı	Milletvekili
CUMHUR İTTİFAKI	%49.39	321
MİLLET İTTİFAKI	%35.14	213
EMEK VE ÖZGÜRLÜK İTTİFAKI	%10.53	66
ATA İTTİFAKI	%2.45	0

Açılan Sandık Oranı: %99.26

*Unofficial results of the parliamentary election (**Source:** NTV)*

Results show that a return to parliamentary system is impossible unless the pro-government bloc is convinced and Türkiye will continue to be ruled by a hyperpresidential system, which is often criticized for being a new form of "*Sultanism*" by many pro-Western political scientists in Türkiye. Furthermore, relatively low success of the opposition might lead to internal problems within the Nation Alliance (*Millet İttifakı*), especially between the nationalist İYİ Parti and the social democratic CHP. Before the election, İYİ Parti leader Meral Akşener insisted on the candidacy of Istanbul mayor İmamoğlu or Ankara mayor Mansur Yavaş, but she was not able to convince Kılıçdaroğlu and other four right-wing parties within the bloc. So, after the second round, polemics might increase between CHP and İYİ Parti circles.

Winners

It seems like the biggest winner of the election is again President Erdoğan. As far as I'm concerned, he will be easily elected once again two weeks later, plus he will a have a strong majority in the parliament. Erdoğan is a tactical genius for political polarization based on the lifestyle and culture and he appeals to average Turkish voters better than other leaders.

Sinan Oğan, with his unexpected 5 % in the first round of presidential election, is another winner. Erdoğan and Kılıçdaroğlu could both offer Oğan an important position in their possible cabinets. However, I think Oğan will stay closer to Erdoğan and might even decide to work with him due to his close ties with the Azerbaijan and ultranationalist rhetoric against HDP. It will not be surprising for me if Oğan becomes for instance the new Foreign Minister of Türkiye in the cabinet of Erdoğan. Moreover, with his increasing popularity, Oğan could play for MHP's leadership in the near future after Bahçeli.

Turkish nationalist MHP and its veteran chair Devlet Bahçeli also could be stated as victorious after these results. Although all polls were showing MHP around 6–7 % before the elections, the party had got more than 10 %, better than their pro-secular equivalent İYİ Parti's 9.8 %. Moreover, MHP was able to pave the way for Erdoğan's victory in the presidential election.

Islamist YRP (New Welfare Party) is another winner, taking almost 3 % of the votes in their first election and proving that anti-Occidentalist Islamism will continue to develop in Türkiye.

Conclusion

Election results show that despite of the huge economic problems and epic failures of management made by the government after the earthquake disaster in February this year, Turkish people continue to vote on the basis of their religious, sectarian, and ethnic identity in elections and populist right-wing politicians like Erdoğan use these identities skillfully. In fact, I call elections in Türkiye as "*census*", since almost all people vote for their identities and lifestyles, not for the projects and visions of the candidates and parties.

Elections might lead to Türkiye's deteriorating relations with the West and a more troubled economic situation. In that sense, Erdoğan's last term might be even shorter than 5 years in case economic problems would grow seriously. In addition, elections will probably cause a leader change in pro-secular CHP since Kemal Kılıçdaroğlu is now old and he used his last chance to become the President. Although he has a center-right background, Istanbul mayor Ekrem İmamoğlu is the favorite candidate to replace him.

Lastly, in my opinion, with Erdoğan in office, Türkiye will now do its best to get Donald Trump elected in the U.S. to change Washington's approach to many issues including the Kurdish Question, democratization, the Eastern Mediterranean, and relations with Russia.

Ozan Örmeci[*]

2023 Turkish Elections: Erdoğan Clinches Victory

Abstract This chapter analyzes the second round results of 2023 Turkish presidential elections and tries to explain the reasons of Erdoğan's victory.

Keywords: *Turkish Politics, 2023 Turkish elections, AK Parti, CHP, Recep Tayyip Erdoğan, Kemal Kılıçdaroğlu.*

Introduction

Turkish people went to ballots for the second round of the presidential election on May 28, 2023. The election took place in a peaceful atmosphere and in that sense it was a free and fair election. However, to be honest, conditions were not completely equal between two candidates as President Recep Tayyip Erdoğan and Islamist/conservative his party (AK Parti) used all state privileges against the opposition's presidential candidate and pro-secular CHP leader Kemal Kılıçdaroğlu during the whole election process. This was observed best in the broadcasting policy of the state's television channel *TRT*, which served as a propaganda machine and almost completely ignored the opposition while praising President Erdoğan at every instance. In the end, President Erdoğan won the second round with 52 % of the votes and gained another 5 years term in the office.

Prior to the Second Round

Before the second round of the election, both candidates tried to reach the voters of Turkish nationalist candidate Sinan Oğan, who unexpectedly had got more than 5 % of the votes in the first round. While President Erdoğan convinced Sinan Oğan himself and secured his support for the second round, CHP leader and the opposition's presidential candidate Kemal Kılıçdaroğlu achieved to take

---

[*] Associate Professor in the department of Political Science and International Relations (English) at Istanbul Aydın University, Istanbul, Türkiye.
   Email: ozanormeci@aydin.edu.tr / ozanormeci@gmail.com.
   ORCID: 0000-0001-8850-6089.

the support of Professor Ümit Özdağ, the Chair of the Victory Party (*Zafer Partisi*), a small and new ultranationalist, anti-immigrant, and xenophobic party that was instrumental in the candidacy of Oğan. Kılıçdaroğlu and Özdağ even signed a protocol for deporting Syrian immigrants as soon as possible (within a year) and the continuation of AK Parti's policies for the appointment of trustees (*kayyum*) to pro-Kurdish HDP-controlled municipalities. In addition, Kılıçdaroğlu and CHP increased the dose of populism and nationalism in their rhetoric as a response to President Erdoğan's promotion of fake videos and exaggerated claims about the opposition's links with the terrorist groups (mainly the PKK). While these policies might have garnered Kılıçdaroğlu a few extra points from the ultranationalist groups, it also caused the risk of losing Kurdish and leftist voters' full support. Lastly, Kılıçdaroğlu participated into a 4 hours tv program on *Babala Tv* during which he showed a very good performance.

President Erdoğan on the other hand underlined the importance of his parliamentarian majority in his speeches and encouraged voters to choose him for a stable and harmonious government. Erdoğan seemed very confident of his victory especially after his unexpected high performance in the first round both in the parliamentary and presidential elections despite of the ongoing economic crisis and corruption scandals. Before the second round, although both sides increased the dose of Turkish nationalism and created an atmosphere of pressure to intimidate Kurds, pro-Kurdish HDP (Peoples' Democratic Party) did not retreat and continued to endorse Kılıçdaroğlu with the hope of making transition into a fully democratic regime. However, many CHP voters as well as some Kurdish groups were disappointed from Kılıçdaroğlu's anti-immigrant and ultranationalist rhetoric, which was not found suitable to a progressive social democratic party.

Results of the Second Round

In the second round, President Erdoğan's number of total votes increased to 27.8 million from 27.1 million in the first round (approximately 700,000 increase). On the other hand, Kılıçdaroğlu's votes rose to 25.5 million from 24.6 million (approximately 900,000 increase). The participation rate on the other hand decreased to 84 % in the second round from 87 % in the first round. In the end, Erdoğan won comfortably with more than 4 % difference.

OY FARKI 2.330.140

ERDOĞAN
KILIÇDAROĞLU

%52.18
AÇILAN SANDIK ORANI
%100.00
%47.82

27.834.692 OY
25.504.552 OY

Results of the second round (**Source:** *NTV*)

However, Kılıçdaroğlu's performance in the second round could be considered as partial success since in the first round he lost the parliamentarian majority to Erdoğan and his bloc by large difference, but was still able to protect and even slightly expand his electoral base in the second round. This shows the strength of the CHP and the Nation Alliance (*Millet İttifakı*) and the loyalty of their supporters. In that sense, Kılıçdaroğlu's strategy of establishing an alliance with right-wing parties worked and provided a real chance for the opposition to win the executive power first time after 21 years. Moreover, 2.5 million vote difference between two candidates in the first round in fact fell to approximately 2.3 million in the second round. However, in the end, both parliamentary and presidential elections were lost and this would not make people from the opposition very happy.

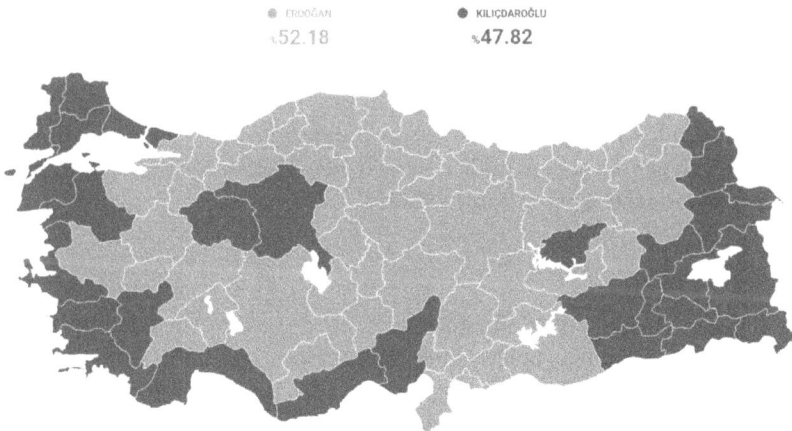

ERDOĞAN
%52.18

KILIÇDAROĞLU
%47.82

Electoral map (**Source:** *NTV*)

Lastly, it should be also stated that Sinan Oğan's votes in the first round were shared between both candidates, but they seem to be headed more for Kılıçdaroğlu rather than Erdoğan. In that sense, Kılıçdaroğlu's alliance strategy with Ümit Özdağ and Victory Party also did not backfire, but did not change the overall picture as well.

What to Expect?

After reaching this miraculous victory in extremely difficult conditions after the terrible earthquake in February 2023 and the deepening economic crisis, it seems like there is no barrier left in front of President Erdoğan to shape the future of his country freely as he wishes. In my opinion, President Erdoğan will now make bolder steps to transform Türkiye into a regional power by increasing the dose of nationalism and militarism. Leaning on developing national defense industry, Turkish President could defend Türkiye's interests in a stricter manner in the new term by adopting harsher stances in the Eastern Mediterranean, Cyprus, the Aegean, and Syria. Results might also encourage Erdoğan to continue with his neutrality policy towards the Russian invasion of Ukraine while trying to form better relations with the West as well.

However, from my perspective, as long as President Joe Biden stays in the Oval Office, it might be more difficult for Erdoğan to straighten out things with Washington. In that sense, Erdoğan, together with Russian leader Vladimir Putin, will do everything to get Donald Trump elected in the U.S. presidential elections in 2024. In the meantime, President Erdoğan might try to redesign the opposition in Türkiye as well by using his full control over the state mechanism. Especially legal restrictions on pro-Kurdish organizations and groups could increase and the dose of Islamism, misogynism, and patriarchalism might reach all time high level with the effect of some radical groups who contributed to Erdoğan's victory including Fatih Erbakan's New Welfare Party (*Yeniden Refah Partisi*) and Islamist and pro-Kurdish Hüda-Par.

Conclusion

To conclude, 2023 Turkish elections were very exciting, but contrary to the popular belief and public opinion polls made prior to the first round, President Erdoğan and his bloc showed a great success and clinched another victory in a relatively easier manner. Erdoğan's success lies in the fact that he is a man of the people with all his improper and exaggerated speeches, behaviors, and gestures and he knows how to grasp power better than anyone in the country. In that sense, President Erdoğan is a great populist right-wing politician, but not a very promising liberal democrat. Finally, Türkiye's economic problems will persist and make the regime fragile unless President Erdoğan changes his approach to economics and liberalize the regime.

Ozan Örmeci*

CHP's Electoral Performance Over the Past Years

Abstract This chapter is about Türkiye's pro-secular CHP's electoral performances in the past and the present.

Keywords: *Turkish Politics, CHP, Mustafa Kemal Atatürk, İsmet İnönü, Bülent Ecevit, Deniz Baykal, Kemal Kılıçdaroğlu, Kemalism, Social Democracy, Turkish Left.*

Turkey's main opposition party, the Republican People's Party (CHP), has been quite popular for many years, thanks to both being the party of Mustafa Kemal Atatürk, the founder of the country, and preserving the modern lifestyle based on secularism, which is heavily advocated by the intelligentsia and culture and arts circles in Turkey. On the other hand, CHP, especially since its re-establishment in 1992, has not shown great success in the general and presidential elections. It is useful to remember the past election performances of the CHP, which is currently on the agenda with the 45 % votes of Kemal Kılıçdaroğlu in the first round of the 2023 Presidential elections.

---

* Associate Professor in the department of Political Science and International Relations (English) at Istanbul Aydın University, Istanbul, Türkiye.
Email: ozanormeci@aydin.edu.tr / ozanormeci@gmail.com.
ORCID: 0000-0001-8850-6089.

After the transition to the multi-party system in Turkey, the CHP lost the 1950 general elections to the Democrat Party with 39.6 % of the votes under the Presidency of İsmet İnönü, thus becoming the opposition for the first time after a 27-year single-party period. The CHP, which decreased its vote rate to 35.11 % in the 1954 elections under the leadership of İsmet Pasha, increased to 41.4 % in the 1957 general elections, increasing the hopes that it could defeat Adnan Menderes' Democrat Party (DP) through the ballot box. However, due to the May 27, 1960 military coup, it was not possible for the CHP to take power through ballot boxes and end the DP administration. Looking at the 1950–1960 period, it is seen that the CHP was a Kemalist/Atatürkist party under the leadership of İsmet Pasha, has not yet made a left-wing expansion, and received votes from the state cadres and the urban modern population as the defender of the state.

The CHP, which entered the 1961 general elections held after the military coup under the Presidency of İsmet İnönü, became the first party with 36.7 % of the votes and came to power again years later through coalition governments. Since this period, right-wing parties and conservative public opinion have criticized the army-supported position of the CHP and claimed that the "CHP + Army = Government" formula is not suitable for democracy. However, the CHP's power did not last long and the party, which had 28.7 % of the votes in the 1965 elections, had to hand over the power to Süleyman Demirel and the Justice Party (AP). In this period, under the leadership of Bülent Ecevit, who was the young deputy of the party (from 1957), the Minister of Labor (1961–1965), and later the Secretary General (1966–1971), starting from 1961, the CHP's left-wing transformation process started and İsmet Pasha also supported this trend. During this period of approval, the party took important steps towards transforming from a state party to a European-style leftist party by creating organic ties with labor movements and other socialist and social democratic actors. However, this transformation, which started with the slogan "left of the center" (ortanın solu) and later became the "democratic left" (demokratik sol) under the leadership of Ecevit in the following years, did not increase the votes for the party in the 1969 general elections and the CHP had to give the power to Demirel again with only 27.37 % of the total votes. The CHP, which entered the 1973 general elections held after the March 12, 1971 memorandum under the Presidency of Bülent Ecevit, became the first party again after years with 33.3 % of the vote, and "Karaoğlan" Ecevit, who formed an unexpected coalition with Necmettin Erbakan's National Salvation Party (MSP), achieved a historic success with the Cyprus Peace Operation in 1974. However, when Ecevit, who hastened to rely on the success of the Cyprus Peace Operation, broke the coalition in hopes of early elections, Demirel established the first National Front (MC) government and removed the CHP from power again. Ecevit and CHP, which showed a successful graph with 41.38 % of the votes in the 1977 general elections, were able to form a *"patchy bundle"* government with the transfers made from other parties because they did not have a parliamentary majority, and could not develop a solution to the deep economic and political problems of the country. In this period, it can be said that the CHP developed close ties with the unions and worker-laborer movements and was very influential on the Kurdish population, thus, presenting a contemporary social democratic/socialist party appearance.

While politics was reset in Turkey with the military coup of September 12, 1980, the left, which took part in the political scene with the Populist Party (HP) and the Social Democratic Populist Party (SHP) instead of the banned CHP, became the first party with 28.69 % of the votes in the 1989 local elections with the SHP led by Erdal İnönü. Apart from this success, the SHP did not show much serious existence. During these years, the left was represented by two different political parties, Erdal İnönü's SHP and Ecevit's Democratic Left Party (DSP). In this period, while the Kurdish political movement gained momentum and became a party, a cooperation environment was formed between the SHP and the Kurdish political movement from the end of the 1980s, and the fruits of this were partially seen in the 1989 local elections. The SHP also became a member of the Socialist International during this period. Despite the fact that the SHP, which was below expectations with 20.75 % in the 1991 elections, served as a junior partner in the coalition government with the DYP in the 1991–1995 period, it could not prevent the increasing radical Islam and Kurdish nationalism in the country and reactions to İnönü's leadership increased.

After the CHP was re-established in a more Kemalist and nationalist line with the leadership of Deniz Baykal and with the contributions of İsmail Cem -in response to the SHP's close stance to the Kurdish political movement- in 1992, the SHP-CHP merger took place. During the merger a strategy known as the *"Hikmet Abi formula"* was implemented and Hikmet Çetin became the Chair of the party for a while. After the temporary Presidency of Hikmet Çetin, Deniz Baykal started to freely redesign the party as a pro-secular and unitary middle-class party. In the 1995 general elections, Baykal's CHP fell short of expectations and lagged behind the DSP with only 10.71 % of the votes. When the CHP, under the leadership of Baykal, reacted with its belligerent attitude during the February 28, 1997 process, the party's voting rate fell below the threshold with 8.71 % of the votes in the 1999 general elections. Thus, the party also lost its representation in the Grand National Assembly of Turkey (TBMM). After this, with Baykal's resignation, journalist Altan Öymen became the Chairman of the party in the 1999–2000 period, while the *"factionalist"* (*hizipçi*) Baykal, who managed to keep his party delegates in place, took over the leadership of his party again in 2000. The party maintained its membership in the Socialist International during these periods; however, it followed a more nationalist and Kemalist policy and tried to appeal to the middle class instead of the working-class. Since these years, the Kurdish support of the party has also decreased considerably.

The CHP, which stood out as the defender of secularism and modern life against Recep Tayyip Erdoğan and the AK Parti, who rose in the second Baykal era, was able to get 19.39 % of the votes in the 2002 elections and 20.87 % in the 2007 general elections, and thus, suffered heavy defeats against Erdoğan. During this period, the CHP again adopted a very nationalist/Atatürkist style and took care to stay close to the Turkish nationalist MHP against the AK Parti. Baykal's strategy in this period, on the other hand, was to come to power with an interim regime period similar to February 28 with the support of the MHP, using the secularism-based problems that the AK Parti and Erdoğan had with the state and particularly with the Turkish Armed Forces (TSK), but these efforts were unsuccessful.

As a result of Baykal's dismissal from the leadership of the party with a sex tape scandal in 2010, the then-rising star of the party, Kemal Kılıçdaroğlu, was elected the new Chairman. Kılıçdaroğlu, who increased the party vote to 25.98 % in the 2011 general elections, entered the 2014 Presidential election together with the MHP by appointing Ekmeleddin İhsanoğlu, the former Secretary General of the Organization of Islamic Cooperation, and despite İhsanoğlu's 38.44 % vote, Erdoğan won the election. Kılıçdaroğlu, who received 24.95 % of the votes in the June 2015 elections and 25.32 % of the votes in the November elections, could not approach the performance of the AK Parti, which was in the band of 40 %, although he succeeded in expanding the party base partially. While the presidential and parliamentary elections were held in 2018, the votes of the CHP fell to 22.65 % in the parliamentary elections, and in the presidential election, CHP candidate Muharrem İnce lost the election to Erdoğan in the first round with 30.64 % of the votes. On the other hand, Kılıçdaroğlu made an effort to open the way to power in the country where the Presidential system was passed by establishing alliances and showed everyone that he was very determined in this direction with the Justice March (*Adalet Yürüyüşü*).

When the unserious administration by the Erdoğan government during the earthquake disaster in February 2023 was added to the economic difficulties that reached an incredible level with the increasing arbitrary administration and corruption in the country, Kılıçdaroğlu's CHP entered the 2023 general and Presidential elections confidently and believed that they could finish the election in the first round. However, despite the alliance policy and the Nation

Alliance (Millet İttifakı) umbrella initiative, the fact that the party had got only 25.33 % of the votes in the parliamentary elections, and that Kılıçdaroğlu was well behind Erdoğan in the first round of the presidential election, where victory was expected, party supporters and cadres fell into despair by considering these results as a defeat. Although Kılıçdaroğlu was able to get approximately 45 % of the votes, it seems like the intra-party conflicts and debates will increase after the election. CHP, prior to the second round, by increasing the dose of nationalism and anti-immigrant rhetoric, opposed Erdoğan regime harshly and hoped to come to power by collecting Ümit Özdağ and Victory Party's (*Zafer Partisi*) ultranationalist votes.

However, despite these efforts, Kılıçdaroğlu lost the election in the second round to Erdoğan with only 48 % of the votes (highest votes taken by a CHP leader). Although we cannot talk about completely equal conditions for the government and the opposition in Turkish elections, mostly caused by the hyperpresidentialism, the fact that the CHP's electoral base in the parliamentary elections still remains at 25 % and the party's difficulties in reaching the votes of workers, Kurds, and conservative-nationalist people living in Anatolian cities make us think that all the stages on the way to turn into a mass party or catch-all party have not been completed yet. We will see how these results will affect and transform CHP and its leadership…

Ozan Örmeci[*]

Erdoğan's New Cabinet: Fresh Names But Low Hopes

Abstract This chapter is about the new government established by President Recep Tayyip Erdoğan following the 2023 Turkish elections. The chapter also discusses what to expect from the new term.

Keywords: *Turkish Politics, 2023 Turkish elections, AK Parti, Recep Tayyip Erdoğan, Hakan Fidan, Turkish Foreign Policy.*

Introduction

After having a clear victory both in the parliamentary and the presidential elections in May, Türkiye's long serving (2014–) President Recep Tayyip Erdoğan (1954–) took his oath and announced his new cabinet today on June 3, 2023. Erdoğan's new cabinet saw the inclusion of fresh names to the forefront, but did not create high hopes among the Turkish people for the future. In this piece, I am going to introduce some important members (secretaries) of Erdoğan's new cabinet and I will try to explain what might happen in the new term.

The New Cabinet: Who Is In?

Since Türkiye's most serious problems are related to its economy in the last few years, Erdoğan's choice of the new Minister of Treasure and Finance was of critical importance. It had been already known for a while that President Erdoğan was trying to convince Mehmet Şimşek (1967–), former Minister of Finance (2009–2015) and Deputy Prime Minister of Türkiye (2015–2018) for this position. Şimşek has always been considered as a trustworthy person for the international finance market since he previously worked 7 years as the chief economist and strategist for the Merrill Lynch Company in London. Coming from Kurdish roots, Şimşek is an internationally accepted professional figure for the finance

---

[*] Associate Professor in the department of Political Science and International Relations (English) at Istanbul Aydın University, Istanbul, Türkiye.
Email: ozanormeci@aydin.edu.tr / ozanormeci@gmail.com.
ORCID: 0000-0001-8850-6089.

market having also a British passport. Now, Şimşek will act like the new savior of the economy and will try to give confidence to international markets. Şimşek's biggest problem on the other hand seems to be President Erdoğan's stubbornness of keeping interest rates low. Moreover, Türkiye's deteriorating democratic status and lack of coherent relations with the West will also create some problems for Şimşek to recover the economy and calm down the anxiety in the business circles. Thus, the most important problem in the country will continue to be the economic hardship.

Another fresh name in the cabinet will be the new Foreign Minister Hakan Fidan (1968–). Having been served as the President (Undersecretary) of Türkiye's intelligence agency-MİT (Milli İstihbarat Teşkilatı) for long years (since 2010), Fidan is a famous, but at the same enigmatic person. Rarely seen in the public and media until now, it will be interesting to see Fidan at the headlines of newspapers and in press conferences very frequently from now on. Fidan is for sure a Turkish nationalist and a loyal bureaucrat to Erdoğan who could create a difference by organizing a more operational Foreign Service with increasing ties with the security bureaucracy. Fidan's presence could be felt especially in Türkiye's struggle with terrorism and influence in some regions (Balkans, Caucasus, Middle East, and North Africa) not only with the hard power methods, but also through soft power instruments and negotiation (diplomacy).

The 30th Chief of the General Staff of the Turkish Armed Forces (TAF) General Yaşar Güler (1955–) is appointed as the new Defense Minister by President Erdoğan in this cabinet. Served almost 5 years as the head of the TAF, Güler will replace Hulusi Akar, former Chief of General Staff. Güler is a serious statesman who rarely makes public statements. However, in this new regime dominated by President Erdoğan, Güler will surely not act as the mighty Turkish Generals of the past.

In addition, by replacing Süleyman Soylu, Istanbul governor (2018–2023) Ali Yerlikaya (1968–) became the Minister of Interior. Furthermore, Yılmaz Tunç (1971–) was appointed as new the Minister of Justice. This was largely perceived as a surprise by political commentators in Türkiye. Professor İbrahim Kalın (1971–) on the other hand was named as the new President of Turkish intelligence organization MİT by replacing Hakan Fidan. Having been served as Turkish Presidential Spokesperson since 2014, Kalın is a conservative/Islamic intellectual having many academic books published. An intellectual at the top of the country's intelligence agency would certainly be a distinguishing factor for Türkiye. Vice President pick of Erdoğan on the other hand was Cevdet Yılmaz (1967–) who previously worked as the Minister of Development (2011–2015, 2015–2016).

Here's the full list of Erdoğan's new cabinet:

Vice President: Cevdet Yılmaz
Minister of Justice: Yılmaz Tunç
Minister of Family and Social Services: Mahinur Özdemir Göktaş
Minister of Environment, Urbanisation and Climate Change: Mehmet Özhaseki
Minister of Foreign Affairs: Hakan Fidan
Minister of Energy and Natural Resources: Alparslan Bayraktar
Minister of Youth and Sports: Osman Askın Bak
Minister of Treasury and Finance: Mehmet Şimşek
Minister of Interior Affairs: Ali Yerlikaya
Minister of Culture and Tourism: Mehmet Nuri Ersoy
Minister of National Education: Yusuf Tekin
Minister of Defense: Yaşar Güler
Minister of Health: Fahrettin Koca
Minister of Industry and Technology: Mehmet Fatih Kacır
Minister of Agriculture and Forestry: İbrahim Yumaklı
Minister of Trade: Ömer Bolat
Minister of Transport and Infrastructure: Abdülkadir Uraloğlu

Expectations from the New Term

President Erdoğan's new term will be very difficult as usual. He will have to face with Türkiye's growing economic problems in addition to negative spillover effects of the recent earthquakes and the Russian invasion of Ukraine. Unwelcoming attitude of Washington and Brussels towards Erdoğan regime due to Türkiye's problems related to rule of law, freedom of opinion, and democracy will also be major risk elements for Ankara in the new term.

The first issue on the agenda in the new term will be the Swedish accession to NATO. Sweden already ratified a new law for satisfying Turkish concerns about struggle with terrorism. However, due to negative approach towards his government especially in the last few years, President Erdoğan might be in expectation of a rendezvous given to him from the White House by the Biden administration. Erdoğan will probably try to use this meeting as a diplomatic success and consolidate his power in domestic politics. Moreover, Türkiye definitely wants to solve the F-16 problem with Washington in order to be able to supply its air forces with new fighter jets and to modernize the already existing ones.

In domestic politics, Erdoğan government might start to work on a new bill to liberalize all kinds of Islamic dresses in public offices, an issue that was already on the agenda before the elections. By doing this, Erdoğan could further strengthen his ties with the pious masses, plus, he can create a cleavage within the opposition since conservative elements from the opposition such as İYİ Parti (Good Party), DEVA Party, Democrat Party (DP), and Future Party (*Gelecek Partisi*) might have to support this bill for not alienating their voters. In addition, Erdoğan government might take steps to legislate a new and completely civilian constitution together with its partners Nationalist Action Party (MHP), the New Welfare Party (YRP), and Hüda-Par. This constitution will certainly not bring a return to parliamentary system, but at least it might increase guarantees for personal freedoms and rule of law within a hyperpresidential system.

In addition, the reconstruction of 10 Turkish cities that were devastated by the huge earthquakes in early February will be at the top of the list for domestic politics. The hybrid regime in Türkiye could also be more courageous in the new term for weakening the opposition. In that sense, party closure case against the pro-Kurdish HDP and political ban on pro-secular CHP's Istanbul mayor Ekrem İmamoğlu could be finalized before the March 2024 local elections to weaken and redesign the opposition. In my opinion, Erdoğan would prefer a classical Kemalist opposition, which would be less dangerous for his regime in terms of electoral performance. Lastly, Erdoğan will continue to support the Turkish defense industry and encourage his country to produce Turkish Army's weapons domestically. By doing this, Erdoğan will try to decrease Türkiye's dependency on foreign powers, primarily the United States.

In foreign policy, one of the most important issues in the new term will be the chaotic situation or the mess in Syria. It is not a secret that PYD/YPG groups are seen as branches of PKK, an outlawed Kurdish political organization and a terrorist group, by Ankara. In that sense, Türkiye might try to organize new military operations into Syria in order to sweep or at least weaken PYD/YPG groups. But it should be mentioned that these groups are well trained and equipped by Washington and it might not a piece of cake situation for Ankara to reach its goals in Syria. Moreover, Russia, Iran, and the United States' approaches to Türkiye's military operations in Syria have been rather discouraging so far and it could be very hard for Ankara to get the green light from these three actors. However, in case Türkiye and Russia could agree on a limited scale operation, Turkish Armed Forces could do this successfully and could relocate more Syrian immigrants into Syrian soil by forcing Kurdish groups to migrate to distant areas.

In foreign policy, other than these stated issues, normalization with Washington, Tel Aviv (Jerusalem), and Cairo might also be on the agenda in the new term. In addition, Erdoğan could start the construction of a new nuclear power plant in Sinop with Russians, to deepen his ties with the Putin regime. Russia and Türkiye could also work on transforming Ankara into an energy transit country that will facilitate Russia's gas supplies to European countries. This will provide Türkiye some advantages in the pricing, but also allow Russia to continue to trade with Europe via Ankara. Russian President Vladimir Putin previously offered this vision to Türkiye to separate Ankara from the Western bloc. In addition to these, the visa liberalization for Turkish citizens going to European Union (EU) countries and the updating of the Customs Union could be other major issues in foreign policy for Erdoğan government. But no one is hopeful in Türkiye right now about a real progress in Turkish accession to the EU. Lastly, Türkiye's efforts of normalization with Armenia and Greece could also continue in the new term, but to be honest, no one expects a miracle on that matters. However, the opening of border between Türkiye and Armenia would not be a big surprise. Armenian Prime Minister Nikol Pashinyan's visit to Ankara for Erdoğan's presidential inauguration was also a positive signal for the future.

Conclusion

To conclude, we should be aware of the fact that although Turkish President Recep Tayyip Erdoğan is a political genius and an electoral winning machine, during his term, in fact Türkiye's distancing from the West accelerated. To put it more concretely, I should say that out of 21 Presidents who personally attended to Erdoğan's oath ceremony, there were only a few (e.g. Bulgarian President Rumen Radev) Western and democratic countries' heads of the states. On the contrary, most of the attendees were from autocratic states. One good thing was the participation of NATO Secretary General Jens Stoltenberg to the ceremony, but this could be related to the Swedish accession to NATO. The lack of interest shown by the Western countries' Presidents to the ceremony should give us an idea about the direction of Türkiye for the future. This should also be considered as a warning for the Western world since I believe Turkish-Russian relations will further develop with this new cabinet unless there is a fundamental change in Ankara's relations with the West.

Ozan Örmeci[*]

What Happens in Türkiye in the Post-Election Process?

Abstract This chapter deals with the contemporary political developments in Türkiye following the 2023 presidential and parliamentary elections.

Keywords: *Turkish Politics, 2023 Turkish elections, AK Parti, Recep Tayyip Erdoğan, Hakan Fidan, CHP, İYİ Parti.*

Introduction

Turkish people decided on the future of their country by overwhelmingly choosing right-wing conservative/Islamist AK Parti's chair Recep Tayyip Erdoğan on May 28, 2023, in the second round of the presidential election with 52 % of the votes. Thus, despite of huge economic problems and Türkiye's authoritarian transformation in recent years, *"election winning machine"* Mr. Erdoğan once again proved his success and legitimacy in the eyes of Turkish people and earned 5 more years in the office. However, Erdoğan's unconventional tactics during the electoral campaign including spreading false videos about the opposition's presidential candidate and CHP chair Kemal Kılıçdaroğlu created some reactions as well. On the night of his electoral victory, Erdoğan set his next target: to win the municipalities of big cities (Istanbul and Ankara primarily) in the local elections that will take place on March 2024. Erdoğan keeps his party's electoral coalition called People's Alliance (*Cumhur İttifakı*) with other right-wing/far right parties and seems to have high chance to be successful in local elections if he could fix the economy. In this piece, I am going to summarize most important political developments in Türkiye in the post-election process.

---

[*] Associate Professor in the department of Political Science and International Relations (English) at Istanbul Aydın University, Istanbul, Türkiye.
Email: ozanormeci@aydin.edu.tr / ozanormeci@gmail.com.
ORCID: 0000-0001-8850-6089.

HDP Leader Selahattin Demirtaş Resigned from Politics

One of the most important political developments taking place in Türkiye following the election was the resignation of pro-Kurdish HDP's jailed chair Selahattin Demirtaş from active politics. In an interview made from prison, Demirtaş announced his decision by stating the reason as *"not being able to put forth politics that are deserving of our people"*. A source close to Demirtaş on the other hand claimed that the politician's decision was affected by the HDP's ignorance of his suggestions. It must not be forgotten that, during the night of the second round, after Erdoğan's victory was declared, Erdoğan's supporters yelled out for the execution of Demirtaş. This might be another reason for Demirtaş's surprising resignation.

Socialist Journalist Merdan Yanardağ Is Imprisoned

More recently, the founder of Erdoğan opponent *Tele 1* tv channel, veteran socialist journalist Merdan Yanardağ was arrested due to his remarks related to the imprisoned PKK leader Abdullah Öcalan. Yanardağ was accused of *"praising the crime and the criminal"* as well as *"making propaganda for a terrorist organization"* due to his statements about Öcalan during a broadcast on the *Tele 1* channel on June 25. Yanardağ's statements could be criticized and refuted, but it is hard to believe that there was a real encouragement for violence. In fact, he only mentioned Öcalan's intelligence and intellectual capacity, which are unusual statements to be used for a terrorist leader from my perspective as well but might not constitute a real reason for conviction. Yanardağ decision shows that the dose of nationalism will increase in Türkiye unless a new peace process is not implemented. Moreover, the decision destroyed the earlier hopes that Erdoğan could soften the regime following his decisive victory in the elections.

CHP in Leadership Race

Erdoğan's biggest rival pro-secular CHP on the other hand has been having hard times since the election night. Awaiting a victory from the presidential election on the basis of public opinion polls, CHP cadres and supporters are extremely disappointed and unhappy after the results. Voices criticizing the party's current chair and presidential nominee Kemal Kılıçdaroğlu are increasing day by day, but Kılıçdaroğlu does not seem willingly to resign. Kılıçdaroğlu's biggest contender is Istanbul Mayor Ekrem İmamoğlu, a rising star of the party, who had defeated Erdoğan twice in 2019 in the Istanbul local elections (the election was renewed due to AK Parti's pressure). İmamoğlu's popularity is still very high, but the current legal system of Türkiye has been harassing and trying to ban him from active politics. Appeal decision is not yet announced, but it is still possible that İmamoğlu might soon be temporarily banned from politics for saying "*idiot*" (*ahmak*) to the people who decided to renew Istanbul local elections in 2019. This seems again a very harsh punishment considering the fact that Turkish people including politicians and statesmen use slang words very often. Without a leadership change, it might be very hard for CHP administration to motivate voters to go to ballots once again in March 2024 after such a huge disappointment. However, İmamoğlu becoming CHP's new chair might mean an easy victory for AK Parti in Istanbul since the party does not have an equally strong and popular candidate. İmamoğlu's possible ban from active politics on the other hand might leave CHP very weak. That is why; CHP's situation is very ambiguous for the moment.

Akşener and İYİ Parti Distancing Themselves from CHP

Another crucial development was pro-secular right-wing İYİ Parti's recent congress. During the congress, the party's leader Meral Akşener criticized her party and showed signals of leaving CHP-led Nation Alliance (*Millet İttifakı*). In fact, Akşener opposed Kılıçdaroğlu's candidacy in March 2023 and openly supported the candidacy of Istanbul Mayor Ekrem İmamoğlu or Ankara Mayor Mansur Yavaş, but had to withdraw from her position upon social pressures coming from pro-secular masses. However, after the loss of the presidential election, Akşener now seems very angry towards CHP and Kılıçdaroğlu. In that sense, without a leadership change in CHP, it might be very difficult for CHP to convince Akşener and her party to join the Nation Alliance in March 2024 in the local elections. Of course, without İYİ Parti's support, the opposition might not win many municipalities including Istanbul and Ankara as well.

New Stars in the New Cabinet

Erdoğan's new cabinet includes some names that drew too much attention from the international public. The new Foreign Minister of Türkiye Mr. Hakan Fidan for instance, was praised for his intellectual capacity and competence. Fidan was the head of Türkiye's top intelligence agency, the MİT (*Milli İstihbarat Teşkilatı*) for long years and is known as a serious statesman. Fidan is not an classical or ordinary right-wing figure and he was the one who started peace talks with the

PKK several years ago in order to end four decades-old violence and terrorism in Türkiye. In this sense, Fidan could be the one who could come up with a solution to Türkiye's PKK problem and could take Washington's full support as well in doing this. However, the first thing to be solved on the table of diplomacy is of course the Swedish accession to NATO, on which Ankara continues to act as a barrier. It seems like Türkiye follows a *"transactionalist"* approach and expects some favors in return from Washington. Some sources state that this might be related to the sale of F-16 jets to Ankara and Erdoğan's reception in the White House by the United States (U.S.) President Joe Biden.

The new Treasury and Finance Minister Mehmet Şimşek was also praised with his foreign experience and skills. However, in a country having serious structural problems related to democracy, rule of law, and free-market economy, it is still unknown whether Şimşek could create a difference or not. Another important fresh name is the new head of MİT, İbrahim Kalın, who could be pointed out as the first Islamist President of Türkiye's top intelligence agency. However, with his foreign experience, intellectual capacity, and good education including his PhD at the George Washington University, Kalın could create a difference and establish new ties with the United States as well as the Islamic world.

Economy Giving Bad Signals

Although the new Minister of Treasury and Finance was largely praised by the press, in fact Turkish lira's free fall continues following the election. American Dollar now worth more than 26 Turkish Lira (TL) and Euro is equal to approximately 28.5 TL. The inflation in the country is still very high and although the state and private firms recently increased the wages of working people, people's purchasing power continue to diminish. Recently, Türkiye decided to hike interest rates to 15 % from 8 %, which could be considered as a U-turn. The decision was taken by the recently appointed new Turkish Central Bank chief Hafize Gaye Erkan. The optimistic view suggests that the interest rates will be augmented even further in the near future and this will stabilize the rapid rise of the value of foreign currencies. The nightmare scenario on the other hand is based on the uncontrolled rise of foreign currencies and the rapid devaluation of Turkish Lira. This might put Erdoğan in a difficult position once again in the 2024 local elections.

Conclusion

In conclusion, as expected, Türkiye's problems continue following the election and there is no sign of relief. However, the inclusion of some new competent names into the cabinet is a promising development. On the other hand, the jailing of opposition figures (Merdan Yanardağ) rings the alarm bells for Turkish democracy. Let us hope that President Erdoğan will try to expand freedoms in Türkiye and will be successful in doing this.

Ozan Örmeci[*]

Secular Opposition Is Weak in Türkiye

Abstract This chapter is on the political developments taking place in Türkiye following the 2023 elections, with a particular focus on the opposition actors. The article discusses a potential leadership change in CHP as well as CHP-İYİ Parti electoral cooperation.

Keywords: *CHP, Özgür Özel, Örsan Kunter Öymen, İYİ Parti, Meral Akşener.*

Özgür Özel and Meral Akşener

Introduction

Türkiye is heading towards local elections set for March 31, 2024, approximately 6 months later. After President Recep Tayyip Erdoğan and his conservative/ nationalist bloc's decisive victory in the 2023 presidential and parliamentary elections, the secular opposition in Türkiye is now very weak, fragmented, and fragile. On the other hand, since this will be President Erdoğan's last term according to the constitution (Erdoğan's tenure in office will end officially in 2028 May), there are also heated debates about his successor. In this piece, I am

---

[*]   Associate Professor in the department of Political Science and International Relations (English) at Istanbul Aydın University, Istanbul, Türkiye.
       Email: ozanormeci@aydin.edu.tr / ozanormeci@gmail.com.
       ORCID: 0000-0001-8850-6089.

going to evaluate recent political developments in Turkish Politics by focusing on the situation of the opposition while leaving aside the discussion about who could replace Erdoğan to another article.

CHP's Congress Will Be Held on Early November

Türkiye's main opposition party, pro-secular and social democratic CHP (Republican People's Party) is in ruins psychologically after the shocking electoral defeat. The party's chair, Kemal Kılıçdaroğlu, was hoping to become Türkiye's new President due to Erdoğan government's poor economic performance and terrible management of crisis following the devastating earthquakes in early February 2023. Although Kılıçdaroğlu was not doing very good in the earlier polls - especially compared to his party's popular Mayors such as Ekrem İmamoğlu and Mansur Yavaş-, as the election approached, almost all polls pointed him as the favorite candidate against Erdoğan. However, Erdoğan, his Islamist/conservative AK Parti (Justice and Development Party), and the right-wing electoral bloc with other small right-wing and far-right political parties *Cumhur İttifakı* (People's Alliance) showed an outstanding performance at the ballots and acquired a decisive victory in May 2023.

This shocking defeat caused despair and apathy among the supporters of the opposition as people stopped talking politics and watching TV channels for several months. Even the party's chair Kemal Kılıçdaroğlu did not appear on media for several weeks to regain his confidence and recover his morale. However, Kılıçdaroğlu's turning back to normal also did not change the anger and despair of the opposition voters. While the party's Istanbul Mayor and rising star Ekrem İmamoğlu showed his intention to replace Kılıçdaroğlu, CHP chair openly stated that he would make necessary changes within the party administration and continue to lead CHP. Kılıçdaroğlu also mentioned that the party needs İmamoğlu as Istanbul Mayor since there will be a tough local election in March 2024 in the economic capital of the country. Kılıçdaroğlu also endorsed Mansur Yavaş as the party's Ankara Mayor for the approaching elections. Eventually İmamoğlu calmed down and accepted Kılıçdaroğlu's leadership temporarily while continuing to make reference to the necessity of change and self-criticism.

But the media and party supporters continued to ask for a change in the leadership of the party. Eventually, the party's young deputy from Manisa and the new parliamentary group leader Özgür Özel (1974–) announced his candidacy for the leadership. Ekrem İmamoğlu also supported Özel's bid for leadership. Another candidate for leadership is Örsan Kunter Öymen (1965–), a Philosophy Professor coming from an important Republican family, the Öymens. Öymen's uncle Altan Öymen is a famous journalist and he was CHP's leader for a short while in the 1999–2000 period. Öymen's close relative and former diplomat Onur Öymen on the other hand was CHP's Vice Chair during Deniz Baykal era.

So, do these candidates have a real chance to replace Kılıçdaroğlu at the 38th Ordinary Party Congress? It seems like Professor Örsan Kunter Öymen does not have a strong base among the party delegates and members. Delegates are important because they will vote at the Congress to choose the leader. Özgür Özel on the other hand could have a real chance to replace Kılıçdaroğlu and become the 8th Chair of the party following Mustafa Kemal Atatürk (1923–1938), İsmet İnönü (1938–1972), Bülent Ecevit (1972–1980), Deniz Baykal (1992–1995, 1995–1999, 2000–2010), Hikmet Çetin (1995–1995), Altan Öymen (1999–2000), and Kemal Kılıçdaroğlu (2010–).

Özgür Özel was born in 1974 in Manisa. He graduated from Bornova Anadolu Lisesi (BAL), a famous state college in Izmir. He later started to have university education in the department of Pharmacology at Ege (Aegean) University in Izmir. As a young Turkish citizen raised in Izmir, Türkiye's third biggest city known for its strong secular and Kemalist tradition, he became involved in social democractic circles and began to support the CHP. Özel finished Ege University's Pharmacology department in 1997 and began to work as pharmacist independently. He became CHP's Mayor candidate in Manisa in 2009, during Deniz Baykal's leadership, but eventually lost the election. In 2011, he was elected CHP's Manisa deputy for the first time. In 2014, he took his chance to become Manisa Mayor once again, but was defeated. He was elected regularly CHP's Manisa deputy in 2015 June, 2015 November, 2018, and 2023 parliamentary elections. He became a member of the party administration in 2014 first time. In 2015, he was elected deputy chairman for the parliamentary group of CHP. Özel drew attention seriously first time in 2014 when he warned the public and authorities about the difficult and dangerous working conditions in Soma Coal Mine in Manisa. A few weeks after his warning, a terrible disaster in Soma Coal Mine caused the death of 301 coal miners and showed the miserable condition of Türkiye in terms of labour safety. Özel continued to appear on TV channels with his heated speeches and rational criticism of the government and achieved to find considerable support among the party members and supporters. Father of a child, Özel is fluent in German and English languages.

Özgür Özel is not the favorite candidate for the moment since party delegates are determined by the party administration and the leadership. However, one should keep in mind that, in case party authorities and delegates realize that they will not have any chance against Erdoğan in the March 2024 local elections without a leadership change, they might decide to support Özel. In that scenario,

Özel could be the party's new chair in a surprising manner. This could bring new hope and dynamism to CHP and could change the overwhelming defeatist psychology. Although I do not have the latest polls and opinion polling companies failed largely at predicting the result of 2023 elections, I think the opposition could have a chance in the approaching local elections only in case of the leadership change. Otherwise, I expect AK Parti victory in many metropolitan cities including Istanbul and Ankara as well. This is because many CHP voters are very angry towards the party leadership and they might not even go to ballots this time in order to punish Kılıçdaroğlu. It is still possible for Kılıçdaroğlu to motivate people within this long 6 months period, but a leadership change could accelerate things and seems to be a more guaranteed solution. That is why, Özel's election as the new chair of CHP will not be a big shock to me although I think Kılıçdaroğlu is still the favourite.

İYİ Parti Trying to Find Its Own Way

Another important political party from the opposition is secular/Turkish nationalist İYİ Parti (Good Party). Split from MHP in 2017, the party's first and current leader is former Turkish Minister of Interior Affairs Meral Akşener. Coming from an ultranationalist background, Akşener tries to find a suitable place for her party on the political spectrum and appeal to secular nationalist, center-right, and Kemalist voters primarily. After Kılıçdaroğlu's insistence of becoming a presidential candidate himself, Akşener reluctantly supported him after a few days of hesitation. However, when the opposition had a terrible defeat at the ballots, Akşener began to distance her party from CHP and follow their own path. After a long break, Akşener severely criticized Kılıçdaroğlu for his decision to force his own candidacy although public opinion polls were favouring other candidates such as İmamoğlu and Yavaş. Thus, we can clearly state that Akşener has now been trying to separate her ways from Kılıçdaroğlu's CHP.

This might be a clever strategy for taking more support from right-wing voters, especially at a time when the ultranationalist MHP (Nationalist Action Party) is weak, President Erdoğan is in his last term, and Turkish economy continues to perform poorly. But now Akşener not only distances herself from the leftist CHP, but also rejects an electoral collaboration/cooperation with CHP under the banner of *Millet İttifakı* (Nation Alliance) as well. This might be very risky for the secular opposition in Türkiye and without CHP-İYİ Parti partnership, I estimate that AK Parti could win almost in all metropolitan cities except Izmir. That is why, Akşener's anti-Kılıçdaroğlu positioning could facilitate the leadership change in CHP as well in the coming days, opening the way for

Özgür Özel's chairmanship. With Özel becoming the new chair, Akşener could be more easygoing concerning electoral collaboration with CHP. In any scenario, 6 months is a very long period for Turkish political life and anything is still possible.

Conclusion

Finally, in my opinion, as Türkiye's democratic backsliding is no joke but a serious problem, opposition parties should act responsibly and continue to cooperate in elections. Otherwise, the emergence of a party-state system similar to 1930s is possible with secular lifestyle and personal freedoms as well as the rights of minorities are getting into danger.

Note: Özgür Özel was elected 8th chair of the CHP in the Congress organized in November 2023.

Ozan Örmeci[*]

Erdoğan's Successor?

Abstract This chapter discusses who could replace President Recep Tayyip Erdoğan in Türkiye as the new leader of the large right-wing conservative bloc after Erdoğan's expected end of tenure in office in 2028. The article focuses on key actors such as Hakan Fidan, Selçuk Bayraktar, and Fatih Erbakan.

Keywords: *Recep Tayyip Erdoğan, AK Parti, Selçuk Bayraktar, Hakan Fidan, Fatih Erbakan.*

President Erdoğan's transformation in years

There is no denying that Turkey's President Recep Tayyip Erdoğan has dominated the political scene and the political life in the country in the last two decades. Erdoğan gained his first important success in Turkish politics by being elected Istanbul's Mayor in 1994 in a very surprising manner from the Islamist Welfare Party (*Refah Partisi*). His leaning towards Islamism, heated speeches, young and dynamic style, struggle with the state elite (e.g. military and the secular establishment), and the use of colloquial language distinguished himself from all other politicians. However, the secular establishment tried to prevent Islamist

---

[*] Associate Professor in the department of Political Science and International Relations (English) at Istanbul Aydın University, Istanbul, Türkiye.
Email: ozanormeci@aydin.edu.tr / ozanormeci@gmail.com.
ORCID: 0000-0001-8850-6089.

Erdoğan's rise by putting him into jail due to a poem he had read. The decision
was unfair; this further impassioned Erdoğan and made him a hero in the eyes
of millions of people who were alienated from the state and Turkey's unjust
and corrupt system. After getting out of prison, Erdoğan established a new and
more moderate and liberal Islamist/conservative party, the AK Parti (Justice and
Development Party) in 2001. He won the very first election he entered in 2002
and became the Prime Minister of Turkey in 2003, a few months after winning
the election due to his electoral ban. Since then, he has been serving as the Prime
Minister (2003–2014), the President of the Republic within the parliamentary
system (2014–2018), and the President of Türkiye (2018–2023, 2023–) within
the Presidential system. He is -without any doubt- the most popular (after
Atatürk), influential, controversial, and polarizing political leader in Turkish
political history. However, due to constitutional limits, Erdoğan's tenure in office
will normally end in 2028. For sure, a strongman like Erdoğan could find ways
to lengthen his term. But if we accept the constitution as the basis of Turkey's
political system, this will be Erdoğan's last term. Thus, discussions about who
could replace Erdoğan as the new leader of right-wing politics have become an
important issue in foreign countries' think-tanks and international media. In
this piece, I will try to respond to this question and analyze who could replace
Erdoğan.

Before getting into a discussion about the potential successors, one can realize
that Turkey's current political system is often labelled as hyper-presidentialism
due to the very strong and central position of the President within the system.
Of course, Turkey still has a democratically elected parliament responsible for
making laws and it implements free and fair elections, but the Western and
pro-Western political scientists often criticize the current political system for
not having any check and balance mechanism against the mighty powers of the
President. However, one should keep in mind that, looking at the world map
starting from North America and going toward the East, it is hard to find any real
functioning democracies after Greece (except for some far East democracies such
as Japan and South Korea). So, Turkey's current political system and Erdoğan's
hybrid or mixed regime between democracy and authoritarianism is also a
direct consequence of Turkey's geopolitical reality; a country stuck between the
West and the East and so close to Russia, which promotes authoritarian rule
and supports authoritarian leaders (Lukashenko etc.) in the region. Thus, unless
Turkey makes a real change in getting rid of this geopolitical curse and develops
better relations with the West, Erdoğanism might stay in the country although
Erdoğan will be gone in the near future.

Hakan Fidan

Now let us look at the potential successors. President Erdoğan has a larger than life personality and obviously it would be very difficult for anyone to replace him. However, as Erdoğan gets older (69), and advances towards his final 4–5 years, there are new candidates appearing in the political scene and media to replace him. Among them, one of the most popular candidates these days is Turkey's current Foreign Minister (2023–) and the former President (Undersecretary) of Turkey's National Intelligence Agency (MİT) (2010–2023) Hakan Fidan. Originally from Van and having Kurdish roots, but born and raised in Ankara, Fidan is still young (55), charismatic for the right-wing nationalist electorate with his enigmatic intelligence background, but lacks the populist politician qualities of Erdoğan. He rarely appears on TV channels and his voice is still unknown for many in the country. It is still hard for many to think of Fidan making populist speeches in crowded public meetings and demonstrations and to enchant the crowd like Erdoğan does. However, his deep connections within the security bureaucracy (Fidan comes from military background, he studied in the United States in Maryland University, he worked as political consultant for the Australian Embassy in Ankara for a while, and he ruled MİT for 13–14 years while collaborating with his American and European counterparts) both in Turkey and among the allies, is a strong asset for him. Fidan could learn petty politics in time and could become successful in replacing Erdoğan although I think he is not a favorite candidate. Fidan's ideology is unknown and he now seems like trying to appeal to nationalist and conservative right primarily; but he was also one of the key figures in Turkey's Kurdish opening in the recent past, which might help him to have more support from Kurdish voters, but also risking the support of Turkish nationalists in the future.

Selçuk Bayraktar

Another potential candidate and one of the most likely successors is Selçuk Bayraktar, Erdoğan's groom. Bayraktar is married to Sümeyye Erdoğan Bayraktar, he is very young (44), and he works in the defense industry, a sector that is supported by almost everyone in the country. Originally from Trabzon, Bayraktar was born and raised in Sarıyer, Istanbul and had a graduate education in the U.S. in the University of Pennsylvania and the Massachusetts Institute of Technology (MIT). As an engineer, he established the Baykar Teknoloji company in 2010 as a successor company of his father Özdemir Bayraktar's old firm producing automobile vehicles and parts. Together with his brother Haluk Bayraktar, Selçuk Bayraktar began to develop and produce high-developed armed drones or unmanned aerial vehicles. Bayraktar, with the help of his father-in-law, became very successful in the drone business and began to make large sums of money in recent years by Turkish drone sales to many countries including Azerbaijan, Qatar, Libya, Ukraine, Turkmenistan, Poland, Morocco, Ethiopia, Pakistan, Kirghizstan, Nigeria, and Mali etc. Turkish drones now have a very good reputation in the world due to their cheapness and high-level of efficiency. Having good relations with Azerbaijan, Bayraktar was recently invited to the U.S. aircraft USS Gerald R. Ford, an important sign of his increasing prestige among the world's only left superpower and Turkey's historical ally. Bayraktar sometimes appears on TV channels and due to his nationalist speeches focusing on the strength of Turkish Armed Forces, the institution that established the Republic of Turkey a century ago, he has considerable support among the right-wing and mainstream voters. However, Bayraktar's rise and central place in the defense industry might be considered risky by Turkey's imminent neighbors and regional countries including Greece, Armenia, Iran, Syria, and even Iraq and Israel. Russia and China, two non-Western countries which have recently become Turkey's most important trading partners might also be abstained from Bayraktar, a defense industry entrepreneur who seems to have open support from Washington. Moreover, American defense industry companies might not also be very happy to see Turkey becoming increasingly independent and self-ordained in the defense industry. In addition, similar to Fidan, Bayraktar as an engineer and businessman, lacks Erdoğan's qualities as a populist politician. However, recently, he has begun to top the list and presented as the likely successor of President Erdoğan. Since President Erdoğan trusts her daughter Sümeyye very much in politics and has a natural affection toward her daughter, his decision might be affected from this emotional aspect and he might choose and point out Albayrak as his successor. Journalist İsmail Saymaz also recently wrote that Erdoğan's successor will be Selçuk Bayraktar.

Hulusi Akar

Hulusi Akar, Turkey's former Chief of General Staff (2015–2018), and Defense Minister (2018–2023) was also presented as a potential candidate to Erdoğan until recently. However, he was recently elected deputy from Kayseri and was not given any Ministerial position by Erdoğan, a sign that he might not be favored by the President as the likely successor. Akar is also a bit older (71) compared to other candidates, which might reduce his chances in a very young and dynamic country. It should be also stated that soldiers are not very successful in Turkish politics in terms of electoral performance and none of the political parties having military leaders (İnönü's CHP, Osman Pamukoğlu etc.) showed a good performance in elections against the populist civilian leaders. But being nationalist, hawkish, and not anti-Western, Akar could still find a chance in the future to serve as the President.

Berat Albayrak

Erdoğan's another groom, Turkey's former Minister of Energy and Natural Resources (2015–2018) and Finance Minister (2018–2020) Berat Albayrak (45) was also a likely candidate a few years ago. Albayrak is married to Esra Erdoğan and had a great chance to replace his father-in-law, but his performance as the Minister of Finance coincided with a terrible economic crisis in the country, which left a bad taste for everyone and reduced his chances. However, Albayrak is still a potential successor due to his inner circle position within the Erdoğan family and his prior success as the Minister of Energy and Natural Resources (Turkey's recent hydrocarbon discoveries in the Black Sea region are made by the ships purchased by Albayrak).

Süleyman Soylu

Another potential candidate who has lost his advantageous position recently is Turkey's former Minister of Interior Affairs (2016–2023) and Minister of Labour and Social Security (2015–2016), Süleyman Soylu (54). Coming from the center-right political tradition, Soylu had once good support among the Turkish nationalists and former center-right elements. Plus, as the head of all police forces, Soylu was very influential in domestic politics a few months ago. However, now it seems like his role in the new term is rather limited as he serves only as an ordinary deputy. Thus, Soylu is not given too much chance actually. However, it should be stated that Soylu is a better politician in terms of dialogue with ordinary people, organizing large demonstrations, and populism in general compared to previous alternatives.

Sinan Oğan

Coming from Azeri background, Sinan Oğan (54) is the new transfer of President Erdoğan to AK Parti prior to the second round of the 2023 Presidential election. He is coming from an ultranationalist (MHP) background and has close ties with Azerbaijani political leadership. Although Oğan now does not have any position in the government, his developing relations with Erdoğan and his alleged endorsement by President Ilham Aliyev in Azerbaijan could give him a chance in the future to replace Erdoğan and become the new leader of the right-wing. Oğan is a better politician compared to all other alternatives as he served previously as MHP's Iğdır deputy and was a presidential candidate himself against Erdoğan in the first-round of 2023 elections. He took around 5 % of the votes, which shows his true potential as a young and hawkish Turkish nationalist leader who could further militarize the country and boost nationalism and the national defense industry. Oğan could replace MHP's Devlet Bahçeli as well in the near future as Bahçeli gets very old.

Numan Kurtulmuş

Born in 1959 in Ordu, Numan Kurtulmuş is an important National Outlook (*Milli Görüş*) politician similar to President Erdoğan and a highly-qualified academic. He is currently the President (Speaker) of the Turkish Parliament and has a leadership potential although he had been staying under the shadow of Erdoğan for many years. However, after Erdoğan retires, despite his old age (64), Kurtulmuş could step forth and try his chance to become the new leader of AK Parti. Kurtulmuş could also get support from Erbakan loyalists and more traditional Islamist circles of the party.

Fatih Erbakan

Being the son of Turkey's famous Islamist politician and the first Islamist Prime Minister (1996–1997) Necmettin Erbakan, Fatih Erbakan has also a considerable chance to lead the right-wing politics in Turkey after President Erdoğan. A very young politician born in 1979, Erbakan has all the qualities to lead the Islamist bloc as he is young (44), a true believer, and has good relations with bureaucratic institutions. He is currently the chair of New Welfare Party (YRP), which had supported President Erdoğan in the previous presidential election in May. Since an Islamist movement growing outside of AK Parti is a real danger for AK Parti and Erdoğan regime as well as the Western powers who are afraid of an anti-Occidentalist Islamism to get strong, the young Erbakan himself and his party members could be given important ranks within the AK Parti in the coming years. This might even create a chance for him to become the new leader after Erdoğan.

In conclusion, replacing a man for all seasons is a tough job and Erdoğan's positive and negative deeds and speeches in Turkish politics will continue to shape the country for long years. But for sure, the graveyards are full of indispensable men and everyone could be replaced. In that sense, the trends in global politics and Turkey's key partners such as the U.S., the EU, Russia, and Azerbaijan, will also affect who will replace Erdoğan. In the meantime, it is still possible for the opposition to gain power with a leadership change and come to government position following Erdoğan's retirement.

Ozan Örmeci[*]

Tragedy in Gaza and the Republican Centennial

Abstract This chapter analyzes the reactions in Turkish Politics especially on the side of the governing bloc and President Erdoğan after Hamas' terrorist attack toward Israel on October 7, 2023 and Israel's harsh response to it.

Keywords: *Recep Tayyip Erdoğan, Turkish Politics, Gaza, Israeli-Palestinian Conflict.*

Turkish people were ready for an enthusiastic celebration of the 100th year anniversary of the foundation of the Republic. However, Hamas' vicious attack on Israel on October 7 and Israel's irrational response based on excessive use of force on civilians by bombing settlements in Gaza caused sadness and anger, especially among the Islamist/conservative circles within the country; thus, overshadowing the joy of the Republican celebration.

It should not be surprising that in a country almost fully composed of Muslims, the death of innocent Muslim children causes despair and anger toward Israel. Wrong military strategies adopted by the Israeli State can be proven by

---

[*]   Associate Professor in the department of Political Science and International Relations (English) at Istanbul Aydın University, Istanbul, Türkiye.
       Email: ozanormeci@aydin.edu.tr / ozanormeci@gmail.com.
       ORCID: 0000-0001-8850-6089.

the statistics as well; almost half of the dead people due to Israeli bombardments were children and babies (3,000 children died among 7,000). For sure, not only Islamists who care about Muslim lives, but left-wing, liberal, and humanitarian right-wing moderate people also feel sad and angry because of witnessing dying children especially when hospitals and sanctuaries are targeted by military forces.

Following Hamas' attack, Turkish President Recep Tayyip Erdoğan kept his calmness and common sense and invited both sides to moderation to prevent further bloodshed. Erdoğan's response was positively received by Israeli diplomats as well. However, as a politician from an Islamist background, and gaining popularity with his fierce criticism of the Israeli aggression in Palestine, Erdoğan could not keep his calm anymore and began to criticize the Israeli administration with harsh words in the coming days after seeing the tragic videos coming from Gaza. Bodies of dead children and babies deeply wounded Erdoğan and Turkish people. In that sense, Erdoğan defended Hamas as a liberation organization and mujahedeen group and blamed Israel for acting like an organization rather than a state. Erdoğan also stated that he cancelled his visit to Israel although he shook the hand of Netanyahu just a few weeks ago at the United Nations General Assembly. In Türkiye, even people who defend Israel's right to self-defense began to criticize the Israeli government and defense forces for such horrific crimes. Western countries' indifference including the United States, the United Kingdom, the European Union, etc. also hurt Turks and Muslims around the world and proved once again the flawed nature of the international order of today.

Was it a coincidence or a deliberate timing we do not know, but the tragic effects of Israeli strikes in Gaza overshadowing Republican centennial ceremonies could be the marker of Türkiye's second century as a more conservative, Muslim-oriented, and self-ordained country. It is obvious that Turkish foreign policy has become more divergent from Western preferences in recent years as proven by Türkiye's continuing trade and good relations with Russia as well as Turkish concerns for Palestinians in addition to Turkish insistence in Cyprus for the recognition of Turkish Cypriots' state; the TRNC (Turkish Republic of Northern Cyprus). Objectively speaking, while the West seems more just in the case of Ukraine, the Turkish position seems more convincing to me in Palestine. That is because in the first case, Russia was the aggressor and started an unnecessary war, and in the second case although Hamas seems to be the aggressor who started the bloodshed, in fact, the lack of a political settlement, Israeli occupation of the Palestinian lands, and Israel's continuous military operations over the years provoked such an attack. Hamas' Islamist nature and barbaric methods should be of course condemned and criticized, but this does not change the fact that these are the results of the lack of a political solution to the decades-old Israeli occupation problem.

So, for all these reasons, we urge the United States to take the lead and come up with a settlement plan in Palestine to stop the deaths of more children and babies. Israeli-Palestinian conflict could be ended with a just, well-thought, and well-negotiated plan that would create a free Palestinian State in addition to the existing Israeli (Jewish) State. This could be done only by a joint U.S. and the United Nations (UN) effort, but so far Biden administration seems very ineffective and indecisive, unlike earlier Democratic governments such as Jimmy Carter and Bill Clinton who struggled for a settlement in Palestine and Arab-Israeli normalization. Biden administration should remember that even Trump administration had a plan for settlement and peace in Palestine and staying behind Trump administration on the Palestinian issue should be a source of shame for all Democrats.

Lastly, I should warn that a free Palestinian State that came out of threats made by nuclear weapons possessed Iran in the coming years would make the U.S., Israel, and democratic regimes in general much weaker and less prestigious in the region. So, that is why, I think it is very timely for the U.S. to take action and solve the problem for good for the safety of Israel as well. Otherwise, I think an Iran-forced settlement in Palestine could be happening in the near future and this will turn Iran into a regional power despite its regime's theocratic and totalitarian character. Turkish people on the other hand will celebrate the centennial of their Republic in a respectful manner to show their respect for Palestinian and Jewish people who lost their lives in a meaningless war.

Ozan Örmeci[1]

Türkiye's Main Opposition Party Elected A New Chair: Özgür Özel

Abstract: This chapter analyzes the leadership change in Türkiye's main opposition party, the CHP, with Özgür Özel becoming the new chair of the party.

Keywords: *CHP, Özgür Özel, Kemal Kılıçdaroğlu, Ekrem İmamoğlu.*

Özgür Özel became the new CHP Chair

Introduction

During the 38th regular Congress of the party, Türkiye's pro-secular founder party, the CHP (Republican People's Party) elected a new chair: Özgür Özel. Young pharmacist (49) became the 8th leader of CHP after Mustafa Kemal Atatürk (1923–1938), İsmet İnönü (1938–1972), Bülent Ecevit (1972–1980), Deniz

---

1   Associate Professor in the department of Political Science and International Relations (English) at Istanbul Aydın University, Istanbul, Türkiye.
     Email: ozanormeci@aydin.edu.tr / ozanormeci@gmail.com.
     ORCID: 0000-0001-8850-6089.

Baykal (1992–1995, 1995–1999, 2000–2010), Hikmet Çetin (1995–1995), Altan Öymen (1999–2000), and Kemal Kılıçdaroğlu (2010–2023). Özel commented on his victory as the *"greatest honor throughout his life".*

Özel's Surprising Victory

Although the CHP had a terrible defeat last May both in the presidential and parliamentary elections, party chair Kemal Kılıçdaroğlu was declared the favorite candidate before the voting. This was related to the delegate system of Turkish political parties, which somehow gave a chance to the headquarters to control delegates and influence the leadership race. However, CHP delegates, after listening to both candidates' speeches carefully and being aware of the risks that the party will face in the approaching local elections in March 2024 in case Kılıçdaroğlu continued to lead the party, decided to choose Özel. Özel took 682 votes in the first round against Kılıçdaroğlu's 664 votes. In the second round, Özel increased his support by 130 votes and reached 812 while Kılıçdaroğlu stayed behind with only 536 votes. Although the Congress in general was peaceful and democratic, Özel's speech before the first round of voting was interrupted by disorder and fights. The overcrowded Congress was nostalgic for those who remember the old and glorious CHP days as the Kemalist/social democratic party is known in Turkish Politics as the *"party of Congresses".*

Özgür Özel's speech during the Congress was oriented toward delegates. Özel criticized the Kılıçdaroğlu administration, especially for its close ties with right-wing groups/parties and the lack of financial support given by the headquarters. He promised more financial support for party branches and he underlined his hardworking personality. Moreover, Özel promised to change the party charter in the coming weeks and make it more democratic. Kılıçdaroğlu on the other hand criticized his young opponent for being disloyal and used the rhetoric of stabbing in the back (*sırtından hançerlemek*). Özel responded to these claims harshly and rejected Kılıçdaroğlu's accusations.

Who is Özgür Özel?

Özgür Özel was born in 1974 in Manisa. He graduated from Bornova Anadolu Lisesi (BAL), a famous state college in Izmir. He later started to have a university education in the department of Pharmacology at Ege (Aegean) University in Izmir. As a young Turkish citizen raised in Izmir, Türkiye's third biggest city known for its strong secular and Kemalist tradition, he became involved in social democratic circles and began to support the CHP. Özel finished Ege University's

Pharmacology department in 1997 and began to work as a pharmacist independently. He became CHP's Mayor candidate in Manisa in 2009, during Deniz Baykal's leadership, but eventually lost the election. In 2011, he was elected CHP's Manisa deputy for the first time. In 2014, he took his chance to become Manisa Mayor once again but was defeated. He was elected CHP's Manisa deputy in the 2015 June, 2015 November, 2018, and 2023 parliamentary elections. He became a member of the party administration in 2014 first time. In 2015, he was elected deputy chairman of the parliamentary group of CHP. Özel drew attention seriously first time in 2014 when he warned the public and authorities about the difficult and dangerous working conditions at Soma Coal Mine in Manisa. A few weeks after his warning, a terrible disaster in the Soma Coal Mine caused the death of 301 coal miners and showed the miserable condition of Türkiye in terms of labor safety. Özel continued to appear on TV channels with his heated speeches and rational criticism of the government and achieved considerable support among the party members and supporters. Father of a child, Özel is fluent in German and English languages.

What to expect from CHP in the 2024 Local Elections?

With Özgür Özel becoming the new party chair, the CHP might have more chances in the March 2024 local elections. That is because Türkiye's economic performance has been terrible in recent months due to hyperinflation and devaluation of the Turkish lira which makes life unbearable for all working people. In that case, a new and young leader with fresh names around him, could attract more people and motivate unhappy but desperate voters to go to the ballots. In that sense, the party's star Mayors including Ekrem İmamoğlu of İstanbul and Mansur Yavaş of Ankara could keep their seats in the two most important metropolitan cities. Moreover, with Tunç Soyer, the CHP's chance in İzmir, the third biggest metropolitan city in the country, is also very high. That is why, Özgür Özel could make a very good start to his leadership period with three over three wins in addition to several wins, especially in coastal cities where the secular opposition is still very strong.

Ekrem İmamoğlu and Özgür Özel could restructure CHP to lead the country after long years

Özgür Özel would definitely need the support of other oppositional parties; primarily Meral Akşener's Good Party (İYİ Parti), a secular nationalist right-wing populist political party as well as the HEDEP, the new name of the pro-Kurdish left-wing political party. The biggest difficulty the CHP has experienced in the last years has been to keep these two groups together within the opposition bloc. Özel, as a young politician coming from the left-wing political tradition, can keep these two large parties (each has around 10 % support) within the People's Alliance (*Millet İttifakı*) bloc with clever tactics as Kılıçdaroğlu did. The popularity of Ekrem İmamoğlu is another chance for the opposition bloc. However, in case these two parties could not be convinced, the CHP might not win the local election in İstanbul and maybe in Ankara as well. On the other hand, after winning the local election in the economic capital of the country in March 2024, İmamoğlu could become the ideal Presidential candidate for the 2028 elections.

Conclusion

Finally, after 13 years of leadership, I think it was timely for Kemal Kılıçdaroğlu to give up leadership right after the lost elections in May. However, he insisted on staying in power and eventually, he lost the election in his party's Congress as well and made an unpleasant farewell to active politics. Although he was a peaceful and bright politician, Kılıçdaroğlu's biggest disadvantage was coming across a period during which President Recep Tayyip Erdoğan dominated the political scene in Türkiye with his support coming from rural areas, Islamist masses, as well as the international Islamist movement. I think if Erdoğan continues to stay in active politics, the same thing might happen to Özel and İmamoğlu as well. However, according to the current constitution, Erdoğan's tenure in office will end in 2028, which is the greatest chance for the opposition. In case Erdoğan continues to active politics or find a strong successor, however, the Turkish political system might evolve into a hegemonic party system similar to the system in Japan, with AK Parti continuing the lead the country without any breaks. We will closely monitor developments in Turkish Politics to inform our international audience.

Ozan Örmeci[1]

Türkiye Is Heading Toward 2024 Local Elections

Abstract: This chapter contains an earlier analysis of 2024 Turkish local elections touching upon recent political developments such as the leadership in CHP, the power struggle within the ruling bloc, worsening economic conditions of the country, and the intraparty struggles in İYİ Parti.

Keywords: *2024 Turkish local elections, Recep Tayyip Erdoğan, CHP, Özgür Özel, Turkish economy, Meral Akşener, İYİ Parti.*

After the decisive victory of President Recep Tayyip Erdoğan and his Islamist/nationalist bloc in Türkiye in the critical presidential and parliamentary elections in May 2023, for a few months, it seemed like politics stopped in the country as the defeated pro-secular opposition bloc dealt with its own power struggles and voters from the opposition felt a deep despair. Due to increasing political apathy, hundreds of thousands of people from the opposition circles stopped watching television programs, buying newspapers, and talking about politics. It seemed like President Erdoğan and his ruling bloc were running for another victory in the approaching local elections on May 31, 2024.

However, things have begun to change rapidly in the last few weeks, increasing hopes among the opposition parties and voters. The first critical change came when the young social democratic politician Özgür Özel had a surprising victory at the 38th Regular Congress of the Republican People's Party (CHP) on November 4–5, 2023. Although Türkiye has been holding democratic elections since 1950, it is often accepted by Turkish political scientists that the political party system in the country is not democratic and makes party chairs mortal gods who cannot be defeated and replaced. The earlier transition of powers also strengthened this view. For instance, unlike the common knowledge, when young Bülent Ecevit replaced the very old war hero İsmet İnönü in 1972 as the new CHP chair, it was not the result of a leadership race, but rather the withdrawal of İnönü from the

1   Associate Professor in the department of Political Science and International Relations (English) at Istanbul Aydın University, Istanbul, Türkiye.
    Email: ozanormeci@aydin.edu.tr / ozanormeci@gmail.com.
    ORCID: 0000-0001-8850-6089.

intraparty election due to his anger to party delegates when he lost the election for the party parliament. Moreover, in 2010, Kemal Kılıçdaroğlu did not become the new chair of the party by defeating Deniz Baykal in a party congress. Instead, Baykal had to resign due to an alleged sex tape containing his inappropriate relationship with a party deputy. In the right-wing parties, the earlier experiences were even worse. MHP's Alparslan Türkeş and Islamist Necmettin Erbakan were leaders of their parties until their death. In the governing AK Parti, Congresses are held regularly with only one leadership candidate: Recep Tayyip Erdoğan, and Ahmet Davutoğlu for a short while. Thus, the replacement of Kılıçdaroğlu with Özel as the new CHP leader is an important progress and novelty for Turkish politics. This change gave new hope to many voters since Özgür Özel is a young, bright, untried, and unknown politician who has a clean sheet.

The second important change in recent weeks was the increasing disagreements between Turkish President Recep Tayyip Erdoğan and his junior partner MHP chair Devlet Bahçeli. It is common knowledge that Turkish Political Islam (*Milli Görüş*) and Turkish nationalism are two very different ideologies taking their roots and inspirations from contradicting sources. It should be remembered that Devlet Bahçeli also was the fiercest critic of Erdoğan until the failed coup attempt in 2016. However, understanding the changing sociological nature of Türkiye as well as the transformation of the state, Bahçeli, with the consciousness of keeping the state strong and stable, decided to support Erdoğan for a smooth transition into the Presidential system in 2017. This marked the beginning of the People's Alliance (*Cumhur İttifakı*), which continued and strengthened after the transition into Presidentialism, with an official electoral coalition between the two parties. Although this coalition helped Erdoğan to stay in power and Bahçeli to employ and emplace trusted Turkish nationalists into critical positions in the bureaucracy, the two partners continued to disagree on many issues. For instance, according to some journalists, the removal of Süleyman Soylu from the Ministry of Interior Affairs after the election was a step against Bahçeli. Moreover, Ali Yerlikaya, the new Interior Minister appointed by Erdoğan after the elections, started legal operations against some criminal leaders (Ayhan Bora Kaplan) who had good relations with the state during Soylu's tenure in office. Bahçeli on the other hand criticized this and openly backed Soylu[2]. This led to an increasingly confrontational political stance between Erdoğan and Bahçeli. The trend was

2 https://www.dw.com/tr/bah%C3%A7elinin-soylu-mesaj%C4%B1-i%CC%87%C3%A7i%C5%9Flerinde-nas%C4%B1l-yank%C4%B1land%C4%B1/a-66956620.

further accelerated when the shooting of a young ultranationalist politician and former Grey Wolfes (*Ülkü Ocakları*) leader, Sinan Ateş, in December 2022 turned into a legal battleground between the MHP and the government[3]. Police investigation showed that some people from the MHP headquarters (Mersin deputy Olcay Kılavuz) had close relations with the murder suspect Tolgahan Demirbaş.[4] In fact, Demirbaş was taken into custody by the police from Kılavuz's house in Ankara.[5] While this investigation turned into a power struggle between AK Parti and MHP, the editor of an MHP-related political website –*Orhun Haber*– Mert Kerim Ejder was recently taken into custody due to threats toward Ankara Chief Prosecutor Ahmet Akça who conducts the investigation of Sinan Ateş assassination. Although I do not believe that MHP could be involved in the murder with its legal entity, it seems like some people from the administration could have been involved in the murder of Ateş. That is why, this issue and power struggle between two critical elements of the People's Alliance give the opposition a chance to convince voters in the local elections.

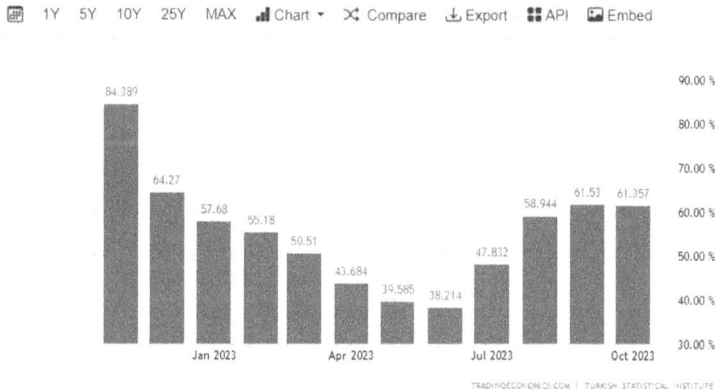

Inflation rates in Türkiye in the last 12 months

---

3 https://www.al-monitor.com/originals/2023/01/murder-former-grey-wolves-leader-divides-turkeys-nationalists.

4 https://www.dw.com/tr/sinan-ate%C5%9F-cinayeti-tutanaktan-mhpli-k%C4%B1lavuzun-ad%C4%B1-%C3%A7%C4%B1kar%C4%B1ld%C4%B1/a-65305518.

5 https://www.dw.com/tr/sinan-ate%C5%9F-cinayetini-anlama-k%C4%B1lav uzu-kim-neyle-su%C3%A7lan%C4%B1yor/a-64317362.

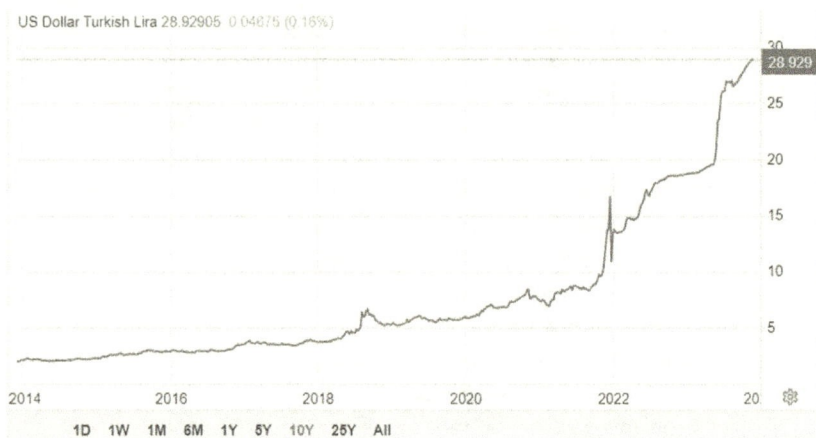

The devaluation of Turkish lira since 2014

The third important advantage for the opposition is the worsening socioeconomic conditions in Türkiye, particularly in expensive big cities. According to *The Economist*, Türkiye struggled with triple-digit inflation rates throughout the year 2022.[6] In 2023, the average inflation is estimated around 51,45 % in the first 10 months of this year and 66 % in the last 12 months.[7] For many people, it has become increasingly difficult to maintain a decent living due to the rapid rise of prices as well as the sharp devaluation of Turkish lira. A U.S. dollar is worth less than 3 Turkish liras in 2014, less than 5 liras in July 2018, less than 8 liras in April 2021, less than 15 liras in March 2022, and less than 20 liras in May 2023. But now, as of November 2023, a U.S. dollar is worth almost 30 Turkish liras, which shows the enormous devaluation of Turkish currency in the last decade. In that sense, the economy is giving a clear message to average voters in Türkiye: do not vote for the government. However, due to sociocultural inclinations, many people voted for the government last May, and many of them might continue to vote for the government and President Erdoğan in next March's local elections as well.

But the opposition also now has a new problem. The second most important party of the opposition's Nation Alliance (*Millet İttifakı*), İYİ Parti (Good Party)

---

6 https://www.economist.com/europe/2022/07/14/turkey-grapples-with-triple-digit-inflation.

7 https://tradingeconomics.com/turkey/inflation-cpi#.

has been having some intraparty struggles recently due to the party's poor performance in the earlier elections. İYİ Parti is a leader-oriented party built around the charisma of the former Minister of Interior Affairs (1996–1997) Meral Akşener. It is a split party from MHP and most of its members are former Turkish nationalists. However, as a popular politician, Akşener was able to open the party to different segments of society and embraced new voters escaping from CHP and AK Parti. By doing this, the party established a 9–10 % solid voter base in the previous elections, an important success for a new political party created in 2017. Akşener, due to the failure of the alliance strategy with the social democratic CHP last May, has been adopting a different rhetoric in recent months and does not want to seem very willing to engage in another electoral election. Akşener wants to reach right-wing conservative and nationalist voters and she thinks that the electoral coalition with CHP prevents her party from expanding. However, this strategy led to increasing criticism of her leadership in the party, and eventually 79 out of 200 founders of the party either resigned or exported from the party.[8] Especially the party's Sakarya deputy Ümit Dikbayır's recent criticism and accusations put Akşener into a difficult position.[9] In addition, the growing popularity of the anti-immigrant Victory Party and its leader Ümit Özdağ is another problem for İYİ Parti to have a successful performance in the elections. Current polls suggest that the party lost a considerable amount of its votes following the election in May, 4 months before the local elections.[10]

Local elections are often classified as different types of elections by Turkish political scientists. It is a fact that the identity, popularity, and image of the candidate can make a difference at the local level since people directly vote for their local governors. According to an expert on Turkish elections, Professor Birol Akgün, in the local elections, four factors play key roles:[11]

1. The potential of political parties in that electorate,
2. The personality and local connections of the candidates,
3. Sociocultural and ethnic composition of the electorate,
4. Electoral moves such as transfer expenditures.

---

8 https://www.memurlar.net/haber/1084086/iyi-parti-de-200-kurucudan-79-u-gitti.html.

9 https://www.aydinlik.com.tr/haber/umit-dikbayirdan-zehir-zemberek-sozler-aksener-ozur-dileyecek-436521.

10 https://artigercek.com/politika/orcden-yerel-secim-anketi-en-dezavantajli-konumda-iyi-parti-var-261695h.

11 For details, see; Birol Akgün (2002), *Türkiye'de Seçmen Davranışı, Partiler Sistemi ve Siyasal Güven*, Ankara: Novel Akademik Yayıncılık.

In that sense, a good candidate by establishing local connections, fitting to the sociocultural and ethnic composition of this electorate, and making clever electoral moves, can reach the maximum potential of his party whereas a wrong choice might reduce the potential. That is why, the choice of candidates especially in metropolitan cities will be very important for party leaders in the coming weeks. It is almost certain that CHP will continue to contest in the March elections with Mansur Yavaş in Ankara and Ekrem İmamoğlu in İstanbul. In İzmir, the current Mayor Tunç Soyer's candidacy is not guaranteed, but I think he will keep his seat in one of the most secure electorates for CHP. In the meantime, CHP decided to organize satisfaction surveys to choose its candidates[12], which will not affect Yavaş or İmamoğlu's candidacy in my opinion.

According to the Turkish press, AK Parti also has recently intensified its research for choosing the appropriate candidate in metropolitan cities and organized tendency surveys within the party. In Istanbul, the party's İstanbul provincial chairman Osman Nuri Kabaktepe, İstanbul deputy and former Minister of Environment and Urbanization Murat Kurum, and President Erdoğan's groom and drone company Baykar's founder Selçuk Bayraktar are referred to as potential candidates.[13] Former Minister of Foreign Affairs Mevlüt Çavuşoğlu was also mentioned by some journalists in earlier weeks. In Ankara, Keçiören Mayor Turgut Altınok and former Minister of Education Ziya Selçuk topped the list in the tendency surveys.[14] In İzmir, party members preferred the party's head of the youth branch Eyüp Kadir İnan, and İzmir deputy Hamza Dağ. While potential AK Parti candidates are strong politicians, they are not very well-known among the public, which might be a big disadvantage. But on the other hand, the success of young and enigmatic Ekrem İmamoğlu in the 2019 local elections in İstanbul, might encourage Erdoğan and other key party officials to choose a fresh name. But whoever is chosen as the candidate, everyone knows that AK Parti enters into all elections with President Erdoğan and he is the main reason why millions of people continue to vote for the party that does not perform very well in recent years, especially concerning economics.

---

12 https://www.ntv.com.tr/turkiye/chpde-belediye-baskan-adaylari-anket-ile-belirlenecek,c9oomL4Kw0GfN6_DM8_X_w.

13 https://www.sondakika.com/politika/haber-ak-parti-de-temayul-yoklamasi-bitti-iste-16571271/.

14 https://www.yenimeram.com.tr/ak-parti-de-temayul-yoklamasi-bitti-iste-ankara-istanbul-izmir-ve-diger-illerde-one-cikan-isimler-kimler-konya-da-surpriz-yok-527655.htm.

To conclude, the 2024 Turkish local elections will not be boring or non-contentious with the recent leadership change in CHP and the worsening economic conditions of the country. However, the opposition has to keep its electoral coalition to be more challenging while Erdoğan also has to solve the problem with the MHP for not losing votes.

Conclusion

In this book, I tried to collect my articles on the most important political developments taking place in Türkiye before, during, and after the 2023 presidential and parliamentary elections. I hope this will be interesting and helpful to those who study Turkish Politics around the world.

2023 Turkish elections were critical and decisive in the making of Türkiye's future for several reasons. First of all, elections took place on the 100th anniversary of the Republic, as a test to decide on which way to go for the future of the country. The struggle between the secular opposition and the conservative governing bloc ended with the clear victory of conservative forces; thus, (at least) temporarily rotating the country toward a more conservative and nationalist political course. Secondly, the elections turned into a power struggle between the Western bloc and the non-West. Although Turkish government did not follow a clear anti-Occidentalist discourse and foreign policy line, it was obvious that Turkish decision-makers were seeking for more autonomy in their decisions and aiming to reshape Türkiye to become a power bloc of itself. The government's close links with Russia and China for instance are developed as a counterbalancing act against the Western tutelage rather than pro-Russian or pro-Chinese foreign policy preference. The opposition on the other hand, tried to stay closer to the West and to defend Western type democracy. In the end, Turkish people decided clearly in favor of a more autonomous and independent country due to lack of trust toward Western powers. Turkish elections in that sense should be understood as the gradual decline of the West against the non-Western world as well.

Then, a new question arises now; what could be the potential consequences of the elections? It seems like President Erdoğan will continue to rule Türkiye for 5 more years. In that sense, if the opposition could not change the mood of voters, 2024 local elections could turn into Erdoğan's glorious victory despite of Türkiye's serious economic problems. Thus, the ruling bloc could regain the municipalities of the metropolitan cities including İstanbul and Ankara, two most important Turkish cities. But the opposition on the other hand could still keep its chance due to Türkiye's unbearable socioeconomic conditions caused by the hyperinflation in the country in the last few months in addition to the rapid devaluation of Turkish lira. In addition, the main opposition party, CHP, had a leadership change recently. With the new and young chair of CHP, Özgür Özel, the opposition has now much better chances against Erdoğan mostly due to the fact that Türkiye has heavy economic problems. However, CHP has to keep its electoral alliance with other elements of the secular opposition because the disappointment felt in the last May might direct many voters to apathy and boycott the elections with the despair that nothing could change in the country through elections.

A clear Erdoğan and AK Parti win in the 2024 local elections will certainly make Türkiye a more conservative and nationalist country. What is more, without a serious challenger and opposition, Turkish government could decide on more adventurist policies on the international stage especially in relation to Cyprus, the Eastern Mediterranean, and Syria. Furthermore, since under ordinary conditions this would be Erdoğan's last term, intragovernment power struggles might also accelerate in the coming years. In my opinion, Foreign Minister Hakan Fidan, Erdoğan's drone-maker son-in-law Selçuk Bayraktar, and the young Islamist leader Fatih Erbakan are three strong candidates to replace him following his retirement from active politics. Erdoğan might choose the path of Putin to stay in his seat for another term, but this would necessitate a constitutional change that will allow a third term and also a grand bargain with MHP and some elements from the opposition.

I should underline the fact that, controlling almost all departments and cells of the state with an enormous power equal to that of Mustafa Kemal Atatürk, Türkiye's founder, if President Erdoğan decides to continue in active politics, I think he could find ways to lengthen his ruling term. To do this, Erdoğan could transform the system into parliamentarism once again and becoming Prime Minister or change the constitution to serve for another (third) term. I am not sure what will be his decision, but I can assure that President Erdoğan is the most powerful Turkish political leader since Atatürk and he -in a sense- recreates or reestablishes Türkiye at the beginning of its second century. I hope President Erdoğan's conservative political choices are correct and his reforms will create a stronger, more prosperous, and more democratic country for future generations.

Lastly, most important political issues in Turkish Politics and Turkish Foreign Policy in the coming years will be Turkish people's economic problems, the situation of Syrian and other immigrants, the clash between Islamist and secular lifestyles, Türkiye's balance of power policy between the West (NATO) and Russia and China, and for sure the situation of Kurds both within and outside of the country.

Ozan ÖRMECİ

27.11.2023
Florya, İstanbul